Islamic Law and the Challenges of Modernity

Edited by Yvonne Yazbeck Haddad and
Barbara Freyer Stowasser

ALTAMIRA
PRESS

A Division of Rowman & Littlefield Publishers, Inc.
Walnut Creek • Lanham • New York • Toronto • Oxford

AltaMira Press
A division of Rowman & Littlefield Publishers, Inc.
1630 North Main Street, #367
Walnut Creek, CA 94596
www.altamirapress.com

Rowman & Littlefield Publishers, Inc.
A wholly owned subsidary of The Rowman & Littlefield Publishing Group, Inc.
4501 Forbes Boulevard, Suite 200
Lanham, Maryland 20706

PO Box 317
Oxford
OX2 9RU, UK

British Library Cataloguing in Publication Information Available

Library of Congress Cataloging-in-Publication Data

Islamic law and the challenges of modernity / edited by Yvonne Yazbeck Haddad and
Barbara Freyer Stowasser.
   p. cm.
  Includes bibliographical references and index.
   ISBN 0-7591-0670-3 (hardcover : alk. paper) — ISBN 0-7591-0671-1 (pbk. : alk.
paper)
   1. Islamic law—Arab countries. 2. Law reform—Arab countries. I. Haddad, Yvonne
Yazbeck, 1935– II. Stowasser, Barbara Freyer, 1935– III. Title.
  KBP144.I83 2004
  340.5'9—dc22   2003021504

Printed in the United States of America

♾™ The paper used in this publication meets the minimum requirements of American
National Standard for Information Sciences—Permanence of Paper for Printed Library
Materials, ANSI/NISO Z39.48-1992.

To
Andy Stowasser and Michael Stowasser
Susan Haddad MacPhail and Ramsey Haddad

CONTENTS

CONTENTS

ACKNOWLEDGMENTS

This book brings together studies on Islamic law as it has been reconceived and applied in the modern world. The essays were delivered at the 2001 symposium, Arab Legal Systems in Transition, sponsored by the Center for Contemporary Arab Studies of Georgetown University Edmund A. Walsh School of Foreign Service. The editors wish to acknowledge with gratitude all those who assisted in the coordination of the effort, faculty and staff at the center, the symposium steering committee, panel chairpersons, and external readers of the papers. Special thanks are extended to symposium manager Anne-Marie Chaaraoui; publication managers Stephen Brannon, Jimmy Bishara, and Laila Shereen; publications assistant Nawaal Durrani; graduate research assistants Dorothea Ewing, Paul Prudhomme, and Julie Eadeh; information officer/administrative assistant Ryan Leeson; and the center's proofreader extraordinaire, Nancy Farley.

INTRODUCTION
ISLAMIC LAW AND THE CHALLENGE OF MODERNITY

I n examining the transformation of traditional Islamic legal culture in
a world of nation-states and tracing the as-yet uneasy relationship of
the culture with Western notions of human rights and civil liberties,
this volume is a contribution to the long-standing debates among scholars both East and West on the nature and functions of *shari'a*, Islamic law,
in the modern age. Both the Western notion of "Islamic law" and the use
of the concept of "shari'a" by the traditionalist and Islamist cadres among
the Muslim authorities have become problematic.

As globalization forces continue to push societies toward streamlining or
standardizing legal norms and international etiquette based largely on Western notions, local populations are asserting their rights to determine their
own laws and to maintain their own traditions. Examples can be found across
the globe at both the local and the regional level. Some of these conflicts have
become bloody, while others are resolved in quiet processes of sociopolitical
change through legal and institutional means. The ideological debates that
would determine the path of the country are often waged between two or
more well-defined populations of citizens that the national government must
attempt to balance while simultaneously facing the demands of international
organizations that insist on democratic processes to determine that the will
of the people is being met (but on occasion, the government refuses to recognize democracy when the popular results differ from its own ideas of the
directions in which the country should be heading).

The following chapters examine the role of laws and legal institutions
in the contemporary Arab world. Where appropriate, the authors situate

their analyses of Arab legal systems within the broader context of the political, ideological, economic, and social changes that have marked Arab history from the onset of Western encroachment on Arab affairs in the nineteenth century to the creation of independent nation-states in the twentieth, the beginnings of globalization, and the age of the Internet. Throughout this long and eventful period of time, the processes of legal modernization in the Arab world have been caught up in a spiraling dynamic of largely contradictory political and ideological impulses that have ranged from partial or wholesale adoption of Western codes of law to mass-based efforts in support of renewed Islamification of laws and legal institutions and that have variously legitimized their activities in the name of "modernity" and "progress," "morality" and "authenticity," or a mixture thereof.

Arab traditional law and legal institutions, including the educational requirements and professional competencies of the clerics and jurists who interpreted and administered the law, were at first indirectly affected by changes enacted in the Ottoman legal system in the nineteenth century. With the growing presence of European colonial powers in Arab lands—earlier in the Maghrib (North Africa), later in the Mashriq (Southwest Asia)—the nineteenth and early twentieth centuries brought increasing pressure from the West to replace or, at least, to modify Islamic laws and legal systems according to Western models. Only small pockets of Arab territory, mainly in the Arabian peninsula, escaped direct colonization and thus retained their traditional legal systems. After independence from Western domination—earlier in the Mashriq, later in the Maghrib—in the twentieth century, the newly emerging Arab nation-states promulgated national codes of law that, to various degrees, perpetuated Western influence in both form and substance while deferring to Islamic law whenever possible. It was primarily in the areas of family law and gender relations that the struggles on how or even whether to maintain the validity of Islamic law have been paramount. Arab Muslim reformist scholarship, both clerical and lay, focused at an early date on matters of the Muslim family and women's Islamic rights and obligations, as represented, for example, by some of the work of the Egyptian lawyer-theologian Muhammad Abduh (d. 1905) and his Syrian disciple Rashid Rida (d. 1935), whose background was in journalism. Reformers were inspired by the need to modernize Islam—mainly in "their region"—in order to restore it to its original strength while crafting the framework for the Islamic renewal in terms that differed from the West. A similar sense of mission continues to inform multiple Islamic discourses in the Arab world that range from the reformist/modernist to the traditionalist and the Islamist. Gender questions remain the battleground on which most of the cultural and legal wars about modernization, authenticity, and divine prescriptions are waged. It is for this reason that the second half of this volume is dedicated to these issues.

In principle though not in fact, the notion of the sovereignty of Islamic law over all spheres of life has continued to prevail in areas such as commercial and penal law that were reframed on the basis of Western models well before the promulgation of the national personal status codes. According to Frank Vogel, most Muslim scholars have long accepted the westernizing changes on the grounds of "necessity" but also have refused to endow them with legitimacy so that "Islamic law remains—in faith if not in legal reality—the criterion for right action in Muslim life."[1]

In the Arab world, especially in the Mashriq, the 1970s marked a popular-based withdrawal of support from state-proclaimed secular ideologies such as nationalism, Arabism, and socialism that was in large part galvanized by the Arab defeat in the 1967 war and the loss of Jerusalem and the West Bank to Israeli control. The 1970s was also the decade that marked both the coming of age of the first generation of young men and women who had attained Arabic literary proficiency in the postindependence government-sponsored schools open to all citizens and the larger availability of television. Starting with the "Islamic resurgence" of the 1970s, it was not only the newly strengthened Islamist cadres who intensified and popularized their demands to "restore the shari'a." Many of the faithful, alienated by an impoverishing modernity that they perceived as inspired by the West and dangerous to their moral as well as economic well-being, sought refuge in leading more religious lives and as a matter of piety focused on earnestly (re)appropriating the shari'a-derived criteria of lawful (*halal*) and forbidden (*haram*) as moral yardsticks, while others supported the call to restore the shari'a as a means toward regaining cultural autonomy and authenticity. State-sponsored legislation responded to these demands in limited ways, such as inserting constitutional provisions that recognized the shari'a as a—or even *the*—principal source of the laws of the land or by promulgating a new civil code in countries such as Jordan and the United Arab Emirates.[2]

Islamic Law, Shari'a, and Fiqh

The English term "Islamic law" serves as translation of both shari'a ("the revealed, or canonical, law of Islam") and *fiqh* ("jurisprudence in Islam"). It therefore covers a wider range of meanings than those attributed to "law" in the modern Western context in that it includes such matters as worship, personal morality, family relations, and public welfare. On the other hand, the constructs of both shari'a and fiqh have over time held different meanings in past and present Islamic discourses. Partly because of its alien pedigree and partly also because of this imprecision, the term "Islamic law" has become controversial. On the whole, twentieth-century Orientalist scholars working in the area of the premodern legal tradition who professed to analyze Islamic law qua shari'a have as a matter of fact focused on classical fiqh. Others who are presently researching new Islamic Qur'an-based legal initiatives can be said to work in the area of "modern fiqh" that differs from the classical in both subject matter and method. The shifting borderline between shari'a and fiqh has historically been a function of the precise meanings attributed to these two key components by Muslim authorities. Exponents of Muslim modernist hermeneutics who strive to rethink the Qur'anic base of canonical law (that is, the shari'a) in general terms are finding contradictions between inherited legal norms (derived from fiqh) and Islamic ethical values (derived from the Qur'an). The question of where and how to draw the lines between "revealed law" and its "juridic formulation" is of paramount importance in all manner of contemporary Muslim discourses on the nature and functions of both. Some schools of thought continue to maintain that the shari'a can be known only by way of fiqh. Others legitimize various far-reaching reform plans by proposing to scrap the institution of fiqh altogether in favor of reestablishing a direct connection with shari'a.[3]

Shari'a ("The Way") stands for the normative order contained within the corpus of the Qur'anic revelation and early Islamic precedent, later reconfigured as the Prophet's example, the Sunna. Theology eventually constructed the latter as an embodiment of the divine command and as an expression of, or inspired commentary on, God's law. Preserved by the Prophet's companions and their successors in the form of discrete reports (*hadiths*) that were transmitted from generation to generation, this sanctified record of the Prophet's inspired words and actions became a sacred text. Islamic jurisprudence developed as the science of interpretation of both Qur'an and Sunna. Especially in the modern period, legal-theological scholarship has defined shari'a as revealed or divine law in order to distinguish it from fiqh (jurists' law) and *qanun* (state law), with the aim to stress the divine origin of the shari'a, whose norms are binding for all times.

Fiqh ("understanding") connotes the efforts and activities, largely on the part of qualified scholars, to discover and give expression to the many facets of Qur'an- and Sunna-derived principles of shari'a law. While shari'a is a focus of the faith, fiqh is esteemed mainly as an intellectual literary tradition and/or the sophisticated product of centuries of Islamic high legal culture. In elaborating the law, religious scholars combined rationalist readings of Qur'an and Sunna with the specialists' knowledge of previous and contemporaneous juristic opinions that incorporated time-specific preferences and public policy options on the part of their framers. The science of interpretation thus came to rest on a scheme labeled the "roots of jurisprudence" (*usul al-fiqh*) that were brought together in a process and methodology called *ijtihad* ("effort"—as a juristic term more precisely signifying "exertion of the utmost possible effort to discover, on the basis of revelation interpreted in the light of all rules, the ruling on a particular juristic question").[4] The resulting body of law (the classical fiqh) was stated and recorded in the form of innumerable details, many of which were contradictory. Even though the classical fiqh schools (*madhahib*, "schools of law") each developed sophisticated general legal principles, the law was "not stated in those terms. . . . The rules and the principles are interconnected at a level rarely made explicit. Moreover, the rules and principles often are not only legal but moral, defeating at times any hope of legalistic precision."[5]

During the many centuries of its florescence (roughly 800–1800), classical jurisprudence thus developed a gigantic corpus of legal opinions the main goal of which was to ensure the morality of the *umma* (Islamic community), itself increasingly a cultural construct. While the jurists' methodology was based on the "roots of law" that underlay the science of ijtihad, the subject matters that concerned them were the "branches of law" (*furu'al-fiqh*), meaning all areas of community ritual and public social life, usually divided into *'ibadat* (ritual) and *mu'amalat* (social relations). Inevitably, the jurists were connected in multiple ways with the political, social, and economic realities of their time and place, so that new problems continued to inform their legal formulations. The jurists' opinions occasioned changes in the body of the fiqh's precedent-driven legal maxims and specific detail. Overall, however, the jurists' purpose in employing their professional monopoly regarding the right to engage in ijtihad was to perpetuate a largely inherited, tradition-based moral vision. For this reason, the classical fiqh literature represents an ongoing moral discourse of scholars of theology and jurisprudence rather than a record of legal practices. The latter were largely left to the know-how of judges (*qadis*) who dealt with issues of family law, endowments, contracts, and the like in civil courts often carried out under state supervision, while whole other areas of law enforcement were left to a separate court structure established by the state. The office of juristconsul (*mufti*) first emerged in part to strengthen the input of fiqh into legal practice, but over time muftis became more susceptible to state control than were the *fuqaha'*.

To the modernizing states of the nineteenth century and their new modern-educated lawyers, the classical fiqh collections presented problems on several levels. In part these derived from the unwieldy, atomistic nature of the traditional legal compendia that only a student of medieval fiqh could be expected to master. Equally or more important was the felt need to bring Islamic jurisprudence into closer relationship with the pressures and aspirations of modernization. The Ottoman *Majalla* (enacted in 1876) was the first Middle Eastern code of law that represented the rewriting of large parts of the Hanafi legal tradition in a modern format, enacted by a committee of lawyers whose activities were also commissioned by the Ottoman government as part of its reform programs (*Tanzimat*).

As the notion of traditional fiqh as a salvageable body of Islamic jurisprudence under modern conditions was losing ground, modernists/reformists such as Muhammad Abduh began to focus on the legal instrument of ijtihad in a manner that disregarded the old differences between law schools; by combining ("patching") the various strands of traditional fiqh to find new solutions to new societal problems, Abduh and others hoped to develop a "new fiqh" that would modernize the laws within established parameters for the purposes of the emerging nation-state. Most Arab legislatures adopted the methodology when elaborating personal status codes, and increasing numbers of individual, traditionally trained legal specialists have since then formulated legal opinions (*fatwas*) on maxims and verdicts derived from a combination of juristic traditions. The overall result of these eclectic approaches to the classical fiqh, however, has been to strengthen patriarchal structures in the new laws rather than to produce more liberal modern alternatives. With regard to the personal status codes that were developed in most Arab states after independence, the reason for this modern trend toward greater patriarchy lies mainly in the nature of the European law that heavily influenced the formulation of the codes. Starting with Egypt, the modernizing paradigm was informed primarily by nineteenth-century French law, which later spread across the region as the Egyptian personal status code was largely copied by other Arab nation-states, Tunisia being a notable exception. These efforts at ijtihad by the scholars within the established methods of inherited fiqh profoundly differ in form, if not always in substance, from the ijtihad now used by a layperson interpreting the Qur'an and parts of Sunna, currently a staple of the scripturalist activities of a wide variety of Islamist groups. Ordinary, concerned Muslims of all ages and backgrounds and of both sexes have also begun to consult the scripture directly in order to fashion an individualized frame of reference for all life questions. These activities represent a "democratization" of the concept of ijtihad as elaborated in the classical legal tradition.

The Subsumation of Fiqh under the Concept of Shari'a

Shari'a and fiqh are the star constructs in any study of Islamic law. Their precise definition, however, is complicated by the fact that over time both terms acquired layers of meaning that encompassed the crafting of laws and legal institutions throughout the Islamic world as well as the politics of their maintenance. Haifaa KhalafAllah distinguishes two different spheres of meaning in the term "shari'a" of which the first refers to "a lawful way of making rules and the many constructs of scholarly ideas that were added to it," while in the second sphere "the term acquires a legendary and vague definition . . . [that implies] a divinely sanctioned and detailed code of rules." The latter definition was used by political and religious establishments "to enforce conformity on the illiterate masses in a multiethnic state."[6] Fiqh is likewise a catchall word as to its sources, manifestations, and sociopolitical functions. The relationship between shari'a and fiqh is similarly complex. Some view the two as inseparable, maintaining that the shari'a can be known only by way of fiqh, while others draw a sharp line between the always time- and place-specific tradition of fiqh on the one hand and the universally valid "revealed law" of the shari'a on the other. While either position is problematic, the confusion can serve to enhance the positive connotation of any existing (fiqh-based) legal system by stamping it with some aspects of sanctity and unchangeability. Conversely, the call for shari'a "signifies the semantics of the people's expectations that shari'a will solve the contradictions emerging under the impact of modernity," even though this vision of the shari'a as better than its traditional construction has remained largely utopian.[7]

The issue has problematized the access to the sacred texts themselves. While many Muslim scholars, especially those of nonclerical background, have lately focused on the area of Qur'anic exegesis in order to "rethink" its fundamental truths for the modern age, governments and also the exponents of inherited legal structures have continued to thwart some of these efforts. Islamic modernists see the path to the rejuvenation or overhaul of Islamic legal institutions largely in a new, more liberal Qur'anic interpretation, even though on the whole their influence on the legislative processes in the Arab world has been limited. The work of modernist intellectuals is essentially informed by what they perceive to be a harmful discrepancy between, on the one hand, the Qur'anic ideals of freedom, equality, and justice and, on the other, the actual sociopolitical norms now operative in Muslim societies that are enforced by legal codes that supposedly rest on Qur'anic foundations. Chief victims of this discrepancy have been Muslim women and non-Muslim minorities. A common theme in the modernist discourse is therefore the need to reestablish the vital link between social practice and legal norms that initially informed the law, in other words, to rediscover that the normative basis of shari'a should always lie in the social norms of the time and place of its application.[8]

Among the many modernist-reformist voices that have proposed to bridge the gap between the Qur'an's extrahistorical, transcendental value system of equal rights and its actual application in Muslim legal tradition riddled with discriminatory practices is the Sudanese jurist Abdullahi An-Na'im, disciple of Shaykh Mahmoud Mohamed Taha (d. 1985), founder of the Sudanese Republican Brothers movement. Taha's approach to the problem, as outlined in his book *The Second Message of Islam*,[9] had been to differentiate between the Qur'an's early (Meccan) message (tolerant and egalitarian) and its later (Medinan) message (seen at least in part as an adaptation to the socioeconomic and political situation of the Prophet's Medinan community). An-Na'im has since developed his mentor's general principles into a framework for the radical reform of Islamic law and legal institutions that invalidates the established historical institution of ijtihad in favor of a new "evolutionary principle" of Qur'anic interpretation; the latter is to reverse the historical process of shari'a positive law formation (which was based on the Qur'an's Medinan verses) by elaborating a new shari'a law (based on the Meccan revelations).[10] This modernist approach, which reflects a sort of revival of the beliefs of the early Muslim jurists in the close relationship between law and culture in Islam, denies all normative powers to the shari'a as presently formulated but maintains the essential validity of the concept.

The problem regarding the position and ongoing normative powers of the shari'a in contemporary Islamic societies has continued to exacerbate polarization between secularist and traditionalist points of view. Secularists have argued that the shari'a has lost its normative power and is no longer applicable. According to Mohamed Charfi, a Tunisian law professor, for example, the shari'a laws relating to business and economy are outdated; other laws, such as those regarding slavery, are no longer valid, and the remainder "is largely contrary to international human rights and individual liberty laws."[11] In diametrically opposed fashion, Islamists are likewise focused on the normative power of the shari'a (as presently constituted) by upholding it in essentialist terms. This means that when the law and social practices diverge, it is the law that is valid and social practice that must change in order to achieve conformity with it. The less society conforms to God's law, the more urgent is the Islamists' demand for change and purification. As exemplified by Sayyid Qutb (d. 1966), chief ideologue of the Muslim Brothers in Nasser's Egypt, Islamism has defined sovereignty largely within a framework of law and authority where the sovereignty of God is synonymous with the sovereignty of the shari'a within an Islamic state. When Islamists, therefore, call for a "return of the shari'a," they do not mean to bring back the traditionalist fiqh (tainted by centuries of 'ulama-state accommodation); rather, they envisage an alternative shari'a based on the Qur'an and, especially, the restoration of the Prophet's Sunna that prominently involves the building of a new state structure and new political institutions under Islamist leadership.

By contrast, when the traditionalists, especially now given a voice by conservative clergy and legal experts, call to restore the shari'a, their demand is generally for the restoration of Islamic fiqh to replace the legal norms and institutions that were created during the colonial period or by the postcolonialist nation-states. So far, only a few of the establishment's religious scholars have used their professional credentials and legalistic expertise to develop innovative opinions within the legal methods of traditional fiqh. Two prominent examples are Muhammad al-Ghazali (d. 1996)[12] and Yusuf al-Qaradawi,[13] both of whom arrived at new formulations of Muslim women's social and political rights during the 1990s by way of the established fiqh: indigenous methods of law finding. In addition, the general public has to some degree begun to participate in the civilizational debate on the role and meaning of Islamic law in their modernizing societies. By way of the new media, especially the new electronic means of communication, nonspecialist Muslim individuals, including women and the young, are beginning to create what may perhaps one day turn out to be a groundswell of scripture-based individual opinions on legal issues that they derive largely from a personal study of the Qur'an.

The contributors to this volume address the processes of change and transformation in the legal culture of the modern Arab world from a variety of vantage points. They focus on such questions as the following: Is the shari'a as a legal system now defunct, as Wael Hallaq asserts? Or does the shari'a continue to inform contemporary constitutional law (Brown and Sherif) and also, potentially, Middle Eastern asylum law (Yakoob and Mir)? What is the role of the traditional Muslim clergy who now find themselves as employees of a nation-state (Skovgaard-Petersen)? How do indigenous formulations of women's rights measure up to the standards of international law on human rights and civil liberties enshrined in international legal documents to which Arab governments are signatories

(Mayer)? How and to what degree do shari'a and/or fiqh underlie present-day family law as enshrined in the new national personal status codes (Stowasser and Abul-Magd)? And what are the pressure points and also the agents for legal reform on gender issues in Egypt (Abu-Odeh) and Jordan (Sonbol)?

While there is a clamor by Islamists in the Arab world for the restitution of the shari'a and an affirmation of its efficacy and eternal validity, Hallaq, in chapter 1, argues that the shari'a is "no longer a tenable reality, that it has met its demise nearly a century ago, and that this sort of discourse is lodging itself in an irredeemable state of denial." Although sympathetic to the desire of the Middle East to distinguish itself from the West, Hallaq is firm in his assertion that the concept of nationalism and the creation of modern nation-states have negated the possibility of living by any comprehensive system of shari'a. He supports his thesis by analyzing the nature of reforms currently under way that he refers to as the "cobbling together" of interpretations of shari'a borrowed from various historical legal schools and other legal-theological traditions. Spurred by international pressure to create a body of laws that will adhere to the conditions of a modern constitution, lawmakers in the various nation-states are now creating hastily constructed legal templates that will satisfy both international organizations and popular ideologies. The only way to achieve such a precarious balance is to adopt the most lenient laws offered by the various inherited legal traditions, those laws that will still receive the support of the population. The only sector of law maintaining any uniformity under these conditions, Hallaq argues, is personal status law. It may, however, be precisely the latter's more Islamic uniformity, as opposed to the heterogeneity of the rest of state law, that will eventually serve to accentuate the larger legal system's incoherence and thus contribute to strain "the intricate connection between the social fabric and the law as a system of conflict resolution and social control." At the root of the problem, Hallaq posits, is the modern state control of *waqf* (the wealth amassed by centuries of private unalienable property contributions formerly administered by representatives of the clerical establishment), the loss of which has undermined the ability of Islamic schools of law, institutions, and officials to function independently of the political establishment and thus has destroyed their tradition of legal innovation and adjustment that informed the formulation and practice of Islamic law in the past.

INTRODUCTION

In chapter 2, Brown and Sherif examine the way in which the Supreme Constitutional Court of Egypt has attempted to balance the Egyptian national constitution (representing a largely man-made set of laws tailored to the interests of the state) against popular Egyptian demands for greater reliance on the shari'a. The writers demonstrate that even though discussion of shari'a has recently become more prevalent than before in Egyptian state courts, European legal customs have in fact long dominated (or at least mitigated) the application of shari'a law in all areas. The very creation of a modern national Egyptian constitution promulgated in the twentieth century is a case in point. At the same time, the Egyptian experience proves that the shari'a can work within a modern constitutional framework: "although this experience has yet to develop, it has sought to prove over the past two decades that Islamic shari'a principles, as a legal system, have met, to a great extent, the needs and wishes of the vast majority of the population, without prejudice to the constitutional rights of minority religious groups in the country."

In chapter 3, Skovgaard-Petersen presents a comparative study of the legal and sociopolitical efficacy of state muftis (official interpreters of Islamic law) in Syria, Lebanon, and Egypt. He demonstrates that state control of waqf funds have to some extent limited the independent power of the official *ifta'* system (the official Islamic system of providing legal interpretation, manned by qualified Islamic clerics), so that on occasion its members have found themselves in situations where they were forced to support state policy that met with popular resistance on religious grounds. Nevertheless, the record proves that, on the whole, state muftis have managed to retain the ability to oppose state policy, something that occurs directly by way of confrontational legal pronouncements or else it can materialize by way of galvanizing popular opinion at the grassroots level, which may, in the long run, influence government action. In times of change and hardship, the populace tends to rely more heavily on their mufti's directives, which serves to secure his position when he would be at his weakest politically. State control of the appointment or election of muftis has thus become an exercise in official politics, meaning that these processes must be handled deftly to avoid public outrage.

Chapter 4 concerns contemporary asylum law in the Arab world. On this topic, Yakoob and Mir find justification for sanctuary, emigration, and *nonrefoulement* (to not be returned to a place where one's life would be threatened) laws in the Islamic legal tradition. Such shari'a-grounded principles are, however, generally overlooked when modern international treaties guaranteeing asylum rights are proposed for adoption by Arab nations, so that the latter have generally gone unsigned by Arab states and regional pacts created to deal with refugee problems have seen little action to match their intent. To apply Islamic principles of protection for refugees and other asylum seekers in the modern context will therefore require that these legal principles be pursued at the national state level by way of their integration into state constitutions and that, even at state level, they be implemented with the aid of international agencies. Yakoob and Mir thus suggest that while the shari'a may provide the basis and justification for creating a working Islamic asylum law, the law remains unenforceable until melded with modern constitutionalism.

In chapter 5, Mayer builds on Hallaq's discussion of the strain presently created by the existence of "Islam-based" personal status codes within the (more clearly heterogeneous) larger legal systems of Arab nations. Mayer avows that this situation has marred international credibility in that it is difficult for international organizations such as the United Nations to accept the claims of Arab governments that they are upholding the shari'a in response to popular will in the arena of personal status law when shari'a is neglected in many other areas. Mayer perceives the various attempts on the part of Arab governments to meld traditional Islamic law with modern constitutional law as a double gambit, meaning that a state's promulgation of a shari'a-informed personal status code is usually intended to appease the traditionalist and Islamist cadres among the citizenry for the purpose that the state may then more freely embrace Western law in other areas. Recent Arab attempts and measures to reinforce traditional Islamic principles in personal status codes are indicative of an anti-Western stance that will only become more apparent should other areas of law undergo further Islamization. Nevertheless, Mayer notes that "even as they resist reforming their laws to bring them into compliance with CEDAW [the Convention on the Elimination of All Forms of Discrimination Against Women], the fact that these [Arab] countries work so hard to portray themselves as compliant with the principles of international human rights law signals that change is afoot."

In chapter 6, Stowasser and Abul-Magd use the issue of *tahlil* (a sort of temporary marriage) to investigate how the legacy of the classical legal tradition of fiqh has been adapted to fit within the framework of modern, largely European-derived personal status codes. Their analysis detects a bifurcation of the classical tradition regarding this aspect of Islamic marriage law into two new paradigms, one of which (represented by the modern national family codes) is on the whole silent on the issue of tahlil, while the other (represented by the voices of individual clerics recorded mainly in the form of fatwas, or legal opinions) employs the most restrictive stance on the issue that can be culled from among multiple classical readings. The evidence therefore suggests that in modern usage, the traditional constructs of Islamic family law have in part been profoundly altered by the processes of foreign-inspired legal modernization; in particular, it is the imported notion of "the family as cornerstone of society" that now underlies both state legislatures and the appropriation of the historical legal tradition by scripturalist specialists.

In chapter 7, Abu-Odeh investigates the modern and contemporary Egyptian debates regarding family law and women's rights while locating her inquiry within the wider context constituted by a new Arab civilizational focus on the relationship between culture and legal systems. She argues that the latter, "legal systems," has come to stand for cultural authenticity, so that its defense now represents an act of defiance against the entrenchment that the European legal system has attained in the Middle East. European law has so completely uprooted the preceding Islamic legal tradition that only family law, even in its new format of European-style codification, has managed to retain some of its Islamic underpinnings. This fact represents the result of a long tradition of ongoing and deliberate negotiations between the conservative Islamic Right and the liberal Europe-embracing Left that over time allowed for the progressive westernization of all areas of the law except for family law. At present, it is this inherited situation that has boxed Egyptian feminists into a corner where they have been forced to engage in debates on the Islamic nature of gender-specific laws before being able to pursue reform in the area of women's rights "on its own merits." Abu-Odeh maps the colliding paradigms of her reading of Egyptian feminism as a triangle where Islam, the West, and patriarchy each represent an angle while Egyptian feminism has been forced to respond to all three simultaneously.

In chapter 8, Sonbol examines the local biases that work against the practical reformation of personal status laws in Jordan. While Sonbol credits the Jordanian monarchy for its efforts as catalyst in driving liberal reforms, sometimes carried out in direct opposition to the Jordanian parliament, she argues that the laws that affect women's freedom of mobility and their right to employment in the Jordanian workforce remain "merely nominal" compared to other Middle Eastern nations. Sonbol attributes this discriminatory situation largely to the tribal/patriarchal system prevailing in Jordan since pre-Islamic times. Yet this old legal system that confines women to the home and their father's or husband's keeping is now sold as "Islamic" to the population at large and by consequence today enjoys a great deal of popularity across class lines and societal groupings. Sonbol demonstrates that there are many passages in the Qur'an as well as hallowed examples ("precedents") culled from Islamic history that would support a woman's freedom to work outside the home by her own will and decision, without having to seek permission from her husband or father. The contemporary Jordanian debate on how to modernize/"Islamicize" these entrenched legal customs, however, is more often than not caught up in a larger discourse that pits Islamic authenticity against Western-inspired changes; by nature, this discourse privileges the status quo.

The concept of shari'a remains a powerful cultural symbol in the Arab world today. Arab governments, state-controlled clerical institutions, Islamist groups, parties, associations, and liberal-minded intellectual elites may profoundly differ on the shari'a's precise nature but largely share in the assumption that the shari'a is an inalienable part of Islamic identity. In many Arab countries (such as Bahrain, Kuwait, Jordan, Lebanon, Egypt, Yemen, Algeria, and Morocco), Islamists have now managed to gain a foothold in the legislative bodies, while their power base remains embodied in the local voluntary associations that provide social services to the community. Emmanuel Sivan recently also noted an "osmosis of radical Islamic ideas into the conservative Islamic establishment," made evident, for example, in the opposition of al-Azhar University's Ulama Front group to granting greater rights to women in Egyptian divorce law.[14] By contrast to the Islamists, Islamic liberals have fared less well in effectively propagating their notion that shari'a law has always been historically contextualized and must therefore be thoroughly reformed and modernized at the present time to remain meaningful. Unlike Islamism, Arab Islamic liberalism is represented largely by elitist intellectuals who lack mass-focused organizational skills, rarely speak in popular language in the mass media, and have thus failed to garner popular support.[15]

A major factor in undermining the position of Arab Islamic liberalism and strengthening as well as radicalizing the positions of Arab Islamism and even Arab Islamic conservatism has lately come from abroad. In the aftermath of 9/11, the Bush administration has ventured on a course that seeks to restructure and reformulate Islamic thought. It is a major undertaking that has been placed under the umbrella of fighting terrorism. As it unfolds, the policy has targeted Islamic school texts, seeking to purge them from anti-American, anti-Western, and anti-Israeli diatribes. This policy has also occasioned the organization of a special bureaucratic structure and program in the U.S. State Department whose mandate is the reform of women's issues in Islam, to be accomplished by empowering Muslim organizations and programs on the ground that propagate a moderate Islam. By adopting this policy, the U.S. government has set itself against the dominant Islamist interpretation of the centrality of Islamic law as divinely mandated. America's declared interest in empowering a moderate Islam is also further weakening the credibility and influence of indigenous Arab Islamic liberalism. For observers from the Arab and Muslim world, it spells hegemonic interference more intrusive and nefarious than U.S. efforts to change the political map of the Arab world.

Notes

1. Frank E. Vogel and Samuel L. Hayes III, eds., *Islamic Law and Finance* (The Hague: Kluwer Law International, 1998), 19–20.

2. Vogel and Hayes, *Islamic Law and Finance*, 20.

3. In *Islamic Law and Finance*, Frank Vogel avowed that "the outsider who wishes to comment on Islamic legal phenomena in history without questioning either the perfection of Divine Law or the truth of Muslim beliefs may find [the distinction between shari'a and fiqh] indispensable" (24).

4. Norman Calder, "Law," in *Oxford Encyclopedia of the Modern Islamic World*, vol. 2, ed. John L. Esposito et al. (New York: Oxford University Press, 1995), 452.

5. Vogel and Hayes, *Islamic Law and Finance*, 28.

6. Haifaa KhalafAllah, "Rethinking Islamic Law: Genesis and Evolution in the Islamic Legal Method and Structure. The Case of a 20th Century 'Alim's

Journey into His Legal Traditions. Muhammad al-Ghazali (1917–1996)" (Ph.D. diss., Georgetown University, 1999), 17–19.

7. Muhammad Khalid Masud, *Muslim Jurists' Quest for the Normative Basis of Shari'a* (Leiden: International Institute for the Study of Islam in the Modern World, 2001), 4–5.

8. Masud, *Muslim Jurists' Quest*, 4–5 and elsewhere.

9. Mahmoud Mohamed Taha, *The Second Message of Islam*, trans. Abdullahi Ahmed An-Na'im (Syracuse, N.Y.: Syracuse University Press, 1987). First published in Arabic in 1967.

10. Abd Allahi Ahmad An-Naim, *Toward an Islamic Reformism: Civil Liberties, Human Rights, and International Law* (Syracuse, N.Y.: Syracuse University Press, 1990).

11. Masud, *Muslim Jurists' Quest*, 5.

12. Compare KhalafAllah, *Rethinking Islamic Law*, on Muhammad al-Ghazali.

13. Compare Barbara Stowasser, "Old Shaykhs, Young Women, and the Internet: The Rewriting of Women's Political Rights in Islam," *The Muslim World* 19 (spring 2001): 99–119.

14. Emmanuel Sivan, "The Clash within Islam," *Survival* 45, no. 1 (spring 2003): 29.

15. Sivan, "Clash," pp. 39–41.

Part One

MODERNIZATION AND LEGAL REFORM IN THE ARAB WORLD

CHAPTER ONE
CAN THE SHARI'A BE RESTORED?
Wael B. Hallaq

D uring the past two decades, the forms of discourse demanding a
return to Islamic values and practices have been many, including
literature in print; radio and television programs; the propagan-
dist activities of Islamic parties, associations, and clubs; and the literature
of medical, financial, and other institutions. Permeating these forms is the
distinct call to reapply or reinforce the shari'a. In the majority of cases, the
shari'a is conceived as a well-defined, wholesome entity; the only problem
is that it has been pushed aside to the backburner, so to speak. The Islamic
book market affords the outside observer an abundance of materials embodying the deontic message as to how to apply the shari'a. A fairly representative example of such a beckoning call is a collection of articles by
distinguished men of Islamic learning, tellingly titled *Wujub Tatbiq
al-Shari'a al-Islamiyya* (The Necessity to Apply the Islamic Shari'a).[1] One
author, for instance, suggests that a means to achieve this goal is for the
political sovereign to spread the religious ethic and to "institute a code to
be promulgated for the benefit of organizations and institutions, a code
that is compiled by an assembly of learned and experienced specialists in
law and Islam."[2] Another essay by a prominent author merely presents an
introductory, even sketchy, discussion of the general principles (*qawa'id*)
of the Shari'a for the benefit of secular lawyers who are "entirely ignorant"
of Islamic law and who have left behind the religious law in favor of the
"importation of western legislation into the Arab countries. They are not
the shari'a jurists but rather the 'other group' which needs to be addressed
with such a simplified manner."[3] The underlying assumption here is the

due admission that the hegemonic and professional legal power lies in the hands of this secular group whose knowledge—and, by implication, appreciation—of Islamic law is virtually nonexistent, a fact that justifies simplification of the shari'a subject matter for the purpose of persuading them to adopt it in legal application. In short, in this discourse the shari'a appears as an extramental object that can be applied or pushed aside, appreciated or marginalized, but it is qualitatively and most certainly a known entity the only predicament of which is that it is capable of being subject to these preferences.

It is my contention here that this pervasive and dominating discourse misses the crucial point that the shari'a is no longer a tenable reality, that it has met its demise nearly a century ago, and that this sort of discourse is lodging itself in an irredeemable state of denial. This chapter, therefore, is concerned with showing the features of this demise and of the crises that still persist in the pursuit of an Islamic legal identity.

I

The demise of the shari'a was ushered in by the material internalization of the concept of nationalism in Muslim countries, mainly by the creation of the nation-state. This transformation in the role of the state is perhaps the most crucial fact about the so-called legal reforms. Whereas the traditional ruler considered himself subject to the law and left the judicial and legislative functions and authority to the *'ulama*, the modern state reversed this principle, thereby assuming the authority that dictated what the law is or is not. The ruler's traditional role was generally limited to the appointment and dismissal of judges, coupled with the enforcement of the *qadi*'s decisions. Interference in legislative processes, in the determination of legal doctrine, and in the overall internal dynamics of the law was nearly, if not totally, absent. The modern state, on the other hand, arrogated to itself the status of a legislator, an act that assigned it a place above the law. Legislative interference, often arbitrary, has become a central feature of modern reform and in itself is evidence of the dramatic shift in the balance of legal power.

A direct effect of this shift was the adoption by the new nation-state of the model of codification that altered the nature of the law. Codification is not an inherently neutral form of law, nor is it an innocent tool of legal practice, devoid of political or other goals. It is a deliberate choice in the exercise of political and legal power, a means by which a conscious restriction is placed on the interpretive freedoms of jurists, judges, and lawyers.[4] In the Islamic context, the adoption of codification has an added significance since it represents potently efficacious modus operandi through which the law was refashioned in structured ways. Among other things, it precluded the traditional means of the law from ever coming into play. But to this significant transformation, which is primarily epistemic and hermeneutical, we will have to return later.

An essential tool—indeed, constitutive component—of the nation-state is centralization. In addition to codification, which could not have been achieved without this tool, centralizing mechanisms were carefully harnessed to confiscate the realm of law in favor of state control. As early as 1826, the Ottoman sultan Mahmud II and his men created the so-called Ministry of Imperial Pious Endowments, which brought the administration of the empire's major *waqfs* under central administration.[5] All rich endowments and their revenues and assets, supervised for centuries by the legal profession in the empire's various regions, came under Istanbul's direct supervision. This ushered a new era during which the jurists gradually lost control over their own source of power and became heavily dependent on state allocations that diminished in a steady and systematic manner.

But this was not all. The chipping away of the powers of the religious elite was bolstered by the creation of alternative elites that began to form during the first half of the nineteenth century. Under Mahmud II, there was already a proliferation of technical schools independent of the religious colleges, schools that eroded the monopoly the religious institutions had over the legal system. As if this is not enough, both the Ottoman sultans and the local Egyptian rulers created a new group of legal professionals, among others, who began to displace the traditional legal elite. With the adoption—indeed, coercive enforcement[6]—of Western-style hierarchical courts and law schools, these new elites were easily incorporated into the emerging legal structures while at the same time the religious lawyers found themselves unequipped to deal with this new reality. These courts operated on the basis of codes, and the lawyers who staffed them had little, if any, knowledge of the workings of religious law, be it doctrinally, judicially, or otherwise. On the other hand, while the foreign elements were incomprehensible to the traditional legal hierarchy, their *madrasas*, which depended almost exclusively on the dwindling waqf revenues, were systematically pushed aside and later totally displaced by the modern, university law faculties. The traditional legal specialists lost not only their judicial offices as judges, legal administrators, and court officials but also their teaching posts and educational institutions, the backbone of their very existence as a profession. This latter loss constituted the coup de grâce, for it was depriving them not merely of their careers but mainly of their procreative faculties: they were no longer allowed to reproduce their pedigree. The ruin of the madrasa was the ruin of Islamic law, for its compass of activities epitomized all that made Islamic law what it is was.

Thus, the demise of the shari'a was ensured by the strategy of "demolish and replace": the weakening and final collapse of educational waqfs, the madrasa, positive Islamic law, and the shari'a court was made collateral, diachronically correlational, and causally conjoined with the introduction of state finance (or, to put it more accurately, finance through the controlling agency of the state), Western-style law schools, European codes, and European court system. If law were to represent the entire spectrum of Islamic culture, it would not be an exaggeration to state that by the middle of the twentieth century, nothing in Islam was saved from a distinctly determined and omnipotent European hegemony.

What has remained of the traditional system in the modern codes is no more than a veneer. Penal law, land law, commercial law, torts, procedural law, bankruptcy, and much else has been totally replaced by their European counterparts and supplemented, in due course, by several other codes and regulations, such as the law of corporation, copyright law, patent law, and maritime law. Traditional rules are still to be found in the law of personal status, but these have been uprooted from their indigenous context, a fact bearing, as we will see, much significance. As is well known, one of the favorite tools of modernists is the method of *takhayyur*, namely, picking and choosing legal rules from a variety of sources. Thus, the principles and rules of the marriage contract, for instance, may draw on more than one Sunni legal school, expediency being the rationale for an arbitrary amalgamation of doctrines. The modern legislators in Sunni countries furthermore resorted to Shi'i law in order to supplement their civil codes where Sunni law was deemed lacking in the fulfillment of their expedient methods. But they were extraordinarily daring not only insofar as the sources on which they drew were concerned but also in the manner in which they drew on traditional doctrine: they combined, in what is known as *talfiq*, several elements pertaining to a single issue from more than one source regardless of the positive legal principles, reasoning, and intellectual integrity that gave rise to the rulings in the first place. This approach is arbitrary in that it does not take into serious account—as should be the case—the subtle and intricate connection between the social fabric and the law as a system of conflict resolution and social control.

These considerations, on the other hand, were ever-present in the minds of the traditional jurists and the system they produced, a fact that explains the constancy and stability of classical Islamic law over the long course of twelve centuries. This lack of sensitivity to social reality among the modern legislators is manifest on a number of levels and in many areas of the law, but revealing examples of it may be found in the tinkering of the Indian and Jordanian legislators: in the Muslim Marriages Act of 1939, British India adopted numerous doctrines of the Maliki school when the country had had a long history of exclusive Hanafi jurisprudence. As Joseph Schacht aptly remarked in this regard, "The whole Act is typical of modernist legislation in the Near East, but it is hardly in keeping with the development of Anglo-Muhammadan law which had followed an independent course so far, nor even with the tendency underlying the Shariat Act of 1937."[7] Similarly, but even more flagrantly, in 1927 a Jordanian Law of Family Rights was enacted on the basis of the 1917 Ottoman Law of Family Rights, but in 1943, in less than a decade and a half, this law was replaced by the traditional shari'a law. Only eight years later, in 1951, the law was again repealed in favor of a codified law of family rights, inspired largely by the Egyptian and Syrian laws of personal status. Here it is difficult to draw any conclusion that Jordanian society had undergone, in the span of only two and a half decades, serious changes—and in different directions to boot. Insensitivity to social structures, arbitrariness, and inconsistency speak for themselves.

The point to be made here is that what little that has been preserved of the shari'a in modern codes has been so flagrantly manipulated that it lost its organic connection with both traditional law and society. This arbitrariness is simply a manifestation of the effects of infrastructural demolition of the traditional legal system.

As the opening paragraph of this chapter attests, the workings of the traditional system are little understood today, as has been the case since the end of the nineteenth century, if not even earlier. In the Ottoman *Majalla*, enacted in 1876, the Drafting Committee acknowledged the inability of the judges staffing the new courts to understand the shari'a law. "In fact," the committee argued,

> Islamic jurisprudence resembles an immense ocean on whose bottom one has to search, at the price of very great efforts, for the pearls which are hidden there. A person has to possess great experience as well as great learning in order to find in the sacred law the proper solutions for all the questions which present themselves. This is particularly true of the Hanafi School. In this school there are many commentators whose opinions differ markedly from one another. . . . One can thus understand how difficult it is to ascertain in all this diversity of opinions the best one and to apply it in a given case.[8]

With the increasing adoption of Western legal concepts and institutions, the difficulties mentioned by the Drafting Committee were also doubled and multiplied. The traditional system was steadily rendered irrelevant, useless, and a thing of the exotic past. It is on this account that the implications and consequences of the methods of takhayyur and talfiq were and still are little understood and appreciated by the modern legislators. It is perhaps telling that a Chief Justice of the High Constitutional Court of Egypt, when queried about his professional interest in the positive legal works of the traditional schools, told this writer that they are archaic and incomprehensible.

II

The rupture, therefore, is certainly one of epistemology and goes deep into the inner structure of legal thinking. The modern Muslim lawyer and judge, by the very fact of their training—which is wholly alien to its traditional counterpart—have lost the epistemological and hermeneutical framework within which their *faqih* predecessor operated. To begin with, the modern lawyer has no understanding whatsoever of what *taqlid*, as an authorizing tool, is all about. One of the functions of taqlid was the defense of the school as a methodological and interpretive entity, an entity that was constituted of identifiable theoretical and substantive principles.[9] The school was defined by its substantive boundaries, namely, by a certain body of positive doctrine that clearly identified the outer limits of the school, limits beyond which the jurist ventured only at the risk of being considered to have abandoned his *madhhab* (legal school). An essential part of the school's authority, therefore, was its consistency in identifying such a body of doctrine that was formed of the totality of the founder's opinions, substantive principles, and legal methodology, be they genuinely his or merely attributed to him.[10] Added to this were the doctrines of later jurists deemed to have formulated legal norms in accordance with the founder's substantive and theoretical principles. In other words, Islamic law represented the total sum of doctrinal accretions beginning with the founder down to any point of time in the history of the school.

The multiplicity of doctrinal narrative resulted in the development of a technical terminology whose purpose was to distinguish between types of legal opinion. The evolution of this terminology was symptomatic of the staggering variety of opinion that resulted from a fundamental structural and epistemological feature in Islamic law, a feature that emerged early on and was to determine the later course of legal development. Its root cause was perhaps the absence of a central legislative agency—a role that could have been served by the state or the office of the caliphate but was not. The power to determine what the law was had lain instead, from the very beginning, in the hands of the legal specialists, the *proto-fuqaha'*, and later the fuqaha' themselves. It was these men who undertook the task of elaborating on the legal significance of the revealed texts, and it was they who finally established a legal epistemology that depended in its entirety on the premise of an individualistic interpretation of the law. This feature was to win for Islamic law, in modern scholarship, the epithet "jurist's law." The ultimate manifestation of this individual hermeneutical activity was the doctrine of *kull mujtahid musib*, that is, that each and every *mujtahid* is correct.[11] The legitimation of this activity and the plurality that it produced had already been articulated as a matter of theory by as early a figure as Shafi'i.[12] It was also as a result of this salient feature that juristic disagreement, properly known as *khilaf* or *ikhtilaf*, came to be regarded as one of the most important fields of learning and enquiry, a field in which the opinions of a veritable who's who of jurists were studied and discussed.[13]

This feature of what we might term *ijtihadic* pluralism had already become part of the epistemology that was integral to the overall structure and operation of the law. Its permanency is evidenced by the fact that, even after the final evolution of the madhhab, plurality could not be curbed: the old multiplicity of opinion that had emerged before the rise of the madhhabs conflated with the plurality that surfaced later at every juncture of Islamic history.

If legal pluralism was there to stay—a fact that the jurists never questioned—then it had to be somehow controlled in the interest of consistency and judicial process, for doctrinal uncertainty was detrimental. Which of the two, three, or four opinions available should the judge adopt in deciding cases or the jurisconsult opt for in issuing *fatwas*? The discourse of the jurists, in the hundreds of major works that we have at our disposal, is overwhelmingly preoccupied by this problem: which is the most authoritative opinion? No reader, even a casual one, can miss either the direct or oblique references to this difficult question. Of course, the problem was not couched in terms of plurality and pluralism, for that would have amounted to stating the obvious. Rather, the problem was expressed as one of trying to determine the most sound or most authoritative opinion, although without entirely excluding the possibility that subjectivity—as is admitted in all legal systems—might influence the decision. It is no exaggeration to maintain therefore that one of the central aims of most legal works was precisely to determine which opinion was sound and which less so, if at all. As in all legal systems, consistency and certainty are not only a desideratum but also indispensable. In short, it cannot be overstated that reducing the multiplicity to a single authoritative opinion was seen as absolutely essential for achieving the highest possible degree of both consistency and predictability. However, it must be emphasized here that plurality was not seen as a problem. To the contrary, and as has been concluded elsewhere,[14] it was viewed as conducive to both legal flexibility and legal change.

The same system that produced and maintained legal pluralism also produced the means to deal with the difficulties that this pluralism presented. Legal theory was based on the premise that the activity of discovering the law was both purely hermeneutical and totally individualistic. The allowances that were given to personal ijtihad created, within the theory itself, the realization that, epistemologically and judicially, pluralism had to be subjected to a further hermeneutical process by which plurality was reduced to a minimum. Different opinions on a single matter had to be pitted against each other in a bid to find out which of them was epistemologically the soundest or the weightiest. This elimination by comparison was in theoretical discourse termed *tarjih*, or preponderance, namely, weighing conflicting or incongruent evidence. Here evidence should be understood as the totality of the components making up the opinion itself: the revealed text from which the legal norm was derived, its modes of transmission, the qualifications and integrity of the transmitters, and the quality of linguistic and inferential reasoning employed in formulating the opinion.

The theoretical account of tarjih represents, in general terms, the methodological terrain in which the jurists were trained to deal with all conceivable possibilities of conflict in textual evidence and in the methods of legal reasoning. Their knowledge of all the issues involved in preponderance equipped them for the world of positive law where theory met with legal practice. It is with this arsenal of legal knowledge of the theoretical principles of preponderance that the jurists tackled the problem of legal pluralism and plurality of opinion. These principles provided the epistemic and methodological starting point for the operative terminology used in the determination of substantive law.

Law treatises are replete with statements declaring certain opinions to be correct (*sahih*), more correct (*asahh*), widespread (*mashhur*), and so on.[15] These terms are emblematic of a complex juristic activity that involves a proficient handling of the fundamentals of preponderance as expounded in works of legal theory. But as an organic part of the environment of substantive law that includes as one of its essential components the school's authoritative and long-established positive doctrine, the authorization of opinion was bound to take into account both the methodological and the substantive principles of the school. Thus, in realistic terms it acquired a complexity that exceeded that observed in the discourse of legal theory.

Despite (or perhaps because of) the fact that a staggering number of opinions are determined in terms of sahih or mashhur, the authors of law books seldom bother to demonstrate for the reader the process by which an opinion was subjected to these processes of authorization. This phenomenon, I think, is not difficult to explain. Authorization usually involved a protracted discussion of textual evidence and lines of legal

29

reasoning whose aim was often not only the justification of rules as such but also the defense of the madhhab. Most works, or at least those available to us, do shy away from providing such self-indulgent detail. The Hanafi Ibn Ghanim al-Baghdadi, for instance, explains the problem in his introduction to *Majma' al-Damanat*, where he states, "Except for a few cases, I have not included the lines of reasoning employed in the justification of the rules, because this book is not concerned with verification (*tahqiq*).[16] Our duty is rather limited to showing which [opinion] is sahih and which is asahh."[17] The task of "verifying" the opinions was not only too protracted but also intellectually demanding. It is precisely this achievement of "verifying" all available opinions pertaining to one case and declaring one of them to be the strongest that gave Nawawi and Rafi'i such a glorious reputation in the Shafi'i school and Ibn Qudama the same reputation in the Hanbali school.[18] This was an achievement of few during the entire history of the four schools.

In his magisterial *Majmu'*, Nawawi sometimes, but by no means frequently, explains the reasoning involved in *tashih*. Consider the following examples, the first of which pertains to the types of otherwise impermissible food that a Muslim can eat should he find himself, say, in a desert where lawful food is not to be had:

> Our associates held that the impermissible foods which a person finds himself compelled to eat are of two types: intoxicating and non-intoxicating. . . . As for the non-intoxicant type, all foods are permitted for consumption as long as these do not involve the destruction of things protected under the law (*itlaf ma'sum*). He who finds himself compelled to eat is permitted to consume carrion, blood, swine meat, urine, and other impure substances. There is no juristic disagreement (*khilaf*) as to whether he is permitted to kill fighters against Islam and apostates and to eat them. There are two *wajh*-opinions[19] [though] concerning the married fornicator (*zani muhsan*),[20] rebels and those who refuse to pray (*tarik al-salat*). The more correct of the two opinions (*asahh*) is that he is permitted [to kill and eat them]. Imam al-Haramayn, the author [Shirazi],[21] and the majority of jurists (*jumhur*) conclusively affirm the rule of permissibility. [In justification of permissibility] Imam al-Haramayn maintained that this is because the prohibition [imposed on individual Muslims] to kill these is due to the power delegated to governing authority (*tafwidan ila al-sultan*), so that the exercise of this power is not

preempted. When a dire need to eat arises, then this prohibition ceases to hold.[22]

Juwayni's reasoning here was used by Nawawi to achieve two purposes: the first to present Juwayni's own reason for adopting this wajh-opinion and the second to use the same reasoning to show why Nawawi himself thought this opinion to be the more correct of the two. Thus, the absolute legal power of the sultan to execute married fornicators, rebels, and prayer deserters is preempted by the private individual's need to eat, should he or she face starvation.

Note here that Nawawi gives only the line of reasoning underlying the opinion that he considers to be more correct of the two despite the fact that the other wajh-opinion is admitted as sahih. This was the general practice of authors, a practice that has an important implication: if another jurist thought the second, sahih opinion to be in effect superior to the one identified by Nawawi as the asahh, then it was the responsibility of that jurist to retrieve from the authoritative sources the line of reasoning sustaining that opinion and to show how it outweighed the arguments of Juwayni and of others. In fact, this was the invariable practice since nowhere does one encounter a reprimand or a complaint that the author failed to present the lines of reasoning in justification of what he thought to be the less authoritative or correct opinion(s).

There was no need to present the evidence of non-sahih opinions because they were by definition negligible—not worth, as it were, the effort.[23] These opinions became known as *fasid* (void), *da'if* (weak), *shadhdh* (irregular), or *gharib* (unknown), terms that never acquired any fixed meaning and remained largely interchangeable.[24] No particular value was attached to any of them, for just as in the study of hadith, a da'if report was dismissed out of hand. A premium, on the other hand, was placed on the category of the sahih and its cognate, the asahh. At first, it might seem self-evident that the asahh is by definition superior to the sahih. But this is not the case. Claiming sahih status for an opinion necessarily implies that the competing opinion or opinions are not sahih but rather da'if, fasid, shadhdh, or gharib.[25] But declaring an opinion asahh means that the competing opinions are sahih, no less. Thus, in two cases, one having a sahih opinion and the other an asahh opinion, the former would be considered, in terms of authoritative status, superior to the latter since the sahih had been taken a step further in declaring the competing opinion(s) weak or irregular, whereas the asahh had not been. In other words, the sahih ipso facto marginalizes the competing opinions, whereas the asahh does not, this having the effect that the competing opinion(s) in the case of the asahh continue(s) to retain the status of sahih. The practical implication of this epistemic gradation is that it was possible for the opinions that had competed with the asahh to be used as a basis for *ifta'*, or court decisions, whereas those opinions which had competed with the sahih could no longer serve any purpose once the sahih had been identified (that is, unless a *mujtahid* or a capable jurist were to reassess one of these weak opinions and vindicate it as being more sound than that which had been declared earlier as sahih; this, in fact, was one means by which legal change took place).[26]

This epistemic evaluation of tashih was usually helpful in assessing opinions between and among a number of jurists belonging to one school. At times, however, it was necessary to evaluate opinions within the doctrinal corpus of a single jurist, in which case the sahih and the asahh would acquire different values. If a case has only two opinions and the jurist declares one to be sahih and the other asahh, then the latter is obviously the more preponderant one. But if the case has three or more opinions, then the principles of evaluation as applied to the larger school doctrine would apply here too. It is to be noted, however, that these principles of evaluation were generally, but by no means universally, accepted. Disagreements about the comparative epistemic value of tashih or *tashhir* (the rendering of an opinion as mashhur) persisted and were never resolved, a fact abundantly attested to by the informative account penned by the last great Hanafi jurist Ibn 'Abidin (d. 1252/1836).[27]

The more important point to be made here is the basis on which opinions were authorized. In some cases, the basis was purely hermeneutical in the sense that doctrinal considerations of established principles dictated a certain extension of these principles. In other cases, it was based on considerations of customary practices (*'ada*) and of social need and necessity. In fact, the latter consideration is cited as grounds for abandoning an otherwise sahih opinion in favor of another that would become on these very grounds the sahih. The Hanafi jurist Ibn 'Abidin argues this much: "Not every sahih [opinion] may be used as a basis for issuing fatwas because another opinion may be adopted out of necessity (*darura*) or due to its being more agreeable to changing times and similar considerations. This latter opinion, which is designated as fit for ifta' (*fi-hi lafz al-fatwa*), includes two things, one of which is its suitability for issuing fatwas, the other is its correctness (*sihhatihi*), because using it as the basis of ifta' is in itself [an act] by which it is corrected (*tashih la-hu*)."[28] These notions of tashih did not remain a matter of theory or an unaccomplished ideal. In his *al-Fatawa al-Khayriyya*, Khayr al-Din al-Ramli offers a substantial collection of questions which were addressed to him and which he answered with opinions that had been corrected (*sahhahahu*) by the leading Hanafi scholars on the basis of considerations having to do with changing requirements of the age and of society.[29]

Needless to say, the basis of tashih may also be any of the considerations articulated in the theory of preponderance. Illustrations of such considerations, especially those related to Sunnaic textual evidence, abound.[30] Obviously, the purposes of authorization through tashih, tashhir, and other concepts fundamentally differ from those of defending the madhhab, but the processes involved in both activities are very much the same: they are offshoots of *tarjih* or adaptations thereof.

Preponderance, as we have seen, depends in part on corroboration by other members of a class, which is to say that it is subject to inductive corroboration by an aggregate body of the same type of evidence. Thus, a tradition transmitted by a certain number of channels and transmitters was considered superior to another transmitted by fewer channels and transmitters. Similarly, a *ratio legis* attested by more than one text was deemed to outweigh another supported by a single text. Consensus itself, epistemologically the most powerful sanctioning authority, depended on universal corroboration. Thus, what we have called inductive corroboration no doubt constituted a fundamental feature of legal thinking, both in the theory of preponderance and elsewhere in the law.[31]

It is perhaps with this all-important notion in mind that we might appreciate the controversy that found its way into the discourse on the sahih. Taj al-Din al-Subki reports that in his magisterial work *al-Muharrar*, Rafi'i was rumoured to have determined opinions to be sahih on the basis of what the majority of leading Shafi'i considered to fall into this category,[32] this majority being determined by an inductive survey of the opinions of individual jurists. Ramli reiterated this perception of Rafi'i's endeavor and added that he did so because maintaining the authority of school doctrine is tantamount to transmitting it, which is to say that authority is a devolving tradition that is continually generated by a collectivity of individual transmissions. He immediately adds, however, that preponderance by number is particularly useful when two (or more) opinions are of the same weight.[33]

Be that as it may, tashih on the basis of number or majority appears to have become a standard, especially, if not exclusively, when all other considerations seemed equal. Ibn al-Salah maintained that if the jurist cannot determine which opinion is the sahih because the evidence and reasoning in all competing opinions under investigation appear to him to be of equal strength, he must nonetheless decide which is the sahih and preponderant opinion according to three considerations in descending order of importance: superior number or majority, knowledge, and piety.[34] Thus, an opinion would be considered sahih if more jurists considered it to be such than they did another. The tashih of a highly learned jurist outweighs that of a less knowledgeable one and that of a pious jurist superior to another of a less pious one. In the same vein, an opinion held to be sahih by a number of jurists would be considered superior to another held as such by a single jurist, however learned he may be. The same preference is given to a learned jurist over a pious one. Thus, tashih operates both within and between these categories.

That number is important should in no way be surprising. The entire enterprise and concept of the madhhab is based on group affiliation to a set of doctrines, considered to have an authoritative core. Reducing plurality through number or any other means was certainly a desideratum. It is therefore perfectly reasonable to find the Maliki Hattab declaring, like many others, that the descending order of number, knowledge, and piety is a denominator common to all four schools.[35]

Tashih and tashhir (the latter having particular importance in the Maliki school) did not alone bear the burden of authorization. The four schools resorted to other means, each of which was labeled with what we have called an operative term. Leaving aside any consideration of their order of importance, these terms were as follows: *rajih, zahir, awjah, ashbah, sawab, madhhab, mafti bi-hi, ma'mul bi-hi,* and *mukhtar.* Together with the sahih, the mashhur, and their derivatives, these constituted the backbone of the operative discourse of substantive law. Of these, two are most relevant to my argument here, namely, the madhhab and mafti bi-hi.

The term "madhhab" acquired different meanings throughout Islamic history. Its earliest use was merely to signify the opinion or opinions of a jurist, such as in the pronouncement that the madhhab of so and so in a *particular* case is such and such.[36] Later the term acquired a more technical sense. During and after the formation of the schools, it was used to refer to the *totality* of the *corpus juris* belonging to a leading mujtahid, be he a founder of a school or not. In this formative period, the term also meant the doctrine adopted by a founder and by those of his followers, this doctrine being considered cumulative and accretive. Concomitant with this, if not somewhat earlier, appeared the notion of madhhab as a corporate entity in the sense of an integral school to which individual jurists considered themselves to belong. This was the personal meaning of the madhhab, in contrast to its purely doctrinal meaning, which was expressed as loyalty to a general body of doctrine.

There was at least one other important sense of the term that deserves our attention here, namely, the individual opinion, accepted as the most authoritative in the collective doctrinal corpus of the school. In order to distinguish it from the other meanings of the word "madhhab," we will assign to it the compound expression "madhhab-opinion."

In this doctrinal sense, the term "madhhab" meant the opinion adopted as the most authoritative in the school. Unlike the sahih and the mashhur, there were no particular or fixed criteria for determining what the madhhab-opinion was since it might be based on general acceptance on the grounds of tashih, tashhir, or some other basis. Yet it was possible that the madhhab-opinion could be different, say, from a sahih-opinion.[37] However, the most fundamental feature of the madhhab-opinion remained its general acceptance as the most authoritative in the school, including its widespread practice and application in courts and fatwas. This type of opinion is to be distinguished from the mashhur, in that the latter is deemed widespread among a majority, but not the totality, of jurists belonging to a school. This explains why the madhhab-opinion could not be, as a rule, outweighed by another, competing opinion.

A distinctive feature of the madhhab-opinion was its status as the normative opinion in legal application and practice. It is precisely here that an organic connection between fatwa and madhhab-opinion was forged—the fatwa being a reflection of litigation and the legal concerns of mundane social life.[38] Hattab's commentary on the matter eloquently speaks of this connection: the term "*al-madhhab*," he remarked, was used by the more recent jurists (*muta'akhkhirun*) of all the schools to refer to the opinion issued in fatwas. He also remarked, conversely, that any fatwa issued on the basis of something other than the madhhab-opinion ought not to be taken into account (*la yakun la-ha'i'tibar*).[39] In these pronouncements of Hattab, two important matters must be noted: first, that the connection between fatwa practice and the term "madhhab (-opinion)" is one that appeared among the muta'akhkhirun, not among the *mutaqaddimun*, that is, the early jurists who flourished between the second/eighth and fourth/tenth centuries, a period in which the schools were formed,[40] and second, that the fatwa practice defines the general body of madhhab-opinion in any given school.

But how did the jurist know which opinion constituted the standard basis of fatwas or the madhhab-opinion? This became one of the most urgent questions, constituting a serious challenge to later jurists for whom the determination of the most authoritative school doctrine was essential. Nawawi provides an answer:

> You ought to know that law books of the school contain significant disagreements among the associates, so much so that the reader cannot be confident that a certain author's opinion expresses the madhhab-opinion until he, the reader, deciphers the majority of the school's well-known law books. . . . This is why (in my book) I do not exclude the mention of any of Shafi'i's opinions, of the wajh-opinions,[41] or other opinions even if they happen to be weak or insignificant. . . . In addition, I also mention that which is preponderant, and show the weakness of that which is weak . . . and stress the error of him who held it, even though he may have been a distinguished jurist (*min al-akabir*). . . . I also take special care in perusing the law books of the early and more recent associates down to my own time, including the comprehensive works (*mabsutat*), the abridgements (*mukhtasarat*), and the recensions of the school founder's doctrine, Shafi'i. . . . I have also read the fatwas of the associates and their various writings on legal theory, biographies, hadith-annotation, as well as other works. . . . You should not be alarmed when at times I mention many jurists who held an opinion different from that of the majority or from the mashhur, etc., for if I omit the names of those constituting the majority it is because I do not wish to prolong my discussion since they are too many to enumerate.[42]

Nawawi did not live long enough to conclude his ambitious project, having completed only about a third of it by the time of his death. Yet for him to know what was the madhhab-opinion was in each case, he felt compelled to investigate the great majority of what he saw as the most important early and later works. Hidden between the lines of this passage is the fundamental assumption that in order to identify the basis of fatwa practice, one must know what the generally accepted doctrine was. Only an intimate knowledge of the contents of the legal works written throughout the centuries could have revealed which opinions remained in circulation—that is, in practice—and which had become obsolete. It is precisely this knowledge that became a desideratum, and this is why the subject of *khilaf* was so important. The study of khilaf was the means by which the jurist came to know what the madhhab-opinions were. Law students, for instance, are often reported to have studied law, *madhhaban wa-khilafan*, under a particular teacher. The Maliki Ibn 'Abd al-Barr emphatically states that for one to be called a jurist (faqih), he must be adept at the science of khilaf, for this was par excellence the means by which the jurist could determine which opinions represented the authoritative doctrines of the madhhab.[43]

Although the determination of the madhhab-opinion was more an inductive survey than a hermeneutical–epistemological engagement, it nonetheless entailed some difficulties, not unlike those the jurists faced in deciding what the sahih and the mashhur opinions were. In his notable effort, Nawawi himself did rather well on this score, which explains his prestige and authority in the Shafi'i school. Nonetheless, he and Rafi'i are said to have erred in about fifty cases, claiming them to be madhhab-opinions when they were thought by many not to be so.[44] The following case from the *Fatawa* of Taqi al-Din al-Subki further illustrates the uncertainty involved:

> Two men die, one owing a debt to the other. Each leaves minor children behind. The guardian of the minors, whose father was the lender, establishes against the debtor's children the outstanding debt in a court of law. Should the execution of the judgement (in favour of the first party) be suspended until the defendants (viz., the debtor's children) reach majority, or should the guardian take the oath (and have the debt be paid back)? . . . The madhhab-opinion is the latter. However, he who investigates the

37

matter might think that the madhhab-opinion is that the judgment should await implementation (till the children reach majority), but this may lead to the loss of their rights. By the time the debtor's children attain majority, the money may well have vanished at the hands of the debtor's heirs.[45]

Note here the ambiguity as to which of the two is the madhhab-opinion. Subki identifies immediate execution of the judgment as the madhhab-opinion, while at the same time he also admits that anyone who investigates the matter will find that the opposing opinion has the same status. Subki does not even go so far as to claim that the one who espouses the latter is mistaken.

Be that as it may, the term "madhhab," when referring to an individual opinion, was used to determine what the law on a particular case was. And the criterion for acquiring this status was general acceptance and the fact of its being standard practice in the school. The madhhab-opinions therefore gained authoritative status because they were used predominantly as the basis of issuing fatwas. The Shafi'i Ramli declares that the jurist's most important task is to determine which opinions in his school are regularly applied (*mutadawala*) in the practice of ifta' since this will determine the authoritative madhhab-opinions.[46] In his widely known work *Multaqa al-Abhur*, the Hanafi Halabi also considered his chief task to be the determination of which opinions were the most authoritative. It turns out that next to the sahih and the asahh, the most weighty opinions were those "chosen for fatwas" (*al-mukhtar lil-fatwa*).[47] In the Maliki school, the authoritative category of the mashhur was in part determined by the common practice of ifta'. Hattab maintains that tashhir is determined, among other things, by the mafti bi-hi, the opinions predominantly adopted by the jurisconsults.[48] At the risk of repetition, it is important at this point to recall Ibn 'Abidin's statement that reflected the centuries-old practice of his school: "Not every sahih [opinion] may be used as a basis for issuing fatwas because another opinion may be adopted out of necessity (*darura*) or due to its being more agreeable to changing times and the likes of such considerations. This latter opinion, which is designated as fit for ifta' (*fi-hi lafz al-fatwa*), includes two things, one of which is its suitability for issuing fatwas, the other its correctness (sihhatihi), because using it as the basis of ifta' is in itself [an act] by which it is corrected (*tashih la-hu*)."[49]

Similarly, the rules that were commonly applied, that is, the maʿmul bi-hi, acquired paramount importance as the authoritative doctrine of the school. Like the mafti bi-hi, the maʿmul bi-hi formed the basis of tashhir in the Maliki school,[50] the assumption being that the authoritative opinions of Malik, Ibn al-Qasim, and those of the later mujtahids make up the foundations of dominant judicial practice. In his commentary on Nawawi's *Minhaj*, the Shafiʿi Ramli purportedly included in his work only those opinions that were in predominant use, and whenever citing weaker opinions, he alerted the reader to this fact by distinguishing between the two types.[51] In the Hanafi school, the madhhab-opinion was organically linked both to fatwa and to *ʿamal* (practice). No fatwa was to be considered valid or at least authoritative unless it was backed by the judicial practice of the community (*ʿalayhi ʿamal al-umma*).[52] Ibn Hajar al-Haytami summed up the entire issue when he said that "ʿalayhi al-ʿamal" was a tarjih formula used to determine which opinions are correct and authoritative.[53] Conversely, an opinion that is not resorted to in judicial practice will become obsolete, and therefore negligible, if not altogether needless. Speaking of authorial practices, Tufi argues that the author–jurist must not, as a rule, record those opinions that are not relevant to practice, for "they are needless."[54]

Since practice varied from one region to another, an opinion thought to have gained wide circulation in one region might not have been regarded as such in another, an added factor in the disagreement over which opinion was deemed authoritative in the school and which not. The Maliki discourse on this matter perhaps best illustrates the difficulties involved. Ibn Farhun states that the commonly used formula "This is the prevailing practice in this matter" (*al-ladhi jara al-ʿamal bi-hi fi hadhihi al-masʾala*) cannot be generalized to include all domains in which a particular school prevailed. Rather, such a formula would have been applicable only to that region or locale in which the practice had prevailed. This explains, he maintains, why the jurists attempted to restrict the applicability of the formula by adding to it expressions like "in such and such region" (*fi balad kadha*). Otherwise, if they did not qualify the formula, then the opinion would be said to be universally applicable. The opinion's purported universality was in itself an argument in favor of its preponderance as the authoritative opinion of the school no matter where the opinion might be appealed to. Ibn Farhun also asserts that the principle of authorization by dominant practice is accepted by the Shafi'i as well.[55] To the Shafi'i, he might as well have added the Hanafi, who, as we have seen and as we will further see in the next chapter, placed great stress on dominant practice as a legitimizing factor. The Hanbali, on the other hand, appear to have laid slightly less stress on it than any of the other schools, if we are to judge by what seems to have been a lower statistical frequency of explicit reference to practice in their works. But this is by no means correct in all cases. In his *Muntaha al-Iradat*, for instance, Ibn al-Najjar considers practice (*'alayhi al-'amal*) to be a preponderating factor, standing on a par with tashih and tashhir.[56]

The foregoing discussion has shown that operative terminology evolved as a response to the plurality and thus indeterminacy of legal rules. All operative terms had in common a single purpose, namely, the determination of *the* authoritative opinion on any given case, a determination that amounted in effect to reducing plurality to a single opinion. Epistemologically, this determination and the varied vocabulary that expressed it stood as the binary opposite of ijtihad. The latter created multiplicity, while the former attempted to suppress or at least minimize it. Ijtihad, then, was causally connected with operative terminology, for it stood as its progenitor, historically, hermeneutically, and epistemologically.

A salient feature of operative terminology that evolved as a response to the indeterminacy of legal rules is its own indeterminacy. Yet juristic disagreement was indeed a blessing, a *rahma*, as the jurists might have said. The very diversity of opinion that resulted from this failure allowed Islamic law to keep up with change, a theme that I have discussed in detail elsewhere.[57] (It is worth noting in passing that recent findings[58] to the effect that the mechanisms of change were integral to the very structure of Islamic law raise the question of why the so-called legal reforms were so massive, drastic, and destructive of the established legal structures.)

III

Thus, the traditional jurists operated within a self-sufficient system in which practice, hermeneutics, and positive legal doctrine were conjoined to produce the legal culture, which largely defined their world. Practice stood in a dialectical relationship with doctrine, informing it and by which it was informed. Practice also formed an integral part of interpretation and was by no means a mere tail-end of a process, a funnel through which justice was disposed. The legal practitioners and jurists constituted likewise an *epistemic* community, which was systematically engaged on a hermeneutical level. Their practice was both pragmatic and discursive and was the direct result of a legal tradition that bound them with the authoritative demands of doctrine and continuity. Their present was primarily the last moment of a historical tradition, integral to and inseparable from it. When a qadi or a mufti adjudicated a case or a question, his engagement epitomized at once horizontal and vertical fields of synchronic and historic legal activity: it brought into play 1) the hermeneutical presuppositions of legal theory and methodology and the exegetical arsenal associated with it throughout centuries of refinement and evolution; 2) the principles of positive law,[59] which had been constructed as part of the founders' authority, which in turn was seen as the founding principle of the school as a doctrinal entity;[60] 3) the aggregate but diverse body of knowledge generated by the authoritative figures of the school in the interpretation of these principles; and 4) the reception of these interpretations by the community of jurists within the school, a reception determined by the extent of the interpretive applications in the social, mundane order.

The coming into play of these diachronic and synchronic elements was integrated into other parts of juristic and pedagogical experiences: The qadi or the mufti (or any legal professional for that matter) engaged himself, at one and the same time, in a tradition in which 1) he acquired legal education through the method of "closed texts," which, together with the *ijaza* (license) system, constituted a fundamentally different sort of training from that which the modern law school offered; 2) he was apprenticed, during and after his graduate study, in shari'a courts where doctrine met practice and where the imposing intellectualism of the law collided, but was always synthesized, with the reality of society and judicial practice; 3) the religious ethic was the sole dominating force and the final arbiter of legal legitimacy; 4) the entire juristic (doctrinal) and judicial enterprise was thoroughly supported by financially and administratively self-sufficient and independent institutions; and 5) the authority of the jurist was individualistic and exclusively personal (ijtihadic).

None of these elements continues to exist in the modern legal systems of Muslim countries, and what remains of the traditional system, as we have already said, are remnants of mutilated doctrine patched up in a disparate and methodologically deficient manner. Even if we submit that these remnants are faithful to the Islamic ethos as it stands nowadays—which we do not—they are, by virtue of their displacement and organic disconnection from the erstwhile dynamic and vibrant school tradition, incapable of further development and change, at least not so in a systematic and coherent manner; on the one hand, they have lost their methodological, hermeneutical, practice-based, and institutional connection with the Islamic legal tradition. If the name *furu'* (branches) is to be taken in any real sense, as it well may be, then their stem, through which they are literally nourished, no longer survives. On the other hand, they have been systematically alienated from the modernist legal system, and their disconnection from it is equally obvious.

To put our argument more plainly, in order to rejuvenate the entire traditional system—in its founding principles, axioms, hermeneutics, and financial, educational, and madhhab institutions—it would be required that Islamic law be more than a dead "branch." And this, in light of the intractable and well-nigh irreversible modernity and its imperatives, is a manifest impossibility.[61] Since traditional shari'a can surely be said to have gone without return, the question that poses itself therefore is, Can a form of Islamic law be created from within or without the ruins of the old system?

Before attempting an answer to this intricate question, an explanation must be provided as to the assumption underlying this question, namely, the posited necessity for today's Muslims to live by a religious law. Since the middle of the nineteenth century, Muslim societies have embarked on a course of identity crisis caused, among other things, by the disappearance from their daily lives of the religious structures that sustained them for over a millennium. One of these structures, and a central one at that, was Islamic law as a religious and pragmatic system. To say that this law was "the core and kernel" of Islamic life is indeed to state the obvious. Thus, for these societies to regain their cultural and religious identities, a form of Islamic law must obtain—and this for two good reasons. First, historically, Islamic societies have lived by a religious law for over twelve centuries, and what made their identities what they have always been was their possession of a particular legal phenomenon. Islam has always been a nomocracy. Indeed, Islamic societies and polities have throughout these centuries exemplified the highest form of what a nomocracy can be. Second, it is at present inconceivable that Muslims can or will want to transform their Weltanschauung into a Western model of rationality and secularism. They view the modernity of the West as incompatible with their vision of morality and ethics, as having miserably failed in maintaining the social fabric and in creating a coherent worldview or a meaningful cosmology. The truth claims of Western reason and modernity seem diametrically oppositional and extremely antithetical to the Islamic ethos. The "return to Islam" that we have been witnessing since the Iranian Revolution is partly caused by this disenchantment with Western culture and its products. The solution for Muslims seems to lie in an institutional and normative revival of Islam. It would appear that the legality and legalmindedness that governed Muslim life for so many centuries is again required to surface in order to redress the havoc that the problems of cultural and religious crises have wreaked.

Joseph Schacht once argued that the problems that modern Muslims face are parallel to those that prevailed during the early formation of Islamic law, namely, the first two Islamic centuries:

> [T]he subject matter of Islamic law is to a great extent not originally Islamic, let alone Koranic; it became Islamic law only through having the categories of Islamic jurisprudence imposed on it. Islamic jurisprudence derived its fundamental attitude from the Koran, elaborated and developed it, and thereby created an integrating principle which made of an agglomerate of various elements a unique phenomenon *sui generis*. During the first two centuries of Islam, Islamic jurisprudence created a central core of ideas and institutions which went far beyond the mere contents and even the implications of the Koran, but which the Muslims considered and have continued to consider specifically Islamic. . . . This assimilating power of the Islamic core over foreign elements anticipated the assimilating power and spiritual ascendancy of Islamic law, as a religious ideal, over the practice, after the two had irremediably separated.[62]

Schacht's views represent a major voice in the discourse that was generated—and is still being generated—by the colonizing cultures. In the spirit of this discourse, he persistently upheld the idea that a fundamental gap had always existed between doctrine and practice in Islam[63] and that if Muslims could live with this gap for so many centuries, then why should they not be able to do so now. In other words, Schacht believes that modern Muslims can construct a new jurisprudence and law, but they must continue to live with the fact that much of what they "assimilate" will always go beyond the dictates of the Qur'an. Just as they initially assimilated Jewish, Roman, and other legal institutions and concepts that had dominated the ancient Near East, they can now do the same with Western norms and institutions.

Be that as it may, Schacht's position fails to appreciate the detail of the two historical situations that he sees as parallel. First, when the early Muslims embarked on constructing a legal system and jurisprudence, they—of course unknowingly—were unencumbered by, and in fact largely free from, restrictive and constricting historical precedents or a binding tradition. This is not the case at present. Their movement therefore is detained, if not also limited, by the fact that departures from traditional, *religious* doctrine must be constantly justified (justification here is taken to be no less than the art of persuasion on which hinges the success or failure of a proposed enterprise). The doctrines of usul al-fiqh constitute a powerful grip over the minds of Muslims today, for they are intimately connected with the holy texts. No refashioning of doctrine or jurisprudence can even take off without due considerations of the imperatives that the usul theory dictates. Second, when the early Muslims embarked on constructing a law and a legal system, they did so from a position of international hegemonic power, a fact that allowed them to speak and act with confidence. Whatever they appropriated from other cultures became theirs, especially in light of the fundamental transformations to which they subjected borrowed concepts and institutions. The present situation is significantly different: modernity is a Western product, a fact poignantly obvious to everyone. On both popular and state levels, today's Muslims perceive themselves, and rightly so, as colonized and dominated subjects, and whatever they adopt of Western ideas and institutions is not, and will never be, theirs. The balance of power, which determines the legitimacy of cultural and other appropriations, is simply not in their favor. Third, and issuing from our foregoing consideration, the balance of legal power does not lie in the hands of the religious–legal specialists who were exclusively, individually and collectively, responsible for constructing early Islamic jurisprudence and law. The modern state's appropriation of legal powers changes the old equation and, as we have seen, totally marginalizes even the potential contributions of the individual shari'a-minded jurists (assuming that these now exist). And as long as the modern Muslim states remain vassal-like entities in relation to the Western hegemonic powers, their dedication to the Islamic imperatives will always remain vacuous, especially in light of the close control that the West, especially the United States, has been exercising over politics and the religious movements in the Muslim world.

IV

If the modern reality of Muslims is unprecedented, then what is the solution? First of all, the traditional theory of *usul al-fiqh* is no longer sufficient to deal with the exigencies of modern life, even if we assume—against all odds—that a professional legal class, qualified to harness it, can be resurrected. This theory is essentially literalist, paying heed to the lexical and technical meanings of the revealed texts. In some cases, central to society and economy, no amount of interpretation can change the dictates of certain revealed texts. This theory therefore has no chance of any revival (much less success) unless a necessary and sufficient condition is met, a condition some recent Muslim intellectuals are arguing for, namely, the abandonment of all things, material and otherwise, that conflict or contradict with the dictates of this theory. In other words, on their view, much of modernity must be thrown to the wastebasket, for it is not only incongruent with Islam but also harmful in the first place. This writer, however, begs to differ with this assessment. Modernity, as intrinsically reprehensible as it may be, is a reality that cannot be pushed aside or in any manner neutralized from the midst of Muslim life. Modernity is not only technology and science, Hollywood, McDonald's, and Calvin Klein jeans but also a psychology, an ethic, a set of values, an epistemology, and, in short, a state of mind and a way of life. Modernity is here to stay, at least for a long time to come. The realistic solution, therefore, is to alter what can be altered: legal theory has in any case been on the back shelf for a century and a half, and it is far more realistic and practical to remold it than to sweep modernity—with all its powerful values, institutions, and epistemologies—aside.

If traditional legal theory cannot provide a solution, then what can? Elsewhere, I have discussed in some detail the reformists' proposals toward fashioning a new theory of law and have concluded that no alternative thus far seems to meet the requirements of the time.[64] What I have labeled the "Religious Utilitarianists" fail to produce a cogent legal theory or methodology and thus offer nothing more than shallow juristic devices that at best attempt to justify the existing arbitrariness of state legislation. Their refashioned concepts of necessity (darura) and public interest (*maslaha*, *istislah*), which are inspired by traditional methodology, are taken so far as to obliterate the very system from which they themselves derive. In addition to the incurable subjectivity into which these proposals fall, they fail to provide any tools that permit a coherent, logical, or consistent development of the law. Their utilitarianist positions are barely appropriate solutions for the present, and the proposals they offer can by no means function as dynamic methodologies, organically tied to the demands of an evolving legal sociology.

The other group of reformers we have identified are the "Religious Liberalists" who offer a diversity of theories that have at their core promising nonliteralist methodologies.[65] The proposals of Fazlur Rahman and Muhammad Shahrur represent two major examples of this group. Their merit lies in the fact that they provide methodologies that maintain a coherent hermeneutical link with the religious texts but, at the same time, manage to escape the traditional literalist approach, which, in light of the drastic changes brought to the fore by modernity, is highly restrictive and leads to tortuous lines of legal reasoning. However, associated with these proposals there remain three main problems. First, none of them has been sufficiently elaborated as to create a comprehensive and structured theory, matching in caliber its traditional usul counterpart. What has been offered thus far is no more than an outline, so to speak. Second, these proposals remain circumscribed, having little appeal to Muslims at large. Rahman's ideas, for instance, were and remain a marginal voice, and Shahrur has been the subject of much negative controversy. Personally, I have yet to meet one Muslim intellectual who has adopted a favorable attitude toward him. In fact, the book market is now replete with works and pamphlets refuting or criticizing his intelligent contributions. Third, even if these proposals were received with great favor by the general Muslim public, which is clearly not the case, they have so far had no effect whatsoever on the centers of power—the state officials and political rulers who have turned a deaf ear to them as they did virtually to all others. And it is unlikely that this situation will soon change.

What we are witnessing therefore is no less than a formidable impasse. The cries of Muslim intellectuals, however promising their ideas may or may not be, are still and will remain marginalized. At the same time, the interest of the Muslim states, with their authoritarian and autocratic regimes, is little served by the adoption of a full-scale program of Islamization. The relatively very few regimes that claim themselves to be Islamic (with the exception of Saudi Arabia and Iran) take this stance as a political device and strategy. The promulgation of the *hudud* penal law hardly constitutes a genuine restoration of the shari'a and fails to mask the political expediency underlying the seemingly legal initiative. As long as the Muslim intellectuals are estranged from state apparatus and as long as the present regimes continue to hold a firm grip over power, there can be no hope for a true Islamic revival.

Yet it is only the state that can bring about a revival of Islamic law, but not without the full participation of Muslim intelligentsia and, more important, not while the present regimes remain in power. The Iranian experience affords an eloquent example of the combination of political and legal governing, but then the Shi'ite religious elite differs from its Sunnite counterpart in fundamentally structural ways. The solution for the Sunnite countries, therefore, is for the *new* Muslim state to incorporate the religious intelligentsia into its ranks. The custody of Islamic law, history has shown, must reside with a learned hierarchy largely dissociated from political power: the independence of law from the concerns of politics is as much an Islamic phenomenon as it is American or European. In fact, this independence has a much longer history in Islam. The state must re-create the necessary conditions for a modern version of Islamic law to be constructed and to evolve largely on its own. It must financially sustain religious institutions, especially shari'a colleges; it must install the religious hierarchy in the respective social and political hierarchy so as to enable the legal profession to sense and reflect societal concerns on all levels; it must be able to give this legal profession a free range in determining what the law is; and finally it must respect its verdict. But none of this can be attained without a genuinely Islamic polity.

Theory, however, is one thing, reality another. A most central and vexing problem remains, and the solution to it seems thus far untenable. The question that today's Muslims must answer is to what extent they are willing to subscribe to modernity and to adopt its products. To reject it completely is obviously out of the question: modernity, we have said, is not merely a material phenomenon but primarily one that effected a systematic restructuring of psychology and epistemology, among many other things. Accordingly, if they were to adopt of it what suits them, what is to be adopted? If commercial, corporate, and other business laws are to be adopted, as they have and as they must, can Muslims do so while escaping the snares of usurious interest?[66] If they are to join the other nations in signing human rights charters and conventions, as they have, can they, or are they willing to, enact religious laws that grant their religious minorities an equal status? If the education of women has become an essential feature of their society, can the religious law forge for the Muslim woman a commensurate status compatible with her new role in society? If this status were to be accorded, can this law, while maintaining its intellectual and religious integrity, deal with the implications and consequences of this new role? And if all this were to take place, how are the revealed texts to be interpreted?

Notes

1. Salih Ganim Sadlan, *Wujub Tatbiq al-Shari'a al-Islamiyya* (1404; reprint, Riyadh: Idarat al-Thaqafa wal-Nashr bi-Jami'at Muhammad b. Sa'ud, 1984).

2. See especially the essay by Muhammad Salih 'Uthman, *Wujub Tatbiq al-Shari'a al-Islamiyya,* 143–82, especially 176.

3. See Mustafa al-Zarqa, *Wujub Tatbiq al-Shari'a al-Islamiyya,* 227.

4. Paul Koschaker, *Europa und das römische Recht* (Munich: C. H. Becksche Verlagsbuchhandlung, 1966), 183.

5. Madeline C. Zilfi, "The *Ilmiye* Registers and the Ottoman *Medrese* System Prior to the Tanzimat," in *Contribution à l'histoire économique et sociale de l'Empire ottoman* (Leuvin: Éditions Peeters, 1993), 309–27.

6. See, for example, Nathan J. Brown, *The Rule of Law in the Arab World* (Cambridge: Cambridge University Press, 1997), 26–29, 33–40. However, the author's view that "the legal reforms of the late nineteenth and early twentieth centuries cannot be seen as an external imposition" (49) is entirely unwarranted. It is based on fragmented evidence and is inconsistent with the indisputable facts of history, including those rehearsed by the author himself (see, for example, 33–40). It also grossly ignores central facts about Islamic legal history, the nature of colonialist ven-

tures, and the pervasive effects of modernity. Furthermore, even if we go by Brown's partial and superficial explanation that the adoption of European law was the Arab nationalists' choice and means of "resisting direct European penetration," it still is the colonialist enterprise that imposed this option on the nationalists and that, wittingly or not, created severe legal ruptures in the Muslim world. The crux of Brown's explanation is the underlying assumption, adopted by a large number of Western scholars, that modernity and modernization are universal phenomena and that it is natural and expected that everyone in the world should want to adopt them. This eccentric assumption has been seriously challenged by Western social anthropologists, critical theorists, as well as others, but our field, instead of pioneering these reassessments, still labors with an archaic nineteenth-century mentality.

7. Joseph Schacht, *An Introduction to Islamic Law* (Oxford: Clarendon Press, 1964), 104.

8. Cited in H. Liebesny, *The Law of the Near and Middle East: Readings, Cases and Materials* (Albany: State University of New York Press, 1975), 67–68.

9. Namely, those principles that were elaborated in legal theory (*usul al-fiqh*) and those that governed the hermeneutical activity of taqlid in substantive law (also known as *usul*). Being fundamentally different from each other, these two types of principles must not be confused with each other. On the function of *taqlid*, see W. Hallaq, *Authority, Continuity and Change in Islamic Law* (Cambridge: Cambridge University Press, 2001), chap. 4.

10. On the construction of the Imam's authority, see Hallaq, *Authority*, 24 ff.

11. Abu Ishaq Ibrahim al-Shirazi, *Sharh al-Luma'*, ed. 'Abd al-Majid Turki, 2 vols. (Beirut: Dar al-Gharb al-Islami, 1988), 2:1043–45; Ahmad b. 'Ali Ibn Barhan, *al-Wusul ila al-Usul*, ed. 'Abd al-Hamid Abu Zunayd, 2 vols. (Riyad: Maktabat al-Ma'arif, 1404/1984), 2:341–51.

12. Muhammad b. Idris al-Shafi'i, *al-Risala*, ed. Ahmad Muhammad Shakir (Cairo: Mustafa Baba al-Halabi, 1969), 560–600; Norman Calder, "Ikhtilaf and Ijma in Shafi'i's Risala," *Studia Islamica* 58 (1984): 55–81.

13. Abu 'Umar Yusuf Ibn 'Abd al-Barr, *Jami' Bayan al-'Ilm wa-Fadlihi*, 2 vols. (Cairo: Idarat al-Tiba'a al-Muniriyya, n.d.), 2:45 ff.; G. Makdisi, *The Rise of Colleges* (Edinburgh: Edinburgh University Press, 1981), 107–11.

14. Hallaq, *Authority*, 166 ff., 236 ff.

15. On the non–sahih-opinions, see note 24.

16. Verification is the activity of the "verifiers" (*muhaqqiqun*), scholars who establish the solution to problems by means of original proof and reasoning. See Muhammad b. 'Ali al-Tahanawi, *Kashshaf Istilahat al-Funun*, 2 vols. (Calcutta: W. N. Leeds' Press, 1862), 2:336 (s.v. *tahqiq*); W. B. Hallaq, *Ibn Taymiyya against the Greek Logicians* (Oxford: Clarendon Press, 1993), 12 n. 2.

17. Ibn Ghanim Muhammad al-Baghdadi, *Majma' al-Damanat* (Cairo: al-Matba'a al-Khayriyya, 1308/1890), 3.

18. In the Hanafi school, Marghinani, among others, acquired a similar status. In Malikism, it was Ibn Rushd, Mazari, and Ibn Buzayza, although in his *Mukhtasar*, Khalil was to bring together the fruits of these and other jurists' efforts.

19. Opinions formulated by *ashab al-wujuh* or *ashab al-takhrij*. See Hallaq, *Authority*, 43 ff.

20. Since, unlike the unmarried fornicator whose punishment falls short of the death penalty, the married fornicator receives the full extent of this punishment. See Sharaf al-Din Muhyi al-Din al-Nawawi, *Rawdat al-Talibin*, ed. 'Adil 'Abd al-Mawjud and 'Ali Mu'awwad, 8 vols. (Beirut: Dar al-Kutub al-'Ilmiyya, n.d.), 7:305–6.

21. Since Nawawi's work is a commentary on Shirazi's *Muhadhdhab*, he refers to him as "The Author" (*al-musannif*), a common practice among commentators.

22. Sharaf al-Din al-Nawawi, *al-Majmu': Sharh al-Muhadhdhab*, 12 vols. (Cairo: Matba'at al-Tadamun, 1344/1925), 9:43–44.

23. For example, in his *al-Majmu'*, 1:5, Nawawi states that he will overlook the lines of reasoning in justification of weak opinions even when these opinions are of the widespread (*mashhur*) category.

24. Taqi al-Din al-Subki, *Fatawa*, 2 vols. (Cairo: Maktabat al-Qudsi, 1937), 2:10 ff.; Jalal al-Din al-Suyuti, *al-Ashbah wal-Naza'ir* (Beirut: Dar al-Kutub al-'Ilmiyya, 1979), 104; Sharaf al-Din al-Nawawi, *Tahdhib al-Asma' wal-Lughat*, 3 vols. (Cairo: Idarat al-Tiba'a al-Muniriyya, 1927), 1:94, 113, 164; 'Ala' al-Din al-Ba'li, *al-Ikhtiyarat al-Fiqhiyya* (Beirut: Dar al-Fikr, 1369/1949), 24; 'Ali b. Sulayman al-Mirdawi, *Tashih al-Furu'*, ed. 'Abd al-Sattar Farraj, 6 vols. (Beirut: 'Alam al-Kutub, 1985), 1:25, 31, 32; 'Isa b. 'Ali al-'Alami, *Kitab al-Nawazil*, 3 vols. (Rabat: Wizarat al-Awqaf wal-Shu'un al-Islamiyya, 1983), 3:6. Abu al-Khattab al-Kilwadhani (d. 510/1116) was said to have held a number of opinions not shared by the members of his school, opinions described as *tafarrudat*. These opinions, also characterized as *ghara'ib* (pl. of *gharib*, lit. unfamiliar, thus irregular), were corrected (*sahhaha*) later by Hanbali. See 'Abd al-Rahman Ibn Rajab, *al-Dhayl 'ala Tabaqat al-Hanabila*, 2 vols. (Cairo: Matba'at al-Sunna al-Muhammadiyya, 1952–1953), 1:116, 120, 126–27. It is to be noted that in some cases the opposite of the *da'if* was the *qawi* (lit. strong) or the *aqwa* (stronger), terms that were rarely used and whose technical meaning remained unfixed. See, for instance, the Hanbali 'Ala' al-Din al-Ba'li, *al-Ikhtiyarat al-Fiqhiyya* (Beirut: Dar al-Fikr, 1949), 11. The same may be said of the term *sawab* or its fuller expression *wa-hadha aqrab ila al-sawab* (this is more likely to be true or correct), which

was used infrequently to designate the status of an opinion. See, for example, 'Ala al-Din al-Kasana, *Bada'i' al-Sana'i'*, 7 vols. (Beirut: Dar al-Kitab al-'Arabi, 1982), 1:31. A very rare labeling of weak opinions is the term *quwayl*, which is the diminutive of *qawl* (opinion). See the Hanbali Shams al-Din al-Zarkashi, *Sharh al-Zarkashi 'ala Mukhtasar al-Khiraqi*, ed. 'Abd Allah al-Jabrin, 7 vols. (Riyadh: Maktabat al-'Ubaykan, 1413/1993), 1:63, 290.

25. It is quite possible that the last two, and particularly the fourth, of this quartet may have referred to opinions lacking in terms of sufficient circulation, without any consideration of correctness or soundness. However, the connection that was made between authoritative status and level of acceptance meant that widely circulated opinions were correct, whereas those that failed to gain wide acceptance were problematic. See further discussion on this issue later in this chapter.

26. See Hallaq, *Authority*, 166 ff.

27. See his splendid discussion in *Sharh al-Manzuma*, printed in his *Majmu'ar Rasa'il*, 2 vols. (n.p., 1970), 1:10–52, at 38 ff., which marshals a myriad of opinions from the early and late periods.

28. Ibn 'Abidin, *Sharh al-Manzuma*, 1:38–39.

29. Khayr al-Din al-Ramli, *al-Fatawa al-Khayriyya*, printed on the margins of Ibn 'Abidin's *al-'Uqud al-Durriyya fi Tanqih al-Fatawa al-Hamidiyya* (Cairo: al-Matba'a al-Maymuna, 1893), 3.

30. See Hallaq, *Authority*, chap. 4.

31. On this theme, see Wael B. Hallaq, "On Inductive Corroboration, Probability and Certainty in Sunni Legal Thought," in *Islamic Law and Jurisprudence: Studies in Honor of Farhat J. Ziadeh*, ed. N. Heer (Seattle: University of Washington Press, 1990), 3–31.

32. Taj al-Din al-Subki, *Tabaqat al-Shafi'iyya al-Kubra*, 6 vols. (Cairo: al-Maktaba al-Husayniyya, 1906), 5:124.

33. Shams al-Din al-Ramli, *Nihayat al-Muhtaj ila Sharh al-Minhaj*, 8 vols. (Cairo: Mustafa Babi al-Halabi, 1357/1938), 1:37.

34. Taqi al-Din Ibn al-Salah, *Adab al-Mufti wal-Mustafti*, ed. Muwaffaq b. 'Abd al-Qadir (Beirut: 'Alam al-Kutub, 1407/1986), 126.

35. Muhammad al-Hattab, *Mawahib al-Jalil li-Sharh Mukhtasar Khalil*, 6 vols. (Tarablus, Libya: Maktabat al-Najah, 1969), 6:91. See also Mirdawi, *Tashih al-Furu'*, 1:51; Nawawi, *Majmu*, 1:68.

36. For example, see Muhammad b. Idris al-Shafi'i, *al-Umm*, ed. Mahmud Matarji, 9 vols. (Beirut: Dar al-Kutub al-'Ilmiyya, 1413/1993), 2:102, 113, 136, 163, and passim.

37. Mirdawi, *Tashih al-Furu'*, 1:50–51.

38. This has been demonstrated in W. Hallaq, "From *Fatwa*s to *Furu*': Growth and Change in Islamic Substantive Law," *Islamic Law and Society* 1 (1994), 17–56, at 31–38.

39. Hattab, *Mawahib al-Jalil*, 1:24; 6:91.

40. This periodization, which is determined by our independent investigation of the madhhab evolution and the construction of authority, agrees with the traditional distinction between the "early" and "later" jurists.

41. Wajh-opinions are those formulated by *ashab al-wujuh* or *ashab al-takhrij*, jurists who flourished mainly during the third/ninth–fourth/tenth centuries. The activity of the *ashab*, however, continued on a smaller scale throughout the next three or four centuries. On these, see Hallaq, *Authority*, 43 ff.

42. Nawawi, *Majmu'*, 1:4–5.

43. Ibn 'Abd al-Barr, *Jami' Bayan al-'Ilm*, 2:43 ff.

44. Ramli, *Nihayat al-Muhtaj*, 1:38.

45. Subki, *Fatawa*, 1:324.

46. Ramli, *Nihayat al-Muhtaj*, 1:36–37.

47. Ibrahim al-Halabi, *Mulatqa al-Abhur*, ed. Wahbi al-Albani, 2 vols. (Beirut: Mu'assasat al-Risala, 1409/1989), 1:10; 2:194, 202, 207, 210, 211, and passim.

48. Hattab, *Mawahib al-Jalil*, 1:36.

49. Ibn 'Abidin, *Sharh al-Manzuma*, 1:38–39.

50. Hattab, *Mawahib al-Jalil*, 1:36.

51. Ramli, *Nihayat al-Muhtaj*, 1:9.

52. 'Ala' al-Din al-Haskafi, *al-Durr al-Mukhtar*, 8 vols. (Beirut: Dar al-Fikr, 1979), 1:72–73. See also Ibn 'Abidin, *Sharh al-Manzuma*, 38.

53. Ibn Hajar al-Haytami, *al-Fatawa al-Kubra al-Fiqhiyya*, 4 vols. (Cairo: 'Abd al-Hamid Ahmad al-Hanafi, 1938), 4:293.

54. Najm al-Din al-Tufi, *Sharh Mukhtasar al-Rawda*, ed. 'Abd Allah al-Turki, 3 vols. (Beirut: Mu'assasat al-Risala, 1407/1987), 3:626; "*idh ma la 'amala 'alayh la hajata ilayh.*"

55. Shams al-Din Ibn Farhun, *Tabsirat al-Hukkam*, 2 vols. (Cairo: al-Matba'a al-'Amira al-Sharafiyya, 1883), 1:49.

56. Taqi al-Din Ibn al-Najjar, *Muntaha al-Iradat*, 2 vols. (Cairo: Maktabat Dar al-'Uruba, 1961–1962), 1:6.

57. See Hallaq, *Authority*, chap. 6.

58. See Hallaq, *Authority*, chap. 6.

59. See note 7.

60. On the later construction of the founders' authority, see Hallaq, *Authority*, chap. 2.

61. Today, some Muslim intellectuals argue that the loss of the religious ethic is the cause of failure to apply the shari'a. They maintain that the restoration of this ethic and the regaining of the religious *Geist* will guarantee the creation of a reality in which Muslims will abandon all that is contrary to the legal ethic, thereby abandoning in the process all the evils of modernity. In other words, their argument amounts to the claim that popular conviction can change the facts on the ground, facts here meaning all that is associated with the nation-state, technology, economic modes of production, finance, consumerism, and much else. This writer, however, begs to differ. Even if this popular conviction were to obtain, there remains the problem of how to accommodate the modernist material reality within the parameters of Islamic values.

62. Joseph Schacht, "Problems of Modern Islamic Legislation," *Studia Islamica* 12 (1960), 100–101.

63. A major doctrine of Orientalist legal scholarship that was required to vindicate the colonialist enterprise generally and, more specifically, the massive legal restructuring to which the Muslim institutions and concepts were subjected.

64. Wael Hallaq, *A History of Islamic Legal Theories* (Cambridge: Cambridge University Press, 1997), chap. 6.

65. Hallaq, *A History of Islamic Legal Theories*, 231 ff.

66. In other words, can modern Islamic banking and finance still operate, as it does, in a global market and still avoid, in a true and genuine manner, engagement in usurious transactions? The experience on the ground thus far has shown this to be untenable.

CHAPTER TWO

INSCRIBING THE ISLAMIC SHARI'A IN ARAB CONSTITUTIONAL LAW

Nathan J. Brown and Adel Omar Sherif

In the vast majority of Arab states, official claims of obeisance to the principles of the Islamic shari'a are inscribed in constitutional texts derived far more from European than Islamic legal traditions. The precise formula varies from state to state, but in most constitutions a juristic paradox is created. On the one hand, the constitution presents itself as the fundamental law of the state and (usually) the expression of the will of a sovereign people; it therefore becomes the law that makes other laws possible. On the other hand, the references to the Islamic shari'a imply and sometimes explicitly state the existence of a higher or prior law.

A similar kind of paradox is quite common in many constitutional traditions. It is not uncommon to argue that the constitution itself is bound by prior or higher principles. In the United States, for instance, the Constitution treats rights as recognized—and not created—by the Constitution; unless specifically limited, those rights continue to apply, as the document itself boldly (if quite ambiguously) was amended to read: "The enumeration in the Constitution, of certain rights, shall not be construed to deny or disparage others retained by the people [Amendment IX]. The powers not delegated to the United States by the Constitution, nor prohibited by it to the States, are reserved to the States respectively, or to the people [Amendment X]." It is also common to argue (drawing partly on a natural-law tradition) that constitutions assume certain constitutional principles (such as reason or limited government) and must be interpreted in their light.[1]

Arab constitutional texts tend to sharpen this paradox for two reasons. First, the Islamic shari'a (especially as it has come to be understood in recent years) entails not merely general principles but also very specific rules.[2] But it does not always do so in a way that determines political structure. Although the Islamic shari'a is commonly referred to for the sake of simplicity as "Islamic law," even by Muslims, its nature is different and broader than this might imply. It is better seen as a method or even a code (based on religious principles) designed to inform and regulate the conduct of Muslims in *all* aspects of life, including social, commercial, domestic, criminal, and political affairs, as well as devotional practices.[3] Yet despite such comprehensiveness, the Islamic shari'a does not provide explicitly for a specific framework or a particular legal and government system. While some might therefore view the Islamic shari'a as incomplete, it is perhaps fairer to view it as flexible, leaving details of the political and legal order—including the procedures as well as substantive details—to be determined by Muslims as circumstances dictate, within the broad basic principles of shari'a.

Second, Arab constitutional texts often sharpen the paradox when they imply not merely that the shari'a must guide interpretation but also that it supersedes all other legal rules—including, perhaps, the constitution itself. The paradox is not merely theoretical or abstract: much contentious political debate (and sometimes violence) has centered on the proper relationship between the legal order devised by human beings and that derived from divine sources.

The purpose of this chapter is to answer two questions: first, how did current Arab constitutional texts take the form of inscribing the Islamic shari'a, and, second, what have been the practical effects of adopting such provisions? The first question will be answered with a broad survey of the development of Arab constitutional practice. The second question will be answered with a special focus on the most developed attempt to work out the meaning of such provisions in practice: the Egyptian Supreme Constitutional Court's interpretation of Article 2 of that country's 1971 constitution.

The Islamic Shari'a in Arab Constitutional Texts

Middle Eastern states began experimenting with written constitutional texts in the middle of the nineteenth century, generally in an effort to confront deep and simultaneous fiscal and international crises.[4] While these constitutions are often portrayed as alien imports, they were generally in-digenously generated. The states involved sought less to impress European states and creditors (the most often cited motive for constitutional reform) and more to practice fiscal discipline and regularize state authority (and thus fend off European control).

Constitutional Roads Not Taken

For a variety of reasons, early constitutional experiments did not al-ways provoke questions of the relationship between the constitutional text and the Islamic shari'a. This was partly because constitutions presented themselves as either consistent with or irrelevant to the application of Is-lamic law. Two constitutional forms emerged early in Arab constitutional history that have generally not survived past the middle of the twentieth century; brief exposition of these alternative forms sheds some light on the problems raised by the more ambitious, comprehensive, and European-style documents adopted by most Arab states in this century.

The first alternative is best exemplified by the first Middle Eastern constitutional document: the *qanun al-dawla al-tunisiyya* (law of the Tunisian state or dynasty) of 1861. This law was understood by Europeans at the time—and by some scholars since—as a mechanical and inappro-priate adaptation of European constitutional forms. A reading of the doc-ument, however, reveals something quite different: an attempt to borrow some emerging constitutional practices within a framework described in familiar (and sometimes Islamic) terms. Islamic political vocabulary was used (members of the newly established Grand Council, for instance, were referred to as *ahl al-hall wa-l-'aqd*, literally, "the people who loosen and bind," and the population was generally referred to as *ra'ayana*, literally, "our flock"). Some European usage was also adopted (the ruler was re-ferred to as the king—*al-malik*—rather than *bey*—perhaps an implicit as-sertion of Tunisian sovereignty) but less than is often supposed. The Grand Council and other councils clearly mixed administrative and judi-cial functions, violating emerging European constitutional norms of the separation of powers.[5] There were some real innovations in the document—such as insisting on designating only a share of the state budget for the king himself or that taxes be levied only on a legal basis—but these were not viewed as inimical to Islamic political practice. (The law did imply civil equality regardless of religion, but this principle had already been proclaimed in Tunisia prior to the promulgation of the law.) In short, the Tunisian constitution presented itself to Tunisians less as a new political system based on non-Islamic sources and more as a new codification of preexisting political practices and institutions. The Tunisian constitution appears to be an attempt to develop a constitutionalist system that is Islamic but not democratic. The point is to render authority accountable to the Islamic shari'a and to an elite that keeps the interests of the community in mind.[6] Yet the attempt to put such a constitutionalism into practice proved abortive not only in Tunisia but also elsewhere. Other Middle Eastern states have occasionally attempted to use Islamic political terminology to present their constitutional reforms, but generally on an ad hoc and isolated basis.[7]

A second alternative constitutional path was to issue modest documents that purported to be not comprehensive bases for the political order but merely procedural guidelines for operating existing institutions. Many early Arab constitutional efforts followed this model. Perhaps the earliest example came with Egypt's 1882 constitution (termed the fundamental ordinance, or *al-la'iha al-asasiyya*). The document was fairly brief, focusing almost all its fifty-two articles on the Consultative Council that was already sitting. An elected body, the Council was given an extensive role in legislation and in oversight of public finances. Ministers were invited to attend the Council sessions; they could also be summoned. While the constitution stipulated that ministers were responsible to the Council, it also mandated new elections if a difference between the cabinet and the Council could not be resolved. If a newly elected Council insisted on the position of the former Council, its opinion was binding. The few rights provisions were directly related to the Council, covering issues such as petitioning the Council or the immunity of Council members.[8] In short, this law is better understood as an organic law for the Council rather than a comprehensive legal framework. It thus provoked little debate about its relationship with Islamic law.

Several other Arab constitutional documents followed this pattern. For instance, the collapse of Ottoman rule in the Arab provinces motivated the composition of short-lived and little-remembered constitutional documents in areas that eventually became part of Transjordan and Libya.[9] Kuwait in 1938 and the Kingdom of Hijaz (after its conquest by the Saudi family in the 1920s) issued brief constitutional documents that are noteworthy in retrospect for their brevity and the modesty of their provisions.[10]

Yet even in the late nineteenth century, a far more ambitious path was opened to constitutional development—one that has provoked controversies and problems regarding how to reconcile it with the prevalence of Islamic legal norms and provisions. The paths described here worked to insinuate constitutional practices by incorporating them into prevailing Islamic vocabularies or by presenting them as modest organizational tools. Emerging European conceptions presented a far more ambitious image of constitutions: they were comprehensive legal and political frameworks emanating from the sovereign will (a sovereign that was either a monarch or a people or some odd amalgamation of the two). The Ottoman constitution of 1876 introduced such views, and it has emerged as the dominant form for Arab constitutional texts over the past century.

The Ottoman constitution of 1876 was drafted by a group of leading officials and members of the *'ulama* and modified by the cabinet before promulgation by the sultan.[11] The draft the committee finally submitted to the sultan most closely resembled the Belgian constitution of 1831; there were also parallels with the Prussian constitution, itself a more royalist version of the Belgian model. The sultan submitted the draft to the cabinet, which made some changes before promulgation.

Because the Ottoman constitution presented itself as a comprehensive governing framework, it provoked some debate regarding the role of Islam and the shari'a in Ottoman governance. Indeed, some members of the 'ulama so bitterly and publicly opposed the entrance of non-Muslims into the Parliament that they were exiled. The constitution seemed partly designed to further legal equality between Muslims and non-Muslims. Yet it stopped far short of establishing a secular state. Islam was clearly established as the state religion in various institutional and symbolic ways. For instance, the sultan was charged with executing provisions of shari'a and *qanun* law. The authors of the constitution most likely sought no more than to further legitimate positive legislation alongside the Islamic shari'a; they also probably wished to wean non-Muslims away from separatist hopes. The constitution implicitly (by the way it was issued as well as its effective implementation[12]) issued from the sovereign and absolute authority of the sultan—a feature affirmed by the decision of the sultan to suspend its operation less than two years after promulgation. Yet the document was reimposed in 1908 and amended the following year to introduce a symbolically critical change: the sultan was now required to swear an oath to the shari'a, the constitution, the homeland, and the nation, thus formalizing the idea that the sultan himself was subject to the will of God and the people.

The Ottoman constitution of 1876 served as a model for constitutional development in the Arab world, which also inherited the controversies and problems connected to its complex messages regarding the role of Islam in politics and governance. These controversies began in fairly muted fashion but have emerged in virtually all Arab countries participating in this Arab constitutional tradition.

Inscribing Islam

In the aftermath of World War I and the collapse of the Ottoman Empire, two Arab states sought to establish their sovereignty and political structure through composing constitutional texts. The first effort was undertaken in Damascus by a new (and abortive) Arab state and turned immediately to the Ottoman constitution for inspiration. While the constitution was not promulgated before the collapse of the state (which occurred with the imposition of the French Mandate), it set the pattern for other documents in the Arab East. Later Syrian, Iraqi, Lebanese, Jordanian, and Kuwaiti documents all drew heavily on the Ottoman constitution. There was a subtle difference in the political context in which these constitutions were written, however. The Ottoman document was issued in an established and recognized state whose leadership was attempting to fend off foreign penetration and fiscal collapse. The constitutions of the Arab East were issued by states that were asserting (or often striving to assert) their independence; this tended to heighten the importance of symbolic elements of the constitution. It is therefore not surprising that the Islamic provisions of the Ottoman constitution—often indirect or connected with the Ottoman sultanate that Arab states were interested in denying—were insufficient for emerging states eager to assert their standing and identity. They thus generally inserted two explicit provisions that were only implicit in the Ottoman constitution. First, Islam has almost always proclaimed the religion of the state. Second, the head of state has been generally required to be a Muslim. In one other case (Iraq), the constitution recognized the shariʿa courts as authoritative in personal status matters for Muslims (Article 76).

The second effort at constitution writing occurred in Egypt with its 1923 constitution. This experience was successful only in comparison with the 1920 Syrian constitution: the king suspended it twice and strained at the limits implied in its provisions even when it was in force. Nevertheless, it proved extremely influential. Not only did all subsequent Egyptian constitutions begin with the 1923 document as their starting point, but the influence of Egyptian constitutional lawyers throughout the Arab world has led to many of its formulations reappearing throughout the Arab world. Those who drafted the 1923 constitution turned to the Ottoman constitution but also drew on their broad familiarity with European constitutional law. As with their Eastern counterparts, the Egyptian drafters were largely satisfied with declaring Islam to be the "religion of the state" with little elaboration. Shaykh Bakhit, the country's former mufti, drafted the language, which provoked little controversy.[13] Indeed, the only controversy involving religion was occasioned by Shaykh Bakhit's objection to a clause stating that "the state will protect morals and feelings of religions and creeds"; he complained that this would offend Egypt's existing religions. The other drafters rejected his argument, motivated not simply by liberal sentiments but likely as well by the desire to avoid giving Great Britain any excuse to intervene protecting foreigners and minorities.[14]

Thus, the early architects of comprehensive constitutions in the Arab world were largely satisfied with symbolic declarations. These provisions had little effect on constitutional and political practice. And even on a symbolic level, the provisions appear fairly modest in retrospect. Two issues that have since emerged as central to debates about Islam and the political order—the source of sovereignty and the relationship between positive and shariʿa law—were not addressed, nor was this failure deemed particularly noteworthy at the time.

Such reticence can be explained by several factors. First, religious institutions (such as shariʿa courts and institutions of learning) at that time tended to focus their attention on maintaining autonomy rather than establishing hegemony over the political system as a whole.[15] Second, most of the constitutions were written in an effort to establish or affirm independence from European rule (and, in some cases, such as Egypt, an effort to end European extraterritoriality). Thus, establishing national sovereignty was hardly seen as inimical to Islamic values. Finally, the constitutions written during the period generally restricted themselves to modest general statements about the political order and specific procedural provisions. The lengthy ideological and programmatic constitutions were a thing of the future.

Yet as Arab constitutional law continued to develop and Arab politics grew increasingly ideological, the symbolic provisions related to Islam often grew. Islamic legal principles were often cited in constitutional debates.[16] It was no longer enough to refer simply to Islam as the state religion, but lengthy catalogs of principles often grew to include references to Islamic values or heritage. The Saudi Basic Law of 1992 cites Islam and Islamic law in numerous provisions. In some cases—such as in the Libyan and Iraqi constitutions—newer provisions were as vague as the older ones. Occasionally, however, new, more specific elements were added. The Moroccan constitution of 1962 barred amendments diminishing the royal or Muslim nature of the state; the 1970 constitution specifically excepted these matters from parliamentary immunity.[17] Algeria invented a Higher Islamic Council in 1996 for its political system, specifically enjoined to exercise *ijtihad*. And specific steps were taken, especially in the states of the Arabian peninsula, to mandate Islamic legal norms in specific areas. In the Kuwaiti constitutions for instance, Article 18 stipulates, "Inheritance is a right governed by the Islamic shariʿa." Yemeni constitutions have probably been most ambitious and specific in this regard. The 1970 constitution, for instance, required enforcement of Islamic law in business transactions. The constitution further provided that "[i]n cases heard by the Courts, the provisions of this constitution and of the State's laws shall be applied. If there is no precedent, the Courts shall pass their judgment in the case they are dealing with in accordance with the general principles of the Islamic shariʿa."[18]

Despite the increased salience of Islamic issues in constitutional debates, the provisions discussed thus far still generally preserved the constitution as the supreme law in the country. There might be symbolic or institutional concessions to Islamic beliefs, practices, and law, but ultimate political authority remains elsewhere: in the constitution, in the people (with popular sovereignty proclaimed in most constitutions), or in the head of state (formally in some royal system and effectively in some republican systems).

Yet there is another set of provisions in some Arab constitutional texts that suggests a different relationship between the political order described in the constitution and the legal system enjoined by Islam. Beginning with the Syrian constitution of 1950, some Arab constitutional systems have cited the Islamic shari'a as a source or, more ambitiously, as the chief source of law. The 1950 Syrian constitution—the first Arab document to introduce long ideological sections and catalogs of social and economic as well as political rights—was in effect for only a few years, and its provision regarding Islamic law had no noticeable effect.[19] In Kuwait's 1962 constitution, a similar provision was introduced in which "the Islamic shari'a is a primary source of legislation." Periodic proposals to amend the constitution to make the Islamic shari'a *the* rather than *a* primary source of legislation have thus far been unsuccessful, though there appears to be considerable popular support for such a change. Similar language has been adopted in other peninsular states (such as the United Arab Emirates and Oman); Saudi Arabia's 1992 basic law has a much more specific and detailed provision: according to Article 48, "The courts will apply the rules of the Islamic shari'a in the cases that are brought before them, in accordance with what is indicated in the Book and the Sunna, and statutes decreed by the Ruler which do not contradict the Book or the Sunna."[20]

The effect of such provisions is to imply a very different basis for the legal order. Rather than the constitution sanctioning Islam as an official religion and observance of the Islamic shari'a in specific areas, these provisions imply that the shari'a itself stands prior to the positive legal order—including, potentially and by implication, the constitution itself. If the shari'a is a primary source—or even the primary source—of legislation, then it becomes possible to argue that it forms the fundamental legal framework. Indeed, it is noteworthy in this regard that constitutional texts tend to refer to the shari'a as a basis of legislation (*tashri'*), which would include all legal enactments (including laws, decrees, administrative regulations, and arguably the constitution), rather than as a basis of laws (*qawanin*), which would refer only to a specific category of legislation (laws passed by parliament or their equivalent).

It is therefore not surprising that these constitutional provisions have emboldened those who seek the Islamicization of the political order. Such language makes it possible to challenge legislation that does not seem to be in conformity with Islamic shari'a principles on constitutional grounds. In short, it makes it possible—through constitutional jurisprudence—to make the principles of the Islamic shari'a a supraconstitutional order.

Making such a challenge successfully is not easy, however, because of more prosaic elements of Arab constitutional orders. In general, constitutional challenges are exceedingly difficult to mount. While the principle of judicial review of the constitutionality of legislation is firmly accepted in most Arab political systems, a host of procedural, legal, and political obstacles obstruct its exercise in most countries.[21] The most significant exception is Egypt, where a strong constitutional court has emerged willing to strike down legislation as unconstitutional with startling boldness.

In 1971, Egypt received its "permanent" constitution to replace the avowedly temporary documents of the Nasser years. That constitution's second article went beyond mere declaration of Islam as the religion of the state; such a formula was deemed insufficient. It more ambitiously described the principles of the Islamic shari'a as "a principle source of legislation." Arguments in favor of still stronger provisions were rejected for the moment.[22] Yet the proponents of a stronger Article 2 won a delayed victory as the constitution was amended nine years later to make the principles of the Islamic shari'a *the* principle source of legislation. As amended, Article 2 of the Egyptian constitution now proclaims, "Islam is the religion of the State, Arabic is its official language and the principles of the Islamic shari'a are the principal source of legislation." Thus, Egypt has joined other Arab and Islamic countries in providing explicitly for a link between the Islamic shari'a and legislation.

Adoption of the new formula set off a debate in which even advocates of a greater role for Islam in political life found themselves divided. Some jurists charged that the change was unnecessary because as long as the constitution provided that Islam is the religion of the state, then the state is constitutionally Islamic. Thus, they argued, all acts of government and public powers were already required to be in line with the shari'a. A further constitutional provision on Islamic shari'a principles, whether as a source or principal source of legislation, did not really add much to this understanding and was occasioned by the desire to appeal to public opinion rather than effect real change.

The counterview, nonetheless, was upheld, and the constitutional amendment was carried out. Supporters of this view believed that elevating shari'a principles to become the principal source, not merely a main source, of legislation carried significant meanings and implications. Before the amendment, Islamic shari'a principles were seen as merely one main source of legislation beside which other main sources did exist. The amended Article 2 elevated shari'a principles to become the principle source. To be sure, other subsidiary sources of legislation remained valid, but they are accorded lower importance.

This debate might have attracted little attention—and the skeptics about the effectiveness of amending the text would have been vindicated—had it not been for a more subtle and then little-noticed change in Egypt's constitutional order. In 1969, President Nasser had moved against the country's judiciary and dismissed a large number of sitting judges. He also constructed by decree a new "Supreme Court" to sit at the apex of Egypt's judicial structure in a thinly disguised bid to establish firm presidential control over the judiciary. That body was renamed the "Supreme Constitutional Court" in the 1971 constitution, but matters of its organization were left to ordinary legislation. Not until 1979 was that legislation enacted, but when it was, it created a far different court than had been envisioned a decade earlier. The sitting judges on the court constituted a "General Assembly" that was to forward nominations for new members to the president. While the president retained his formal appointment authority over the judges of the court, he effectively exercised it according to the wishes of those judges already members. In effect, the law created a largely self-perpetuating body, relatively free from executive interference.

Thus, since the amended Article 2 of the constitution came into force, it has attracted attention from scholars and activists. Surprisingly, there is probably greater attention to the issue—at least in its constitutional form—outside Egypt and the Arab world. This should not be taken to mean that jurists in Egypt and the Arab world have not yet realized the potential impact of the amended text. Rather, it means while others believe that this amendment is an unprecedented constitutional transformation in the country, jurists in Egypt view this amendment as a revival of Islamic norms that have always been inherent in their religious tradition and society. A gradual return to such tradition is thus perceived as an expected and logical step in the march of development of a religious society and a part of a peaceful process of incorporating religious norms into a constitutional system. Hence, such developments may not encourage a noticeable debate by nonspecialists within the region at the short run.

The Religious Nature of the Society in Egypt

The level of religiosity in Egyptian public life is high, and Egyptians generally cast their understanding of relations not only between individuals and God but also among individuals in terms of religious concepts and obligations. The dominance of Islam in Egyptian society (with perhaps over 90 percent of the society professing to be Muslims) is acknowledged in all Egyptian constitutional texts in the twentieth century. Nevertheless, those same constitutional documents insist that non-Muslim Egyptians are to be accorded the same status as Muslim Egyptian citizens.[23] Such provisions can be—and are—understood not as antithetical to a shari'a-based order but as intrinsic to it, founded on provisions for freedom of religion and belief.

The political order in Egypt has presented itself as Islamic since the arrival of Islam to the country almost 1,400 years ago. With the majority of the Egyptian population turning to Islam, the shari'a became the accepted basis not only for governance but also for social relations. While total obeisance to shari'a principles was probably never the norm, the Islamic shari'a still held ideological dominance until the late nineteenth century. At that point, new and comprehensive law codes, derived mainly from the European codes, began to be introduced in the Ottoman Empire and its affiliated Arab countries, including Egypt.[24] The result was to restrict the applicability of shari'a-based legal principles in almost all fields, with the exception of the family status issues field, in which Islamic shari'a principles continued to prevail. Non-Muslims continued to be governed by their own religious rules, a practice itself in accordance with Islamic principles guaranteeing followers of divine revelations (Christians and Jews) the right to apply their own religious laws.[25]

In fact, the process of transformation has left its impact on these countries since then up until now. Today, legislation in most Arab countries, including Egypt, generally is not drawn from the Islamic shari'a but is grounded in those European codes. For instance, civil and criminal codes now applied in Egypt are ultimately derived from French codes and have in turn inspired a multiplicity of the substantive and procedural legal rules in the region.[26] This state of affairs has become increasingly controversial in recent years not only in Egypt but throughout the Arab world as well. Increasing calls are heard from various Islamic movements for an Islamic state based on shari'a. Such calls seem to strike a strong resonance in predominantly Muslim societies, and Egypt has seen remarkable intellectual ferment concerning the issue. It is not surprising, therefore, that Egypt has, along with many other Arab countries, moved to attempt to adopt a shari'a-based constitutionalism.

Despite this trend, and despite the fact that the constitutions of Islamic countries—to which the constitution of Egypt belongs—ensure their religious nature, the recent movement to accommodate religion has not yet resulted in a noticeable change to the system of government and the practices of public authorities in these countries, which remain essentially secular. This, in fact, presents a conflict between state and religion in Islamic countries that these countries are now attempting to address in various ways. The struggles that have gained the most international attention have taken violent form. Yet a constitutional and legal struggle, occurring far less in the (especially Western) public eye, has also led to a remarkable effort to diminish the gap between law and governance on the one hand and shari'a derived principles and practice on the other. In Egypt, the country's Supreme Constitutional Court has found itself in the forefront of that effort, largely because of the attempt to give life to the very general wording of Article 2. The understandings and rulings of the Court, the highest judicial institution in the country and one of the most influential in the Arab world, will help determine the extent to which the Islamic shari'a serves as a sound base for a constitutional democracy in the contemporary world.

The Supreme Constitutional Court's Interpretation of Article 2 of the Constitution

Article 2 of the constitution of Egypt is potentially quite influential, depending not only on the explicit words of the text (which are strong but general) but also on the judicial interpretation given to them. The impact of such interpretation is not confined to Egypt. Rather, it extends to other Arab countries in the region. The pioneering role of Egypt's legal system means that the Egyptian experience in legal and judicial areas is closely observed by other judicial systems and governments within the region.[27]

On the national level, it is worth mentioning, however, that attempts to challenge the constitutionality of legislation for its unconformity with Article 2 of the constitution began shortly after the constitution was adopted in 1971 and even before this article was amended in 1980. The Supreme Court (SC), the predecessor of the Supreme Constitutional Court (SCC), addressed the issue of Islamic shari'a principles in Article 2 on several occasions before the text was amended. The SCC later upheld some of its reasoning in this area after the constitutional amendment.[28] In fact, the SC's rulings in this area presented the SCC with an important source for judging future cases.

A comprehensive view on Article 2, however, was not developed until the text was amended and the SCC was called on to give its binding interpretation to what is meant by this text in a number of constitutional cases. Here, we will try to have a look at the Court's rulings on Islamic shari'a principles as the principal source of legislation.

The SCC has established three foundations in developing its jurisprudence and binding interpretation of the meaning of Islamic shari'a principles within a constitutional framework. The first of these is that Article 2, together with the rest of the articles in the 1971 constitution, form a unified organic unit. The second is that the constitutional obligation imposed on the legislature to adhere to Islamic shari'a, in accordance with Article 2, is prospective and not retrospective in nature. The third base asserts that the application of shari'a principles in constitutional litigation must be based on a distinction between its definitive and indefinite sources.

The Egyptian Constitution as an Organic Unit

Unity of the constitution is a prevailing theme running throughout the jurisprudence of the SCC. The Court believes that the exercise of the power of judicial review requires a rigid constitution ensuring the supremacy of its provisions over other, inferior rules. In principle, a constitution is perceived as a viable instrument coping with an advanced democratic system, protecting individual liberties, laying down grounds for their development, balancing power between the different branches of the government within the framework of checks and balances, advancing societal values, and promoting openness, talented behavior, and scientific research. A constitution does not simply reflect norms of mandatory character but substantiates advanced concepts that, in their entirety and taken together, are expected to enhance new patterns of behavior, subject in all their forms to the rule of law. Constitutional limitations, if adequately observed, shall base all aspects of power on the public will, further their effectiveness, and eliminate deviations therefrom. A constitution may ensure a better understanding of the relationship between the state and its citizens. It may also fail to match their expected aspirations. However, in both cases, the constitution shall remain at the apex of all other rules, being the paramount law of the land. This principle has been incorporated into the preamble of the 1971 constitution, which declares the determination of the people to vigorously ensure its protection and that no authority may abstain from yielding thereto.[29]

This view of the constitution leads the SCC to deny the supremacy of a particular constitutional text over the rest of the constitution. Instead, the Court has insisted that constitutional provisions do not collide with each other but collectively form an interrelated, organic unit, accomplished by coordinated methods of construction that conserve society-oriented values. In Case No. 23 of the fifteenth judicial year, decided February 5, 1994, the Court assured that these constitutional provisions are to be understood as a coherent, harmonized body of rules, reconciled and brought together to the extent that none of them is to be viewed as standing in isolation from the other.

This rule undoubtedly extends to Article 2 of the constitution, and therefore the Islamic shari'a should always be perceived in a way that assures its harmony with other constitutional commands. Article 2 can therefore not be taken to undermine the rest of the text; instead, the various provisions of the Egyptian constitution must be viewed together. This same understanding was advocated by the drafting committee for the 1980 constitutional amendment. The committee's report stated that it "is evident that any provision in the Constitution should be interpreted in harmony with, not in isolation of, other provisions. This is also applied to the interpretation of the amended Article 2 of the Constitution."

The Prospective Nature of Article 2

The SCC has ruled that the binding obligation to derive legislation from the principles of the Islamic shari'a applies only to the future. Legislation passed before the amendment cannot therefore be contested on constitutional grounds as a violation of Islamic shari'a. The Court laid down this principle in early constitutional litigation in the 1980s. The constitutional issue in question in this case was whether charging the University of Al-Azhar interest on commercial debt violates Islamic shari'a and hence contradicts the constitution.[30]

Legal observers expected that the Court would either uphold the provision in question or declare it unconstitutional. Instead, however, the Court issued a ruling rejecting the claim of unconstitutionality while avoiding a ruling based on its interpretation of the Islamic shari'a. The SCC's judgment, issued on May 4, 1985, included an important legal principle within its apparently narrow ruling.[31] The critical point involved the Court's perception of the chronological applicability of Article 2 and whether it could be applied retroactively. The Court reviewed the drafting committee report defining the meaning of the draft 1980 amendment and concluded that the requirement that all legislation be consistent with the shari'a was prospective only from the date of adoption of the constitutional amendment, that is, May 22, 1980. All legislation passed after that date must be consistent with the shari'a as well as other constitutional commands. The Court held that Article 2 is a limitation on the legislature, which must determine for itself whether legislation adopted before May 22, 1980, is consistent with the Islamic shari'a. By implication, the Court would review all contested legislation adopted after that date for consistency with the Islamic shari'a and hence the constitution.[32]

Based on this conception, the Court ruled that the true purpose of the amendment was to limit the legislative power of the legislature, which logically could be exercised only for future legislation.[33] Yet the Court did not free the legislature of any responsibility for ensuring that pre-1980 legislation conformed to shari'a principles. On the contrary, the SCC imposed a political responsibility on the legislature to initiate new legislation to amend such texts where they were clearly in contradiction with principles of Islamic shari'a. Eventually, both existing and future legislation have to be consistent with Islamic shari'a.

The nonretroactivity application of Article 2 was first decided on the Al-Azhar case in 1985 but since then has become a well-established principal of judicial review, echoed in all subsequent cases dealing with this article, especially those pertaining to legislation adopted prior to the 1980 constitutional amendment.

Distinguishing between Definitive and Indefinite Norms

The final and most complex principle developed by the Court involves the nature of shari'a principles. In essence, the SCC has held that shari'a-based norms have different value: such norms are either definitive or indefinite. The *niqab* case presents the clearest example of the Court's understanding of the distinction between the two kinds of norms. In defining Islamic shari'a principles, in this case, the Court relied on an unshaken chain of precedents that clearly stated that definitive principles are Islamic norms that are not debatable with respect to either their source or their precise meaning. Such definitive norms must be applied.[34] All other Islamic norms are indefinite in that they are susceptible to different interpretations and—because of their nature—changeable in response to the exigencies of time, place, and circumstances. Such flexibility reflects not a defect in the shari'a in the Court's eyes but a strength because it allows the principles to be adapted to changing realities and ensures their continued vitality and elasticity. Only in the realm of Islamic indefinite norms may the legislature intervene to regulate matters of common concern and achieve related interests. It must do so consistent with basic Islamic norms, the aim of which is the preservation of religion, reason, honor, property, and the body. The legislature might develop different practical solutions to satisfy variable societal needs. The SCC regards the bulk of Islamic indefinite norms as highly developed, intrinsically in harmony with changeable circumstances, repulsive of rigidity, and incompatible with absoluteness and firmness. In no way may an Islamic indefinite norm that is fading—whether because of time, place, or pertinent situations— be mandated by the Court or the constitution.[35]

The niqab ruling, along with many similar SCC judgments, has always upheld this distinction between definitive or peremptory provisions or norms of the shari'a on the one hand and its indefinite or nonperemptory provisions or norms on the other. After the 1980 amendment of the constitution, all newly enacted legislation must adhere to definitive or peremptory norms of Islamic shariʻa. Where no such definitive norm exists, the legislature should adhere to the ijtihad most favorable for the people, selected from among indefinite or nonperemptory norms of the Islamic shariʻa.

Thus, ijtihad governs the process of determining the best applicable rule within indefinite norms. Ijtihad within the nonperemptory provisions in shariʻa is a process of reasoning to deduce practical rules to regulate the life of the people and achieve their interest. It should, therefore, cope with the context of events prevailing at the time. While the legislature might choose a specific interpretation as the basis of legislation, it cannot give that interpretation the status of binding doctrine, except on those who accept it. The Court's jurisprudence is based on viewing such multiple possibilities as a sign of divine mercy that encourages Muslims to think and discuss, diminishing the possibility of human error. The existence of indefinite norms is also taken to ensure that the Islamic shariʻa always develops and displays flexibility to accept ijtihad of responsible people to achieve the public interest.[36]

When invoking Islamic shariʻa, the Court, therefore, first searches for peremptory norms and, if finding none, looks at ijtihad that is consistent with the challenged legislation and achieving the interest of the people. Then the Court examines the purposes of this legislation. And at the outset, the Court determines whether the challenged provision is consistent with the interests of the people and decides its constitutionality on the basis of this conclusion.

Conclusion

In 1971 and 1980, Egypt took steps toward sharpening the apparent paradox between an Islamic legal order and a constitutional one. While the Egyptian constitution presents itself as based on popular sovereignty and borrows much of its language from European constitutional traditions, the amended Article 2 seems to promote a higher and prior law, the Islamic shariʻa. The matter of how to resolve this paradox in practical legal terms has been thrown to Egypt's SCC because it is charged with the task of resolving constitutional disputes in an authoritative manner. There are some within Egyptian society who view large elements on the existing legal order not simply as imported but also as hostile to and incompatible with Islamic law, and they have resorted to the Court with some regularity. This has compelled the SCC to develop an approach to melding shari'a principles with constitutional interpretation.

The SCC's approach to Article 2 has already had considerable influence in Egypt because the Court has pursued it consistently for the past sixteen years. But it is also likely to have influence outside Egypt for several reasons. First, similar language exists in some other Arab constitutional texts, and there is considerable pressure in many Arab societies to deepen the Islamic nature of the constitutional order. Second, Egyptian legal thinking and jurisprudence is widely followed in many Arab countries; indeed, some Arab countries consciously modeled their own legal orders (and sometimes their legal education) on Egyptian models. Third, the SCC's jurisprudence is likely to appeal to those who seek practical guidance on how to bring shari'a principles to bear on a modern society. The approach of Egypt's SCC may be summarized in general terms as follows.

The Court began with a fairly conservative approach toward the amended Article 2. It took the SCC almost five years (after the 1980 amendment) to exercise its power of judicial review on legislation alleged to violate Islamic shari'a. Even when it did so, at the time, it was not willing to address the issue in question substantively and opted to cast its argument in procedural terms. While the SCC has a reputation for boldness, the Court's policy on this issue is best understood within the theory of judicial self-restraint. Given the sensitivity of the issue and the potential impact resulting from any ruling on the merits, whether by holding the challenged legislative provision or declaring it unconstitutional, the Court found it wiser not to rule on the substantive part of the case because other grounds to decide the case, without invoking the constitutional issue, were available. This is, in fact, the essence of the theory of judicial self-restraint. To avoid undesirable attacks from the judiciary on the legislature, a court with a power of judicial review, within this theory, would not strike down legislation unless it is absolutely necessary and no alternative basis for judgment is available. This is, in fact, what the SCC followed in this particular case.

Despite such self-restraint and the decision to review only legislation coming into force after the 1980 constitutional amendment, the Court has found itself gradually giving increasing attention to shari'a issues. The pressure of public opinion and the steady growth in cases related to the Islamic shari'a lodged in the Court's docket left the SCC no alternative. Having been unavoidably confronted with the necessity of measuring Egyptian legislation against the constitutional provisions on the Islamic shari'a, SCC judges took up the task. Trained both in law and in Islamic shari'a, they find themselves fully competent to deliver opinions based on shari'a. Following their conservative ruling in the Al-Azhar case, they have, in reality, been dealing with Islamic shari'a issues comfortably. They have managed to strike a balance between Islamic shari'a principles on the one hand and the constitution on the other. To provide litigants with effective legal remedies, they invoked Islamic shari'a principles largely not only in cases wherein the amended Article 2 was applicable but even in other cases within which violations of Islamic shari'a were not initially alleged.

The SCC views Islamic shari'a principles mainly as a legal system. This is evident from the distinction the Court adopted to determine what norms of Islamic shari'a are definite and what are not. In accordance with the Court's policy in this area, since the space occupied by the definite norms of shari'a is considerably limited, the majority of shari'a rules would be derived from its indefinite norms. This is, in fact, a discretionary power basically left to the ruler. But this power is not absolute: it finds its limitations in the public welfare of the society. If the ruler misuses this power or selects an ijtihad that is not consistent with public interest in a specific time, his legislation becomes in violation with Islamic shari'a. The Court may therefore decide whether the selected ijtihad is consistent or in contradiction with societal needs and interest. Therefore, despite its initial reticence, the Court has the potential to play a significant role in determining what is meant by Islamic shari'a principles.

Deference to Islamic shari'a principles, within the limits prescribed by the SCC, does not mean these principles have become the sole source of legislation. Nor does this deference elevate them to a higher status than that of the constitution itself. Rulings of the SCC are clear that other sources may be employed and consulted in the legislative process. They also adhere to the principle that the amended Article 2 bears the same binding force as other articles of the constitution. The unity of the constitution requires this comprehension, which consequently presumes that the applicability of Islamic shari'a principles would eventually be understood in the context of other commands enshrined in the constitution.

From the beginning, the SCC has sought to use the power of judicial review in a restrained manner, but it has also taken up the task of assisting the peaceful integration of Islamic shari'a principles in the constitutional order and daily life of the Egyptian citizen. Although this experience has yet to develop, it has sought to prove over the past two decades that Islamic shari'a principles, as a legal system, have met, to a great extent, the needs and wishes of the vast majority of the population, without prejudice to the constitutional rights of minority religious groups in the country.

Notes

1. John Finn makes this argument for constitutional emergencies in *Constitutions in Crisis: Political Violence and the Rule of Law* (New York: Oxford University Press, 1991).

2. For a general examination of this shift, see Nathan J. Brown, "Shari'a and State in the Modern Middle East," *International Journal of Middle East Studies* 29, no. 3 (1997): 359–76.

3. In Islam, all rights can be viewed as bestowed by God and divided into two categories: the "rights of God" and the "rights of worshipers." Whether a right falls within the former and not the latter category depends on the extent to which that right is related to the public interests of the society. Rights granted in the public interest are considered rights of God, while rights bestowed to protect private interests are deemed rights of worshipers.

4. See Nathan J. Brown, *Constitutions in a Nonconstitutional World: Arab Basic Laws and the Prospects for Accountable Government* (Albany: State University of New York Press, 2002), chap. 1.

5. The mixture of such functions in a single body was quite common in Europe at the time, of course, but those states that were devising written constitutions did so partly to avoid such a practice.

6. For a general articulation of the ideology behind the constitution by one of its primary advocates, see the writings of Khayr al-Din al-Tunisi. His major treatise on the subject has been translated into English by L. Carl Brown, *The Surest Path: The Political Treatise of a Nineteenth-Century Muslim Statesman, a Translation of the Introduction to "The Surest Path to Knowledge concerning the Condition of Countries" by Khayr al-Din al-Tunisi*, Harvard Middle Eastern

Monographs 16 (Cambridge, Mass.: Harvard University, Center for Middle Eastern Studies, 1967).

7. For instance, the addition of an upper house to the Egyptian parliament in 1979 was given some Islamic coloration by designating it the *majlis al-shura* (consultative council). The Saudi Basic Law of 1992 uses such vocabulary more extensively.

8. The text of the document can be found in *Al-Dasatir al-Misriyya 1805–1971: Nusus wa-Tahlil* (The Egyptian Constitutions 1805–1971: Texts and Analysis) (Cairo: Markaz al-Tanzim wa-l-Mikrufilm, 1976). See also Juan R. I. Cole, *Colonialism and Revolution in the Middle East: Social and Cultural Origins of Egypt's 'Urabi Movement* (Princeton, N.J.: Princeton University Press, 1993), 105, and Alexander Scholch, *Egypt for the Egyptians! The Socio-Political Crisis in Egypt 1878–1882* (London: Ithaca Press, 1981), 213.

9. Eugene Rogan mentions a 1920 "Constitution of the Arab Government of Moab" in *Frontiers of the State in the Late Ottoman Empire* (Cambridge: Cambridge University Press, 1999), 251. The constitutional efforts of the Tripoli Republic, partly negotiated with Italy, are treated in Karim Mezran, "Constitutionalism in Libya," in *Islam and Constitutionalism*, ed. Sohail Hashmi and Houchang Chehabi (forthcoming).

10. The most comprehensive source for constitutional documents can be found at www.uni-wuerzburg.de/law/home.html.

11. Scholarly writings on the Ottoman constitution of 1876 are reasonably extensive, but because of the declining interest among scholars in legal and political history, the most comprehensive works tend to be older. The account here depends primarily on such older works, including Robert Devereux, *The First Ottoman Constitutional Period: A Study of the Midhat Constitution and Parliament* (Baltimore: Johns Hopkins University Press, 1963); Roderic H. Davison, "The Advent of the Principle of Representation in the Government of the Ottoman Empire," in *Essays in Ottoman and Turkish History, 1774–1923: The Impact of the West* (Austin: University of Texas Press, 1990); Roderic H. Davison, *Reform in the Ottoman Empire 1856–1876* (Princeton, N.J.: Princeton University Press, 1963); and Stanford J. Shaw and Ezel Kural Shaw, *History of the Ottoman Empire and Modern Turkey, Volume II: Reform, Revolution, and Republic: The Rise of Modern Turkey, 1808–1975* (Cambridge: Cambridge University Press, 1977). See also Bernard Lewis, *The Emergence of Modern Turkey* (Oxford: Oxford University Press, 1968), and Nader Sohrabi, "Historicizing Revolution: Constitutional Revolutions in the Ottoman Empire, Iran, and Russia, 1905–1908," *American Journal of Sociology* 100, no. 6 (May 1995): 1383–447.

12. Not only did the Ottoman sultan promulgate and suspend the constitution at will, but he also made clear that he did not regard his authority as bound by

the constitution. For instance, he claimed the right to issue legislation completely outside the constitutional framework, insisting that the constitutional procedures governed only legislation that went through the parliament. Few current rulers would be so bold in doctrine, but many executives in the Arab world have retained constitutional mechanisms for bypassing parliamentary and other institutions.

13. The minutes of the drafting committee have been preserved, allowing us some insight into the intentions of the drafters. See the discussion of Article 149 in Majlis al-Shuyukh, *Al-dustur: Ta'liqat 'ala Mawadihi bi-l-A'mal al-Tahdiriyya wa-l-Munaqashat al-Barlamaniyya* (Cairo: Matba'at Misr, 1940), pt. 3.

14. Majlis al-Shuyukh, *Al-Dustur*, pt. 1, discussion of Article 13.

15. See Brown, "Shari'a and State."

16. In the debate over the adoption of the first Moroccan constitution, for instance, the opposition was able to cite the opinion of a leading Islamic scholar criticizing the document because it assigned a greater right to legislation to the state than should exist in an Islamic system. See Charles F. Gallagher, "Toward Constitutional Government in Morocco: A Referendum Endorses the Constitution," American Universities Field Staff, North Africa Series, vol. 9, no. 1 (Morocco), 1963, 7. For a very different example, see the discussion of women's suffrage in "Women in the Constitutional Committee," *Ruz al-Yusuf*, October 19, 1953, 13. At that time, a committee drafting a constitution for Egypt considered the right of women to vote. Some committee members unsuccessfully cited Islamic grounds for opposing this right.

17. Ahmad Majid Binjalun, *Al-Dustur al-Maghrabi: Mabadi'uhu wa Ahkamuhu* (Casablanca: Dar al-Kitab, 1977), 151–52.

18. Article 153. For the text, see Albert P. Blausetien and Gisbert H. Flanz, eds., *Constitutions of the World* (Dobbs Ferry, N.Y.: Oceana Publications, updated periodically).

19. On the Syrian constitution of 1950, including Article 3, which described the Islamic shari'a as the chief source of legislation, see Majid Khadduri, "Constitutional Development in Syria," *Middle East Journal* 5, no. 2 (spring 1951): 137–60. Ironically, Syria later made Arab constitutional history when a constitution was proposed that removed the requirement that the head of state be a Muslim.

20. A translation of the Saudi Basic Law is available at www.oefre.unibe.ch/law/icl/sa00000_.html (accessed December 20, 2002).

21. On this point more generally, see Nathan J. Brown, "Judicial Review in the Arab World," *Journal of Democracy* 9, no. 4 (October 1998): 85–99.

22. See Jamal al-'Utayfi, *Ara' fi al-Shari'a wa-fi al-Hurriyya* (Opinions on the Shari'a and Freedom) (Cairo: Al-hay'a al-misriyya al-'amma li-l-kitab, 1980); Joseph

P. O'Kane, "Islam in the New Egyptian Constitution: Some Discussions in *al-Ahram*," *Middle East Journal* 26, no. 2 (1972): 137–48; and Minutes of the Preparatory Committee for Drafting the Constitution [for the Arab Republic of Egypt, 1971] (held in the library of the Majlis al-Sha'b, Cairo).

23. In Constitutional Case No. 74 for the seventeenth judicial year, decided on March 1, 1997, the SCC held that the constitution and the Islamic shari'a recognized that other major religions represented in the population had the right to the application of their own religious norms the same as Muslims.

24. Islamic shari'a, however, occupied an important position under the Civil Code. This code considered shari'a the third general source to which judges resort in case they do not find a legislative provision or customary rule applied to the litigation they are handling. In addition, a great number of legal rules in this code were derivative from Islamic shari'a principles. See Enid Hill, "Al-Sanhuri and Islamic Law," *Cairo Papers in Social Science* 10, no. 1 (1987): 1–140.

25. For more details, see Adel Omar Sherif, "An Overview of the Egyptian Judicial System and Its History," *Yearbook of Islamic and Middle Eastern Law* 5 (1998/1999): 3–28.

26. The legal system of Egypt is based, therefore, on Islamic law and civil law (particularly French codes). For a more extensive treatment, see Nathan J. Brown, *The Rule of Law in the Arab World: Courts in Egypt and the Gulf* (New York: Cambridge University Press, 1997).

27. Because Egyptian experience has always been available for other Arab systems, many attempts by other Arab countries over the years to adopt the Egyptian system have taken place but met with varying results.

28. For example, in the Constitutional Case No. 10 for the fifth judicial year, decided on July 3, 1976, the SC ruled that when providing for Islamic shari'a principles as a main source of legislation, Article 2 meant to guide the legislator to derive legislation from these principles. In doing so, and if no definitive provision of shari'a is applicable, the legislator will then have a discretionary power to choose the proper rule to follow, from among the various ijtihads available in various juristic schools, know as *madhahib*. This understanding, to a great extent, carries a vital distinction: one between definitive and indefinite provisions of Islamic shari'a, on which the SCC soon after, as we will shortly discuss, laid down its own interpretation of Article 2 of the constitution.

29. See Constitutional Case No. 23 for the fifteenth judicial year, decided on February 5, 1994.

30. A judgment of the Administrative Judicature Court of the Council of the State had ruled against Al-Azhar University during the 1970s, charging the university interest on commercial debt. The proceedings in this action had seen the rec-

tor of the university, together with the minister of *Waqfs* and the dean of the university's Faculty of Medicine, ordered to pay a creditor the balance of the price of surgical instruments supplied to the university. The trial court had also ordered the university to pay interest on this amount at the rate of 4 percent, starting from the date of filing the action. The ruling was based on Article 226 of the Civil Code, adopted by the Parliament in 1948, which imposed postjudgment interest on non-payment of debt. When this ruling was appealed before the High Administrative Court, the rector of Al-Azhar challenged the constitutionality of Article 226 and received permission from the appellate court to file his constitutional allegation before the SCC. He then filed Constitutional Case No. 20 for the first judicial year, advancing the claim that charging this interest was *riba* (or usury) prohibited by the Qur'an and therefore contradicted the principles of the Islamic shari'a.

31. Although the SCC failed to reach the riba issue in the Al-Azhar case, it had with it substantively, soon after, in Constitutional Case No. 93 for the sixth judicial year, decided on March 18, 1996. In this case, a company was late in payment of its taxes and was, therefore, assessed a late penalty in the form of interest on its obligation. The tax agency proceeded to confiscate the company's property in order to pay the obligation and late penalty, then the company claimed that this interest is riba, prohibited by the Qur'an. The Court determined that Article 2 was applicable and that the agreed peremptory norm of shari'a was that riba is defined as "an agreement between a creditor and debtor to extend payment deadline in return for additional interest money." When the Court examined the transaction in question, however, it found that there was no agreement between creditor and debtor. The company had not borrowed money for which an extension had been requested. The Qur'anic prohibition, therefore, did not apply to this transaction, which led the Court to reject the unconstitutionality allegation.

32. A preparatory committee to the draft amendment explained in a report, dated July 19, 1979, as the Court highlighted, that Article 2 had obliged the legislature, in its quest for the rule of law, to have recourse to the rules of the Islamic shari'a to the exclusion of any other system of law. If it did not find a clear rule in Islamic shari'a, it should then apply the approved methods of deducing legal rules from the authorized sources of ijtihad in Islamic jurisprudence. This process, the committee added, would help the legislature in reaching a ruling that is consistent with the principles and general framework of the Islamic shari'a. This report was also confirmed by the drafting committee and approved by the People's Assembly on April 30, 1980.

33. This understanding, in fact, was supported and confirmed by a statement from the Report of the General Committee of the People's Assembly, dated

September 13, 1981, presented to and approved by the Assembly on September 15, 1981, in which the committee explained that the amendment meant to require the revision of laws in effect before the application of the constitution of 1971 and to amend these laws in such a manner as to make them conform to the principles of Islamic shariʻa. Nonetheless, the departure from the present legal institutions of Egypt, which go back more than one hundred years, and their replacement in their entirety by Islamic shariʻa require patient efforts and careful practical considerations. Consequently, the change of the whole legal organization should not be contemplated without giving the lawmakers a chance and a reasonable period of time to collect all legal materials and amalgamate them into a complete system within the framework of the Qur'an, the Sunna, and the opinions of learned Moslem jurists and *Imams*.

34. The definitive norms of Islamic shariʻa are usually called "*al-nusus al-qatʻiyyat al-dalala wa al-thubut*," which is an old terminology of *fiqh* with its classical meanings and usage. This term refers to texts of the shariʻa sources (that is, Qur'an and Sunna) that are definitive and indisputable both in their meaning and in their authenticity. Such texts are beyond doubt. They must be historically accurate and authentic and have only one meaning.

35. See the niqab case, Constitutional Case No. 8 of the eighteenth judicial year, decided on May 18, 1996.

36. See the niqab case, Constitutional Case No. 8 of the eighteenth judicial year, decided on May 18, 1996.

CHAPTER THREE
A TYPOLOGY OF STATE *MUFTIS*

Jakob Skovgaard-Petersen

espite their obvious political and social relevance, no one has ever made any systematic comparative study of state *muftis* (interpreters of Islamic law). Judging from the scant literature on the phenomenon of state muftis in general, the reason for this lack of study seems to be that this office is seen as self-explanatory: a state mufti is the state's mufti, a religious instrument of the state, producing or at least promoting a kind of religious culture that accepts the state and its policies.

There is a lot of truth in this premise; a state mufti is an employee of the state, a bureaucrat, and a key figure of its religious administration. In practically any Arab country, one would be able to point to an instance when the state mufti was apparently mobilized to support elements of state policy that were unpopular and met with resistance on religious grounds. But precisely this political utilization is well worth studying, as it will give us useful practical information on the relationship between state and religion in the various Muslim countries—pieces of information that could be used for interesting comparisons. Studying the *fatwas*, public appearances, and administrative dealings of state muftis should give us some indications of how states have been striving to make their policies religiously acceptable and may in some cases give a rare glimpse of the awareness of autocratic regimes of the degree of legitimacy—or lack thereof—of their authority and policies. Moreover, it is not always so easy to identify what the state wants and who is running it. Under certain circumstances, the state mufti may be less a representative of the state as such and rather an ally of a faction of the regime, and it will be important to study his activities in that light.

Finally, not surprisingly, state muftis tend to see themselves as something more than, if not indeed opposite to, the instrument of the state. What they tend to stress is their role as spokesmen for the religious sector of society, as defenders of the shari'a and its norms in a society moving toward secularization. They contend that it is they themselves who use the state as an instrument for their pious and devout religious policies, a claim that has some elements of truth in that very often the state muftis have the budget and the authority to convene conferences, publish information, institute policies, and in other ways influence the public on issues where they perceive a threat to religious norms, values, and rules. And there is also the rare occasion when a state mufti actually stands up against the government and demands that it change its policy on a specific point.

This dual role of the state mufti is similar to that of the 'ulama (Muslim religious scholars) at large as it has been described in earlier Muslim societies. Modern biographies of state muftis come across as much akin to the traditional tabaqat (biographies of the 'ulama) literature, highlighting the few instances of direct opposition and generally stressing their appropriately distant relations with the powers-that-be.

The role of the state mufti may vary quite considerably from state to state. While in some cases he is under tight control and very actively used by the state, in others he appears to have some leeway in following his own course and is able to take initiatives of his own, and in still others he is a fairly marginal person, of little interest to either the state or the public at large. Obviously, the role of the state mufti is dependent on factors such as the nature of government, state ideology, the composition of the 'ulama, and the degree of autonomy of the religious sector. But it is also influenced by the role and importance of religion in each society, including the phenomenon of the rise of Islamism (here understood as the ideology of nonseparation of state and Islam) and of the legal nature of Islam.

Given this variety, it might be useful to establish a typology of state muftis. This chapter is an attempt to do this on a minor scale in order to discuss some of the variables that may be considered in such a typology. To do this, I will compare three state mufti offices, namely, those of Syria, Lebanon, and Egypt, drawing on my own work on the Egyptian Mufti (Skovgaard-Petersen 1997) and on recent works, especially those on the Syrian mufti by Lina al-Homsi (1996) and Annabelle Böttcher (1998). The Syrian and Lebanese state muftis are of particular interest because both stem from the same office, that of the provincial mufti of the Ottoman Empire, and were subject to the same administrative laws in the early period of the French Mandate but have nevertheless developed in fairly different directions. They are thus evidence to the proposition that it is not so much local tradition as state ideology and organization that will determine the role of the state mufti in a given state.

In order to compare the three offices, I have selected a number of variables to be identified in each case: appointments and tenure, administrative tasks and position in bureaucracy, backgrounds of the individual muftis, the numbers and topics of their *fatwas*, involvement in Islamic internationalism, role in the national media, and competitors and response to the rise of Islamism.

The Ottoman Mufti

To understand the modern office of state mufti, it is important to examine its historical precedent during the late Ottoman period. As is well known, the Ottoman Empire developed a hierarchical religious administration with the mufti of Istanbul, the *Shaykh al-Islam*, at its head.[1] The Shaykh al-Islam had wide-ranging powers and was usually closely linked to the sultan and his *wazir*. He was appointed by the sultan and, in most cases, held the position for life. At least until the nineteenth century, his fatwas had great influence in courts, where they were often referred to in the verdicts given by the judges. It was therefore an established practice that litigants, in order to strengthen their case, asked for a fatwa from the Shaykh al-Islam in advance. His administration would rewrite the petition, erasing all particular information on time, place, and persons, thus formalizing it as a legal principle that the mufti would then endorse or reject. Some of the more important of these fatwas were collected in books and circulated, thus becoming legal precedence to be taken into account by judges while adjudicating similar cases.[2] In addition to this important and time-consuming task, the Shaykh al-Islam was also the head of the 'ulama and appointed the head judges and muftis of the empire.

While the Shaykh al-Islam operated out of Istanbul, on the local level (in our case in Damascus and Beirut and until some point in the nineteenth century also in Egypt), there were local muftis of each *madhhab* (school of law), the Hanafi mufti being the most important, as this was the madhhab of the Ottoman government. These muftis were in control of some *awqaf* (pious foundations) and were consulted by the courts, but their fatwas never developed into a standardized legal instrument, as did those of the Shaykh al-Islam. Instead, these muftis were often well-known scholars who devoted much of their time to studying and teaching, and the fatwa collections they left behind seem to have been intended for the study of *fiqh* and its methods rather than as legal manuals.

Two laws of the late Ottoman Empire, dated 1913 and 1917, gave these local Hanafi muftis great discretionary powers, as they were entrusted with giving fatwas, heading the 'ulama, supervising religious schools, and heading the council of *waqf*.[3] In addition, they were often members of local administrative councils. The appointment of these muftis was a compromise between local and central interests inasmuch as the Shaykh al-Islam would appoint one of three locally elected candidates.[4]

Syria

With the collapse of the Ottoman Empire, the role of the mufti of Damascus passed on to the Faysal administration in 1918 continued under the French mandatory administration in 1920. Because of the importance of the office in terms of honor and control of appointments and awqaf, it had been the object of rivalry between a small number of 'ulama families who had, by the late nineteenth century, given up their hostile attitude toward the Ottomans and pursued a strategy of incorporation into the Ottoman bureaucracy and intermarriage with the leading political families.[5]

In November 1918, immediately after the conquest of Damascus, Faysal appointed a new mufti of Damascus, Muhammad Ata al-Kasm (1844–1938), and gave him the title "general mufti of Sham."[6] And in the territorial Syria that gradually emerged, as the French mandatory administration gave up its attempt at dividing it into smaller statelets, the general mufti of Sham became the mufti of the Republic of Syria. It was unclear, however, what exactly would be the role of a "mufti of the Republic" when this republic was in fact secular.

The role of fatwas in courts disappeared, and with the establishment of a Parliament, not to mention the very powerful French administration, the mufti no longer had any direct role in politics. The French administration also took an interest in religious affairs, especially waqf, which they tried to bring under control with the establishment of a special administration, the "Controle Général des Wakfs Musulmans," in 1921.[7] This administration had its seat in Beirut and was headed not by a mufti but by a local *qadi* (judge) in the shari'a court. In 1930, the Syrian and Lebanese awqaf administrations were separated from each other. In independent Syria, a decree in 1947 affirmed the separation of the state mufti from the affairs of awqaf.[8]

The mufti of the Republic did, however, retain some control over the 'ulama, and in the previously mentioned decree of 1947, he was placed at the head of a central administration of *ifta'* (issuing fatwas) with branches all over Syria. There were forty-eight provincial muftis, a few of them representing the Isma'ili and Shi'a schools of jurisprudence. These muftis were not, however, appointed by the state mufti himself but rather by the prime minister.[9]

In 1961, a new law on the religious administration of Syria was promulgated, and it is essentially still in place. It set up a Ministry of Awqaf and made the minister the highest authority of the Sunni religious sector. The mufti retained a number of very important functions but now through a collective body, the "Higher Council of Ifta'," with six members and the state mufti as its head. This Higher Council of Ifta was made responsible not only for issuing and registering fatwas but also for administering the religious sector as a whole: it administered the mosques, religious schools, and religious cultural institutions, including the hiring and firing of personnel.[10] When the Baath Party came to power in 1963, it did not abolish this quite important body but added extra members to it and began transferring parts of its function, especially the right of promotion, to the minister himself.

The political importance of the state mufti is reflected in the many attempts by the various Syrian regimes at influencing his election by altering the laws of appointment to the office.[11] When Muhammad Ata al-Kasm died in 1938, he was simply followed by his aide (the *amin al-fatwa*), Muhammad Shukri al-Ustuwani (1869–1955). When the latter died, however, a new law had come into force whereby a committee consisting of provincial muftis agreed on three candidates from whom the prime minister chose the new mufti. This law was followed when the new

85

mufti, Muhammad Abu l-Yusr Abidin (1890–1981), was elected in 1954. The law of 1961 established a new electoral procedure whereby an electoral college consisting of the members of the Higher Council of Ifta', the provincial muftis, the qadis of Damascus and Aleppo, and a further ten 'ulama actually elected the new mufti by secret ballot. This in effect made the mufti a representative of the 'ulama. However, when Mufti Abidin was dismissed in 1963 and this procedure was adopted for the first time in 1964 (after a period with an interim mufti), the election of the current mufti, Shaykh Ahmad Koftaro (b. 1915), with a majority of one vote, seems to have come as a surprise to many of the thirty-six members of the electoral body who had congregated in the offices of the minister of Awqaf.[12] In 1967, the electoral law was changed again, so that whenever Mufti Koftaro dies, the Ministry will list three candidates from whom the mufti will be selected by the Council of Ministers.

Despite the political bickering around the appointments—or perhaps because of it—most muftis have held the position for life, sitting on average for twenty years. This contrasts sharply with the Ottoman period, when the average tenure was around four years. Particularly during the late Ottoman period, the office of mufti of Damascus was inscribed in an elaborate hierarchy of religious positions. The muftis had made their career in the courts, and some of them went on to become, for instance, qadi of the holy cities. In modern Syria, the mufti of the Republic is the top position, it is not related to the courts, and the incumbents are more likely to have had a career in preaching and teaching. And only one of them has been dismissed, namely, Muhammad Abu l-Yusr Abidin, who was removed from his position in 1961 because of his opposition to state confiscation of private property.[13] After the demise of the United Arab Republic that same year, he was appointed again, apparently only to be dismissed once again in 1963 with the coming to power of the Baath Party. This, at least, is the interpretation of Annabelle Böttcher, who also points out that the fact that his successor, Ahmad Koftaro, was a Kurd and a Shafi'i weakened the latter's power base among the Damascene 'ulama and made him an attractive candidate for the Baath.[14]

I have not been able to obtain the precise number of the fatwas given by the various muftis in their official capacity. According to Lina al-Homsi, the *Da'irat al-Ifta'* has lost the fatwa registers for the first half of the twentieth century, but apparently the fatwas of the first mufti,

Muhammad Ata al-Kasm, now kept by his son, number more than 14,000.[15] This is a very high number but not wholly unlikely given the drastic social and legal changes during the French Mandate; it may well be that many Syrian Muslims considered the mufti the authority to turn to in matters of how to live and deal with the many novelties introduced during this period. However, it is also quite likely that, in independent Syria, to many Muslims the mufti is no longer seen as an independent moral authority, and they may prefer to consult other 'ulama outside the state bureaucracy.

It seems safe to say that with an office headed by the amin al-fatwa, who actually prepares the fatwas, the state mufti today cannot be much burdened with ifta. Instead, the twentieth-century muftis have been much involved in teaching. In contrast to his predecessors, the current mufti, Ahmad Koftaro, has had an impressive travel program, participating in more than fifty international Islamic conferences around the world, often explicitly to promote interreligious understanding.[16] With state support, in 1972 a huge six-story religious center, the Abu Nur Mosque, was built for his teaching activities, and here he has succeeded in building up a significant following who attend classes and lectures and participate in his particular branch of the Naqshbandiya Sufi order. With the rise of Islamism in the 1970s, the position of a state mufti in a secularist, Alawi-dominated state was bound to be precarious, and there has been much opposition against him within the Islamist movement. But anyone who has visited the Abu Nur Mosque can testify that he has succeeded in diverting a substantial part of the broader phenomenon of the Islamic awakening toward religious activities of a less political nature.

To sum up, we have seen that, in independent Syria, the state has taken great efforts to control the appointment and activities of the state mufti. The many important tasks of the Ottoman provincial Mufti have gradually been removed from it. And with the establishment of the Ministry of Awqaf, the regime has taken control over mosques and religious schools, including their financial administration. Today, the mufti is a religious functionary in the Ministry with few administrative powers and little independence. He remains, however, an important figure as the official embodiment of Islamic law and morals. Especially in the era of the Baath Party, there have been attempts at instrumentalizing the office to legitimize the regime and its policies. Ahmad Koftaro has taken part in this, of course. But he has also pursued a strategy of withdrawal—or perhaps privatization of his religious functions—preferring to act through his teaching, thereby successfully tapping in to and furthering the Islamic awakening in Syria.

It is a difficult game: his official biographers, including the previously mentioned Lina al-Homsi, stress the few times that he actually resisted and criticized government policies; for example, in 1967 he threatened to resign if an atheist article in the journal of the Syrian army was not officially withdrawn.[17] One could argue that such stories emphasize the moral and religious integrity of the man in office and only serve the interests of the powers-that-be in affirming that the mufti is a "great intellectual" who can certify that the social order is religiously acceptable and morally right. On the other hand, one could also argue that these stories deceive no one but that they do affirm a general skeptical worldview of at least parts of the Syrian population that the state and religion are in a basic conflict and that any decent state mufti will be operating in a perpetual conflict of moral dilemmas.

Lebanon

Turning to the Lebanese case, we initially see the same basic pattern followed by the French administration that stripped the office of provincial Mufti of some of its functions, most importantly the control of awqaf. But very quickly, the story moves in a different direction. This is due to the nature of the Lebanese state that emerged in the 1920s. First of all, the establishment of the position of mufti of Lebanon was rather more controversial than in the case of Syria, as probably the majority of Sunnis, and especially the 'ulama, for decades rejected the idea of territorial Lebanon. Consequently, the mufti of Beirut, Mustafa an-Naja, declined to take part in the preparation of the constitution of 1926, and he did not accept the title of mufti of the Lebanese Republic but insisted on being just mufti of Beirut right up to his death in 1932.[18] By then, however, the confessional power sharing system of the Lebanese state was in place, providing each of the religious confessions a great measure of autonomy in the religious and educational sphere. A mufti of the Republic was thus indispensable for administrative and confessional guidance, if not for his fatwas. Even the control of awqaf, which, as mentioned, was reorganized and taken away from the muftis in 1921, was partly placed under his authority again with the establishment of a "Supreme Legal Council" in 1931 with the mufti at its head.[19] The following mufti, Muhammad Tawfiq Khalid, strove to use the new title and powers to act as a general spokesman of the Sunni Muslims in religious matters. What we have left from him is a collection of political speeches and sermons directed mainly against the French. After the war, in independent Lebanon, he built the Dar al-Fatwa complex in western Beirut, which houses the mufti's office and administration of mosques and their staff as well as an institution of higher Islamic studies. When Khalid died in 1951, he was succeeded by Muhammad Alaya, a less political mufti.[20]

In 1955, a law was passed instituting the Sunni Muslim religious administration in independent Lebanon. The aim was to secure for the Sunnis an absolute independence from the state by setting up an institution with legislative powers within the field of Sunni religious and internal affairs. This meant that a new and powerful Supreme Legal Council was erected with the participation of all Sunni ministers, ex-ministers, and members of Parliament but still headed by the mufti.[21] The inclusion of all important Sunni political leaders meant, of course, that their political rivalry was also played out in this body, which had, moreover, an important role as employer of staff in schools and mosques and was thus a major source of patronage. In addition, an electoral committee for the Council was set up consisting not only of 'ulama but also of the politicians and members of the Sunni professional elite.

Article 2 in Law 18 of 1955 reads, "The Mufti of the Lebanese Republic is the religious head of the Muslims, and in this capacity, he represents them vis-à-vis the authorities. He is entitled to the same respect, rights and privileges that are enjoyed by the other superior heads of religion, without modification or exception."[22] Article 3 makes him the direct head of all Muslim men of religion and the highest authority in matters of waqf and ifta', and he is in charge of all Muslims' religious and social affairs. Article 6 gives him life tenure. The powers of the mufti of the Lebanese Republic are thus very considerable, and, once elected, he is very difficult to get rid of. With this law, he is constituted not only as a religious administrator but as a kind of behind-the-scenes Sunni politician with great influence.

As is the case in Syria, the political importance of the state mufti is clearly reflected in the ever-changing rules of his selection. The interesting thing in Lebanon—and this is a general feature of Lebanese politics—is not the question of appointment versus election, for the electoral principle is not in doubt, but the question of the composition of the electorate. In 1932, the French administration left the election of Muhammad Tawfiq Khalid entirely to an electoral college consisting of thirty-two high 'ulama. With the adoption of the Law of 1955, on the other hand, the mufti was not really the representative of the 'ulama anymore but rather of the Sunni community at large. Consequently, his election was no longer seen as the prerogative of the 'ulama, but he was to be elected by a much larger committee consisting of all eminent Sunni representatives in politics and the administration and professions. A decree of 1967 further enlarged this electoral body, rendering the 'ulama a clear minority.[23] The problem with the Law of 1955, of course, is that the election of the mufti of the Republic is turned into a quite direct and dangerous competition for influence by the leading Sunni politicians. This happened for the first time in 1966, when the two leading conservative Sunni politicians in Beirut at the time, Saib Salam and Abd Allah al-Yafi, invested great efforts in promoting a relatively unknown judge, Hasan Khalid, in order to avoid the nomination of a left-leaning populist preacher, Shafiq Yamut.[24] Hasan Khalid was assassinated in 1989, and his appointed successor, Muhammad Rashid al-Qabbani, acted as interim mufti for seven years, pending a decision by the leading Sunni politicians to go ahead with new elections, a potentially dangerous and divisive procedure in the aftermath of the civil war. When elections were finally held, once again a new law had to be passed, reducing the number of electors from more than 1,000 to 96. This made it easier to convene and control the electorate. The law was passed in the morning on December 26, 1996, and in the afternoon the electorate convened and elected Qabbani mufti of the Republic.[25] Two days prior to that, it should be added, he had been received in audience by Syrian President Hafez al-Asad. This can be seen as the end of a long process whereby the election of the mufti has been removed from the men of religion and relegated to the Sunni politicians.[26]

The only group to protest against the election and its procedure was the Jama'a Islamiya, the Islamist party of Lebanon, which saw this as political interference in religious affairs. Another critic of al-Qabbani who seems to have nurtured ambitions for himself, the political leader of the group known as al-Ahbash, Nizar al-Halabi, was shot down in August 1995. It seems fair to assert that a main reason for the final promotion of al-Qabbani to full mufti of the Republic was the need among the leading Sunni politicians for an institution that could represent a non-Islamist version of Sunni Islam to the public and ensure the promotion of non-Islamist preachers in the mosque hierarchy. On the other hand, it also seems fair to assert that the reason why it took seven years to promote al-Qabbani was that the leading Sunni politicians, primarily Prime Minister Rafiq al-Hariri, had little interest in reviving a strong mufti of the Republic. Although Hasan Khalid had been the candidate of the leading politicians in 1966, he had soon demonstrated a capacity to carve out a power base for himself, partly through establishing contacts to Islamically oriented regimes abroad, and during the Lebanese civil war, when the militias of the Sunni political leaders were defeated by the militias of the other confessions, the mufti and the Dar al-Fatwa had evolved into a central Sunni political institution.

To conclude, the figure of Hasan Khalid, in particular, chosen for his political views and pursuing a political strategy, demonstrates well the transformation of an essentially religious office into a predominantly political one in the Lebanese case. The mufti of Lebanon gives few fatwas, according to the amin al-fatwa, perhaps fifty per year, and these are private ones, prepared by the amin and not by the mufti himself (interview, Dar al-Fatwa, March 1996). There are other muftis much more respected for their knowledge of fiqh and consulted by the Sunnis of Lebanon. But Qabbani is often in the news, representing a Sunni view on social and religious issues and, like the heads of the other confessions, a symbol and sometimes affirmer of the confessionalist system. This is also expressed in the new constitution of 1990, which calls for the abolition of the confessional system and the establishment of a second chamber where the heads of religion will have permanent seats in addition to a special authority to raise issues directly with the Constitutional Court.[27]

Egypt

The office of "mufti of the Egyptian lands" took form in the late nineteenth century, parallel to a number of legal reforms that abolished the

role of fatwas in courts. Instead, the mufti became involved in state reformist policies, especially under the muftiship of Muhammad Abduh
(1899–1905), who found a new role for the mufti as a public service institution, giving fatwas to the administration and the public at large, sometimes to help out-of-court settlements.[28]

In contrast to the Ottoman Empire and its successors in Syria and
Lebanon, the state mufti in Egypt is not involved in the administration of
religious education, which is the preserve of al-Azhar. Neither is he involved in the awqaf, which have their own ministry. The mufti is employed by the Ministry of Justice but is only vaguely related to the court
system, primarily through the task of scrutinizing death sentences that
have to be in conformity with the rules of fiqh. With the abolishment of
the shari'a courts in 1955, some minor tasks, previously the preserve of the
chief qadi, were transferred to the state mufti, the most important of
which today is the announcement of the beginning of the Islamic lunar
months based on the observation of the new moon.[29]

The question of selection is very different from the Syrian and the
Lebanese cases. In Egypt, the mufti is simply appointed by the president,
formerly by the king, and there has been no prior nomination of candidates by the 'ulama. In general, the selected man has had a distinguished
career at al-Azhar and, until recently, in the shari'a courts. He is considered to be loyal, reasonable, and capable by the president: his usefulness
will be enhanced if he is also respected as a scholar by the 'ulama and the
public at large. For most of the twentieth century, there had been a retire-
ment age for state employees in Egypt, and this is one reason why the
muftis have been in office for much shorter time than is the case in Syria
and Lebanon. Another reason is that a few of them chose to resign after
political disagreements with the king. Yet another reason, especially characteristic of the past two decades, is that the mufti, having demonstrated
his loyalty and general capacities, has been promoted to the even higher
position of shaykh of al-Azhar, the highest religious dignitary in the country. Since World War I, there have thus been fourteen state muftis in
Egypt, in contrast to Syria's four and Lebanon's five. This is why they are
not listed here.

The Egyptian mufti of the Republic could perhaps be described as a
kind of religious handyman for the state. He can point out discrepancies
in legislation and administration that might cause problems with the reli-

gious sentiments of parts of the population. He can sit on committees, for instance, preparing new legislation on family law and similar Islam-related issues. He can address and answer the religious anxieties and questions of the public, thereby affirming the religiously acceptable nature or at least the good religious intentions of the state and its administration. Finally, he can be an important counterweight to the shaykh of al-Azhar if the latter develops too independent and oppositional ideas. This was witnessed in the early 1990s.[30]

Apart from these tasks, the mufti of the Republic has his own agenda. He can arrange conferences and sometimes act behind the scene to promote Islamic issues. But most important, he can raise issues directly with the public through a special type of longer, more studied fatwa that has either been requested by a state agency or simply prepared by himself as a kind of report or press statement. Some of these fatwas may be fully in accordance with the wishes and priorities of the government, for instance, his fatwa on the Camp David peace accord or his fatwas on family planning. But there are others that are less closely related to government policies and seem more to reflect a strategy of asserting Islamic values in the face of a threatening secularization.

That the mufti must have preserved a certain religious integrity in at least some people's eyes is evidenced in his ifta', which is on a much larger scale than in Lebanon and probably also Syria today. The mufti of Egypt issues around 500 fatwas per year, mainly to ordinary Egyptian *mustaftis* (those seeking his opinion) but also as a response to inquiries from the administration and from abroad.[31] Many of these fatwas are later published by the Dar al-Ifta', especially the longer important ones, for instance, on current medical and economic issues. More than his Syrian and Lebanese counterparts, the mufti of Egypt thus represents an important voice in the debates on Islamic solutions to modern challenges, especially in the field of law. In this, he can be seen as a competitor also to the international fatwa-issuing bodies, such as the Muslim World League's fiqh committee or al-Azhar's own Academy of Islamic Research.

These are not his only competitors, however. Especially since the 1970s, the state mufti has come up for criticism by the new Islamist groups who generally have their own muftis to rely on. They have criticized him for being a puppet of the state who gives Islamic credence to its anti-Islamic policies. The mufti has had to respond to these accusations, which, because of a relatively free press, are formulated and circulated much more widely in Egypt than in Syria.[32] The idea of being a defender of Islam against the onslaught of secularization is, of course, more difficult to uphold for the mufti when he is criticized openly on Islamic terms. In short, while the general Islamic awakening may have multiplied the questions for fatwas and done much to make the state mufti an important figure in the Egyptian public today, the Islamist criticism has rendered the very position of state mufti in a country like Egypt quite precarious. His response has been to affirm his authority and mastery of the Islamic authoritative texts and expose Islamism as an ill-informed and misguided political exploitation of Islam. Since the 1970s, the state mufti of Egypt has been at the forefront of the government campaign against Islamism. He has been rewarded with an enlarged administration and a new office building in neo-Islamic style, symbolically overlooking al-Azhar at ad-Darasa.

In more substantive and concrete questions, he has identified himself with a pious pragmatism, a kind of Salafi modernism where modern life and thought can be given its due as long as this does not infringe on basic Islamic principles. Hence, in the 1980s, the mufti chose to redirect some of the more difficult questions posed to him to specialists on the issue involved (finance, for instance), thus in effect transforming himself into a concerned mustafti who will evaluate the answer from the point of view of Islamic law and ethics. This, to me, is an interesting attempt at disclaiming some of the authority vested on him and opting for a more modest role as a kind of model conscience, discussing the issue rather than settling it. I have not come across anything similar in Syria or Lebanon.

Conclusions: The Role of State Muftis in an Age of Islamism

We have seen three different developments of the office of state mufti from the late nineteenth century and until today. Both the Syrian and the Lebanese cases have preserved the essentially administrative identity of the provincial mufti but in different ways. In Syria, he is still formally the head of the 'ulama, but now through the body of the Higher Council of Ifta', which has little to do with actual fatwa giving. This body, however, has gradually been emptied of its political importance, and especially since the early 1960s, a tendency toward greater state control and instrumental-ization can be observed. In Lebanon, on the other hand, the mufti of Beirut has developed into a political figure of potential importance, with an institutional power base and considerable control over the Sunni reli-gious sector, which, in turn, enjoys considerable independence from the state. In Lebanon, the mufti of the Republic is certainly not a representa-tive of the state but rather the formal head of an interest group that he represents vis-à-vis the state and the other confessions. In Egypt, finally, the mufti has no administrative tasks or political power base or indeed for-mal independence. But there is an established tradition of the mufti act-ing as an Islamic conscience in society, and his longer fatwas directed at the public at large have sometimes set the agenda for public debate. While the Egyptian mufti is clearly a legitimizing instrument of the state, he is also more of an intellectual than in the Syrian and Lebanese cases and has to debate important issues in public. In contrast to the others, his ifta' is central but contested.

The three impressive administrative buildings of the muftis of Syria, Lebanon, and Egypt say it rather well: all of them built at a high point of state gratitude for the services rendered by the mufti. As will be clear by now, the general inference that the role of state muftis is to sanction state policies and mobilize public support is generally correct. But it is not an adequate explanation. Political fatwas there are, but they are relatively few, and other fatwas reveal a certain independence and sometimes a more par-ticularist agenda. It seems fair to say that, while he certainly has to serve the state, the individual state mufti also has some room for maneuvering himself. And where state pressures are most massively felt, as in Syria of the 1970s and Egypt of the 1980s, the state mufti can also adopt new strategies, such as Koftaro's privatization of his functions and concentra-tion on education or the Egyptian mufti Sayyid Tantawi's sometimes al-most open-ended fatwas where material is put forward and discussed and several solutions are suggested.

It is interesting to note that precisely these two muftis, who have been particularly singled out for criticism by the Islamist oppositions, have re-tained a certain popularity in non-Islamist circles—some of them also af-fected by the general Islamic awakening. They have been admired for their courage to speak up against, or at least present an alternative to, what in these circles is seen as a rigid and conformist version of Islam. It is my impression that many non-Islamist Muslims are well aware that the state mufti is under pressure from the state and that they may disagree profoundly with the regime on many other issues—that they, in other words, sympathize with the mufti not for representing the state but for the views he expresses. Whether in Syria, Lebanon, or Egypt, it seems that a state mufti's authority cannot rest solely on being vested with the authority of the state. As the status of the independent postcolonial state has dwindled in the eyes of its citizenry, a state mufti is perhaps increasingly seen not as someone who should automatically command respect, as the state would have it, or disrespect, as the Islamist opposition would insist. Rather, it seems that today, above anything else, the state mufti is faced with the task of legitimizing himself.

Notes

1. On the history of the Ottoman Shaykh al-Islam, see Richard Repp, *The Mufti of Istanbul* (London: Ithaca Press, 1986).

2. Haim Gerber, *State, Society, Law in Islam: Ottoman Law in Comparative Perspective* (Albany: State University of New York Press, 1994), 88–92.

3. Adnan Ahmed Badr, *Al-Ifta' wa 'l-Awqaf al-Islamiya fi Lubnan* (Beirut: al-Mu'assassa al-Jama'iyya, 1992), 14–15. On the transition from Ottoman to Republican muftis in Syria and Lebanon, see Jakob Skovgaard-Petersen, "Levantine State Muftis—An Ottoman Legacy?," in *The Ottoman Intellectual Heritage*, ed. Elizabeth Özdalga (in press).

4. Badr, *Al-Ifta wa 'l-Awqaf al-Islamiya fi Lubnan*, 15.

5. Ruth Roded, "Ottoman Service as a Vehicle for the Rise of New Upstarts among the Urban Elite Families of Syria in the Last Decades of Ottoman Rule," *Asian and African Studies* 17 (1983): 63–94; Philip Khoury, *Urban Notables and Arab Nationalism* (Cambridge: Cambridge University Press, 1983).

6. Lina al-Homsi, *Al-Muftun al-'Ammun fi Suriya* (Damascus: Dar al-'Asma' 1996), 29.

7. Badr, *Al-Ifta' wa 'l-Awqaf al-Islamiya fi Lubnan*, 17–22.

8. Annabelle Böttcher, *Syrische Religionspolitik unter Asad* (Freiburg: Arnold Bergsträsser Institut, 1998), 19.

9. Böttcher, *Syrische Religionspolitik unter Asad*, 49.

10. Böttcher, *Syrische Religionspolitik unter Asad*, 63–65.

11. Böttcher, *Syrische Religionspolitik unter Asad*, 54.

12. Böttcher, *Syrische Religionspolitik unter Asad*, 56.

13. al-Homsi, *Al-Muftun al-'Ammun fi Suriya: Damascus, Dar al-'Asma'*, 35.

14. Böttcher, *Syrische Religionspolitik unter Asad*, 55–58.

15. al-Homsi, *Al-Muftun al-'Ammun fi Suriya: Damascus, Dar al-'Asma'*, 25, 29, n. 5.

16. al-Homsi, *Al-Muftun al-'Ammun fi Suriya: Damascus, Dar al-'Asma'*, 80–92.

17. al-Homsi, *Al-Muftun al-'Ammun fi Suriya: Damascus, Dar al-'Asma'*, 117–18.

18. Badawi Swaid, "As-Sunna fi Lubnan," *Ad-Diyar* 18–25: 10 (1990).

19. Decree 157/1 of December 16, 1931, § 23. Al-Hut, Abd al-Rahman, *al-Awqaf al-Islamiyya fi Lubnan* (Beirut: N.p., 1984), 18–20.

20. Swaid, "As-Sunna fi Lubnan," 24/10.

21. Badr, *Al-Ifta' wa 'l-Awqaf al-Islamiya fi Lubnan*, 159–70.

22. Badr, *Al-Ifta' wa 'l-Awqaf al-Islamiya fi Lubnan*, 248.

23. Badr, *Al-Ifta' wa 'l-Awqaf al-Islamiya fi Lubnan*, 90–94.

24. Swaid, "As-Sunna fi Lubnan," 24/10.

25. *Al-Hayat*, December 30, 1996, 3.

26. Jakob Skovgaard-Petersen, "The Sunni Religious Scene in Beirut," *Mediterranean Politics* 3, no. 1 (1998): 69–80.

27. Lebanese Constitution (1990), § 22, 19. See *Beirut Review* 4 (1994): 119–60 for the full text of the constitution in English.

28. Jakob Skovgaard-Petersen, *Defining Islam for the Egyptian State* (Leiden: Brill, 1997), 375–76.

29. Skovgaard-Petersen, *Defining Islam for the Egyptian State*, 196–97.

30. Skovgaard-Petersen, *Defining Islam for the Egyptian State*, 286–89.

31. Skovgaard-Petersen, *Defining Islam for the Egyptian State*, 387–78.

32. Skovgaard-Petersen, *Defining Islam for the Egyptian State*, 298–315.

CHAPTER FOUR

A CONTEXTUAL APPROACH TO IMPROVING ASYLUM LAW AND PRACTICES IN THE MIDDLE EAST

Nadia Yakoob and Aimen Mir

The approach in the Middle East toward asylum and refugees, like many other areas of law and society in the region, provides an example of the tension between culturally appropriate practices and the applicability of international notions of human rights. On the one hand, the states in the Middle East enjoy a rich history of offering protection to forced migrants. On the other hand, these states face pressure to adopt the international legal framework that developed in the West for the protection of "refugees." Middle Eastern states and human rights advocates are, as a result, faced with the challenge of reconciling the regional history and custom of protecting forced migrants in the Middle East with the internationalization of legal standards governing the protection of refugees.

We begin by presenting a snapshot of the current refugee flows in the Middle East. By looking at these numbers, we ask on what basis are these individuals permitted to enter and remain in the host states. This chapter explores the relevance of international legal obligations, regional frameworks, Islamic teachings, and domestic mechanisms for the reception and protection of forced migrants. We seek to identify the bases on which protection is offered in order to find a way by which to hold these states accountable, thereby making protection less arbitrary and ad hoc while preserving the fundamental right to seek asylum and not to be returned to a place where an individual faces persecution.

Through this examination, we found that the most realistic approach to building and strengthening existing regimes for the protection of forced migrants in the Middle East is at the individual state level. We also note that improving mechanisms for protection is ultimately related to and dependent on addressing more fundamental human rights violations in the region.

Identifying the Bases for Protection of Forced Migrants in the Middle East

States highly value their sovereign right to "control the entry, residence, and expulsion of aliens."[1] Yet despite this jealously guarded right, states—including those in the Middle East, as reflected in table 4.1—permit the entry of aliens, even where the entry is primarily a source of burden rather than benefit for the host state. Most states recognize some obligation to assist those fleeing persecution and have taken some measures to formalize such an obligation. Many states have chosen to bind themselves internationally, with the 1951 Refugee Convention being the primary instrument and the foundation of modern international refugee law.[2] Surprisingly, most states in the Middle East have not ratified the 1951 Convention or its 1967 Protocol.[3] The only Arab countries to accede to the Convention are Yemen and Egypt.

Some states that have not bound themselves to international instruments nonetheless bind themselves under domestic law. Constitutional provisions of most Arab states prohibit the extradition of political refugees. Several of them explicitly mention the right to political asylum. Very few Arab states, however, have passed domestic legislation that guarantees the right to seek asylum. Iraq, Lebanon, and Yemen are the only three countries in the Middle East to have passed laws concerning refugees.

These generally weak laws and the absence of legal mechanisms to protect refugees in the remaining states of the Middle East cause concern to many refugee and human rights lawyers. This concern is amplified by the large-scale forcible displacement that has occurred in the region, for example, after the Gulf War in 1991. Typically, the Middle Eastern states have been urged by the United Nations to remedy the situation by ratifying the 1951 Convention and the 1967 Protocol and establishing some form of regional framework for the protection of refugees. While such recommendations are justifiable, we argue that building national capacities for

Table 4.1. The Number of Forced Migrants in the Middle East[a]

Country	Population of Concern to UNHCR	Number of Asylum Seekers	Origins of Refugees
Egypt[b]	22,900	15,655	Sudanese
			Somalis
			Yemenis
Iraq	130,500	393	Iranians
			Turks
			Palestinians
Jordan	6,400 (1,263,000 Palestinians)	5,297	Iraqis
			Sudanese
			Somalis
			Syrians
			Libyans
			Former Yugoslavians
Kuwait	139,300	80	Stateless Bedouins
			Afghanis
			Iraqis
			Somalis
			Palestinians
Lebanon	6,500 (350,000 Palestinians)	3,680	Iraqis
			Afghanis
			Sudanese
			Somalis
Libya	11,700	15	Palestinians
			Somalis
			Eritreans
			Sudanese
			Ethiopians
Saudi Arabia	245,500	234	Iraqis
			Afghanis
Syria	4,000	605	Iraqis
			Yemenis
			Somalis
			Sudanese
United Arab Emirates	900	361	Somalis
			Ugandans
			Iraqis
			Iranians
Yemen[b]	72,000	2,361	Somalis
			Eritreans
			Ethiopians
Totals	639,700 Individuals of Concern to UNHCR 2,252,700 total displaced populations including Palestinians		

[a] Numbers based on UNHCR's *Statistical Yearbook 2001* (available at www.unhcr.ch).
[b] Countries that are party to the 1951 Refugee Convention and 1967 Protocol.

the protection of refugees should come first. Efforts by the international community to date have focused primarily on creating a regional mechanism under the auspices of the League of Arab States, though political divides within the region have tempered the effectiveness of such efforts. The League's draft declaration relating to the status of refugees, issued in 1994, has no legal effect. The development of national laws and national institutions, however, could bypass the need to overcome political divides in the region and reflect domestic political realities for states in a region that is marked by conflict. Such a politically realistic approach is necessary to surmount the enormous obstacles that relate to the very basic tension between international law and state sovereignty that is captured by refugee law.

Is There a Right to Protection?

International refugee law is based on the idea that a person who is persecuted or oppressed in his or her country of origin has the right to leave and seek protection in another state. The right to seek asylum is a principle of international law that challenges the sovereignty of a state because it requires that an outsider be permitted to enter a sovereign state and ask for protection.[4] Thus, the state's fundamental right to control the entry of aliens (to the ultimate aim of preserving its community) is modified.

An asylum seeker can exercise the right to asylum if he or she meets the definition of refugee established by the host state—that is, he or she is recognized as worthy of protection.[5] The right to asylum necessarily encompasses the right not to be returned to a place where one faces persecution or oppression. In certain situations, a state will resettle a recognized refugee in another country where he or she will be free from persecution. Resettlement provides protection for the refugee and also allows a state to exercise some measure of discretion in choosing who can stay within its borders. According to the UN High Commissioner for Refugees (UNHCR), resettlement is one of three durable solutions to the plight of refugees, the other two being voluntary repatriation and integration into the host state.[6]

Unlike the right to seek asylum, the right to asylum and the right to not be returned to a place of persecution are subject to certain overriding state interests, such as national security and the public interest. The 1951

Refugee Convention specifically enumerates categories of individuals that are per se unworthy of protection, such as war criminals and persons who have committed serious nonpolitical crimes before arriving in the host state.[7] A state can also expel or return refugees who have committed a particularly serious crime in the host state or constitute a danger to the community of that country, even if the refugee's life or freedom would be threatened on return.[8] National security interests clearly permeate the Refugee Convention and trump the right of refugees to enduring protection. Encouraging the Middle Eastern states to promulgate domestic asylum laws while recognizing national concerns is, therefore, also compatible with the principles of international refugee law.

Furthermore, analyzing refugee flows from a security paradigm reveals that an influx of refugees can threaten a host state's sociopolitical stability. Myron Weiner identified four principal ways in which refugee populations can destabilize a host state.[9] First, the host country's decision to grant refugee protection can create or reinforce an adversarial relationship with the refugee-producing country. Second, refugee populations may become so strong as to function independently of the host state, often at the host state's detriment. The Palestinians in Jordan during the 1960s are a case in point. Third, large refugee communities can challenge a cultural identity. Finally, host states often perceive refugees as social or economic burdens. The economic costs associated with protecting refugees, the additional competition in tight job markets, and the resentment experienced by local impoverished communities toward the international assistance given to refugees exacerbate tensions. Security[10] concerns, therefore, lead states to grant refugee protection with caution. Some states even fear that giving protection to a small number of individuals "might open a flood-gate and lead to the entry of more immigrants than society is prepared to accept."[11] As such, states prefer restrictive criteria in order to keep the influx small.[12]

The 1951 Convention Relating to the
Status of Refugees and Its Protocol

We have chosen to emphasize the development of domestic asylum law not only because it allows each state in the Middle East to address its domestic political interests but also because we recognize the valid concerns held by these states regarding the 1951 Refugee Convention and regional frameworks, specifically under the League of Arab States. The 1951 Refugee Convention was formulated in the immediate post–World War II period in response to the flow of European refugees. The Convention's scope was limited in both time and territorial application. First, the Convention applied only to individuals fleeing persecution on account of events occurring before January 1, 1951.[13] Second, the Convention allowed state parties to limit the territorial application to Europe. Under Article 1(B), "the words 'events occurring before 1 January 1951' in Article 1, Section A, shall be understood to mean either a) 'events occurring *in Europe* before 1 January 1951'; or b) 'events occurring in Europe or elsewhere before 1 January 1951.'" State parties had to specify at the time of signature, ratification, or accession which meaning they intended to follow.

Furthermore, the Convention excludes Palestinian refugees from its mandate under Article 1(D), which states, "This Convention shall not apply to persons who are at present receiving from organs or agencies of the United Nations other than the United Nations High Commissioner for Refugee protection or assistance." Since Palestinians were receiving assistance from the UN Relief and Works Agency (UNRWA), created specifically to assist them, they could not fall within the scope of the 1951 Refugee Convention.

The 1951 Convention was thus a Eurocentric instrument designed to deal with European-defined problems. Professor Khadija Elmadmad observed, "This Convention did not take into consideration the traditions, laws and values relating to asylum and forced migration in other parts of the world, and very few Moslem States participated in the drafting."[14] It is therefore not surprising that Arab states have been reluctant to sign it. Of the twenty-one member countries of the Arab League, only nine have ratified the 1951 Convention relating to the status of refugees, the majority of which are in Africa: Algeria, Djibouti, Egypt, Mauritania, Morocco, Somalia, Sudan, Tunisia, and Yemen.[15]

The 1967 Protocol, however, lifted both the time and the territorial limits.[16] Under Article I(2), the term "refugee" would no longer be limited to those individuals fleeing persecution as a result of events occurring before January 1, 1951.[17] Article I(3) provides that "the present Protocol shall be applied by the State Parties hereto *without any geographical limitation.*"[18] The Protocol removed the European orientation of the 1951 Convention, making it a more universal document. While such a document should be more appealing to the Arab states, the continuing resistance to it is understandable in light of its historical origins.[19] Moreover, the exclusion of the Palestinians continued in the Protocol. The Arab states were generally frustrated with the United Nations and the international community for failing to implement the numerous General Assembly resolutions passed concerning the Palestinians refugees' right to return,[20] which influenced and reinforced their skepticism toward human rights instruments issued by the United Nations.

Regional Frameworks: The League of Arab States

Efforts to create a regional framework for the protection of refugees have been under way since the 1980s, culminating in the Arab Convention on Refugees in 1994 under the auspices of the League of Arab States.[21] To date, no country has ratified it, and only Egypt has signed it.[22] It is, therefore, not yet in effect. While the Arab Convention incorporates language from the 1951 Convention, it adopts a much broader definition of refugee. Curiously, although the Preamble of the Arab Convention refers to the Universal Declaration Human Rights, the two International Covenants of 1966, and the Cairo Declaration on the Protection of Refugees and Displaced Persons in the Arab World, it does not mention the 1951 Convention or the 1967 Protocol.

The Arab Convention, under Article 1, defines a refugee as anyone who, owing to a well-founded fear of being persecuted on account of race, religion, nationality, or membership of a particular social group, is outside the country of his nationality and is unable or, owing to such fear, unwilling to avail himself of the protection of that country.[23] This language effectively mirrors that of the 1951 Refugee Convention except for one omission. The Arab Convention omits *political opinion* as a ground for having a well-founded fear of persecution. This gap, however, could be filled by the League of Arab States' 1952 Arab Convention on Extradition, which forbids the extradition of political offenders except for crimes against kings and heads of state and their families (Article 4).[24]

In addition, the Arab Convention recognizes the following reasons for flight that warrant refugee protection: 1) foreign aggression, occupation, or domination; 2) events seriously disturbing public order in whole or parts of the country; and 3) natural catastrophes. The first two categories reflect the expanded definition of refugee found in the Organization for African Unity's Convention Governing the Specific Aspects of Refugee Problems in Africa.[25] The third category recognizes that oppression leading to forced migration does not necessarily need to be man-made. Environmental degradation, droughts, famines, and floods can also threaten a person's existence and compel flight. Such a broadened definition of refugee is clearly commendable. Yet it runs counter to valid security concerns that stem from large flows of refugees. This tension may explain why no country has ratified the Arab Convention, leaving it to be an ambitious regional declaration.

Much like the 1951 Refugee Convention, the Arab Convention excludes certain criminals from protection and enumerates conditions that permit the termination of refugee protection. It guarantees certain human rights to the refugee, such as nondiscrimination, *nonrefoulement* (that is, to not be returned to a place where one's life would be threatened), non-expulsion, and freedom of movement.

Aside from the basic definition, the Arab Convention differs from the 1951 Convention in two further aspects. First, it grants the right to temporary asylum for asylum seekers whose life might be in danger if returned. Second, it prohibits the refugee from engaging in any "acts against" the refugee's country of origin (Article 13). Article 13 serves as a restriction on freedom of speech, but it may stem from the earlier omission of persecution for political opinion as a basis for protection, revealing a general wariness of political dissidents. In addition, one could argue that the national security or public order grounds for revoking refugee protection under the 1951 Convention could be interpreted to possibly justify such a prohibition.[26] While the abridged right to free speech granted to a refugee is clearly problematic in light of prevailing norms concerning democracy and human rights, it may reflect a certain political reality in which the majority of refugees are fleeing conflict in neighboring states, and hosting them could mean some level of involvement in that conflict. For example, the Palestinians often launched attacks from Jordan or Lebanon, ultimately drawing their host states into the Palestinian conflict with Israel.[27]

Despite the particularized contents of the Arab Convention on Refugees, it still has no force. As mentioned earlier, this may simply be a function of the broad definition given for a refugee, which may be impractical or threatening for states to accept. More important, it reveals that efforts at the regional level are not yielding effective results.[28] This is not so surprising in light of current trends in other parts of the world. Attempts to harmonize asylum law in Europe have met with difficulty, as each state has markedly differing interpretations of the 1951 Refugee Convention.[29] Similar efforts in the Americas to coordinate burden sharing of refugee flows also face challenges.[30]

Islam

Another possible source of authority in which to ground refugee protection is Islam. Historical Islamic jurisprudence is replete with discussion of persecution and migration. Indeed, central to Islamic history is the persecution of the Prophet Muhammad and his companions and their Hijra, or migration, to attain a state of security. The Qur'an and Sunnah can, therefore, be read as being extremely sympathetic to the plight of those who face oppression on account of their beliefs and who, therefore, choose to flee to a place of greater security—particularly where the oppression is based on religious belief.[31]

Several modern writers have looked at these basic Islamic notions of concern for the oppressed and for migrants, taking note of various Qur'anic verses and historical practices where Muslims granted protection to the persecuted and based on such sources and practices have contended that a long-standing right to asylum exists under Islamic law.[32] However, while the shari'a and historical Muslim practice may not preclude, may be consistent with, or may even—in today's context—mandate the modern notions of asylum reflected in the 1951 Refugee Convention and other recent regional instruments, such a notion of asylum received little attention, if any at all, for the major part of Muslim history.

The purpose of this section is to examine historical Islamic institutions of protection, their textual bases, their similarity or dissimilarity to modern notions of asylum, and the applicability of the underlying principles to the current context.

The Three Institutions of Protection in Islamic Tradition

Sanctuary. The tradition of protection literally begins at the core of the Islamic world and history—the *Ka'ba*, the focal point of Islamic worship in Mecca. The Qur'an establishes the Ka'ba and the precincts of the surrounding mosque as the *haram*, or sanctuary.[33] Therein, every person is deemed safe, even those who have committed a crime, until they emerge from the sanctuary. Similarly, the Prophet Muhammad identified the city of Medina as a sanctuary.

Hijra. The second institution that has historically been associated with protection in Islam relates to *Hijra*, or migration from one's home. Hijra is considered an obligation on able Muslims when they are persecuted and oppressed such that they are unable to practice their religion.[34] The obligation of Hijra and the conditions necessitating Hijra have historically been the subject of extensive discussion in large part because of the prominent role Hijra has played in Islamic history. The earliest example of Hijra was the migration of a group of early Muslims to Abyssinia to seek the protection of the Christian king and to escape the persecution being inflicted on the Muslims by the Quraish, the ruling clan of Mecca. The second and undoubtedly the most important instance of migration in Islamic history was Muhammad's migration from Mecca to Medina. The significance of this later migration from a place of persecution to a place of safety is reflected by the numerous changes that accompanied the Hijra: the Muslims moved from a position of subjugation to a position of control, from a period of developing inner strength to a period of outward expansion, and from a religious community to a religious state. Indeed, this Hijra is the reference point for the Muslim calendar.

The relevance of Hijra to asylum, however, is found in the obligation of Muslims in a place that can offer security to receive the Muslims making Hijra from their home on account of religious persecution. The Qur'an does not explicitly establish any such obligation. This obligation, however, has been presumed by some modern writers to exist as an implied obligation concomitant to the obligation to make Hijra.[35] Even if such an obligation can be presumed, for reasons we address later, there has historically been very little explicit discussion regarding the obligation of Muslims to receive other Muslims fleeing persecution or even more generally regarding rules governing the movement of Muslims between or into Muslim territory.

Aman. The third institution of protection, *Aman*, is perhaps the most similar to the modern institution of asylum. Aman is a grant of security from a Muslim to a non-Muslim. The textual source for such an action is Sura 9:6, which states, "If one amongst the Pagans asks thee for refuge [*is-*

tijarak], grant it to him, so that he may hear the Word of Allah; and then escort him to where he can be secure. That is because they are men without knowledge." The most apparent meaning of this verse gives Muslims permission to grant Aman to non-Muslims. Aman is the "practice of refraining from opposing [belligerents] through killing or capturing, for the sake of God."[36] Aman was, therefore, initially understood as a form of quarter, or clemency to be granted to enemies. The refuge provided for in the Qur'an entails securing the subject of the Aman, or *musta'min*, from any immediate threat that he might be facing and later returning him, but only to another place of safety. Subsequently, the institution of Aman was expanded to mean granting safe conduct or protection generally for purposes of trade or travel in Muslim territory.[37]

As discussed by jurists, little differentiation was made between the rules of Aman as a grant of quarter and Aman as grant of safe conduct.[38] Aman could be granted by any sane and mature Muslim, male or female, including the poor, sick, and blind, and, according to some jurists, even by slaves, and the grant would be binding on the entire state. The grant could be official (that is, the result of a peace treaty or general amnesty) or private. The grant could be the result of an individual request from a non-Muslim, or it could be given without request. Acceptance of a request for Aman could be inferred from any sign of assent, even if nonverbal. A grant of Aman entitled the musta'min (the person seeking safety) to move safely in or through Muslim territory. While in Muslim territory, the musta'min was subject to the civil and criminal laws of the territory but could also avail himself of the judicial system. Commission of certain crimes could result in revocation of the grant. A grant of Aman is theoretically temporary, with the time limits and other conditions established at the time of the grant. Permanent residency could be established only by accepting Islam or by accepting "*dhimma*" status, which legally referred to the entitlement of a non-Muslim to an indefinite Aman, though not full citizenship, in return for the payment of a poll tax referred to as the "*jizya*."[39]

Limitations on the Continued Relevance of the
Three Classical Institutions of Protection

For Islamic notions of protection to be useful to advocates today and for such notions to gain any acceptance, they must also be compatible with and capable of addressing the modern geopolitical context—one in which the entire world is organized into territorially defined states, where cross-border traffic and immigration are potentially subject to the complete control of the central government, and where citizenship is based on place of birth or blood relations.

The relevance of the historical Islamic institution of sanctuary has limited applicability in today's world because the Muslim world has expanded far beyond the reaches of Mecca and Medina, because access to the two sanctuaries is restricted to Muslims, and because, even for Muslims, access is tightly controlled by the Saudi government. Furthermore, sanctuary, whether in a mosque, a church, or any other place of peace, offers a protection of a sort different from asylum. Sanctuary clearly is not a durable solution to the fears of a person seeking protection. Eventually, that person must venture out of the sanctuary.

The institution of Hijra also appears to have limited relevance today since the primary focus of Hijra is on the duty to migrate rather than on any duty to receive or offer protection. Furthermore, even if one were to presume that a right to seek asylum is derived from the obligation to make Hijra, such a right would exist only to the extent that Hijra is an obligation. Today, despite many glaring injustices in the Middle East, there exists relative freedom to practice Islam, even if only privately. Under such circumstances, few would consider Hijra—and therefore the concomitant duty to receive the migrant—to be an obligation.

Classical jurisprudence on Aman, by contrast, has several elements that would be familiar to modern human rights advocates and would offer some refugees protection approaching that offered under the Refugee Convention. First, for example, the Qur'anic verse cited as the basis for Aman explicitly provides that the musta'min, at the end of the period of Aman, must be delivered to a place of safety, meaning that the mustamin cannot be returned to the place from where he came if he would not find safety there. This prohibition on returning a refugee to a place of insecurity is similar to the modern principle of nonrefoulement. Second, a grant of Aman, similar to the recognition of refugee status under the Refugee Convention, does not automatically entitle the protected individual to permanent residence or citizenship in the host community.[40] Finally, the musta'min is subject to the laws of the host state, and violation of those laws may be the basis for revoking protection and expulsion from the host state.

Aman as traditionally understood, however, also has several elements that are seemingly irreconcilable with the modern context and with precepts of human rights that, for better or for worse, have been accepted as fundamental among most human rights advocates and have shaped the modern context. First, for example, the right of each individual to grant Aman to another would be impractical in the modern context, where immigration is usually subject to the strict control of the central government and where an individual generally has the ability to bind the entire state only if he or she has sufficient government credentials. Second, Aman has been traditionally viewed as a grant of protection to non-Muslims, and there is little evidence to suggest that it was used as an institution to offer protection to Muslims. Therefore, even if Aman were otherwise viable as an institution for protection of refugees today, it would only be a partial solution, as many forced migrants in the Middle East—and the world—today are Muslim. Third, even for non-Muslims, durable status was available only on conversion to Islam or acceptance of dhimma status—requirements that would be likely to find little acceptance today, even in the Muslim world.

Application of the Underlying Islamic Principles of Protection to the Modern Context

While the classical notions of protection may not be suited for direct application to the modern context, the underlying Islamic principles may continue to be relevant. The classical notions of protection were the result of interpretation of the underlying Islamic principles within the particular historical context, which included the growth of the Muslim empire that extended from the Atlantic Ocean in the west and the Indus River in the east. Because of the vast expanse of the empire, many functions that later became the exclusive domain of the government, at that time, were fulfilled by individuals acting in their private capacity. One such function was the granting of Aman.

Furthermore, despite the great expanse of the Muslim world, it was for a time, at least nominally, a unitary state. And reflecting the Qur'anic notion that Muslims form a single community or brotherhood, a Muslim in one area—even if not within the Muslim empire—was considered to be a member of the same community as a Muslim many hundreds of miles away.[41] Therefore, there seems to have been little need for jurists to engage in discussion of or to develop rules for Muslim movement, whether for purposes of seeking refuge or for trade. Related accounts of Muslim travel from one part of the Muslim world to another seem to suggest that the movement was generally accomplished without the need for any special permission and without significant restriction.[42]

The classical Muslim worldview divided the world into *dar al-Islam* (the abode of Islam) and *dar al-harb* (the abode of war).[43] The default relationship between dar al-Islam and dar al-harb was a technical state of war. Thus, in the absence of a treaty, a person from dar al-harb was liable to be killed if he or she entered Muslim territory without some special grant of protection. Verse 9:6 of the Qur'an easily lent itself to an interpretation permitting the grant of protection to someone who was fleeing dar al-harb. However, some form of protection was also needed for those who were not fleeing dar al-harb but were entering dar al-Islam for purposes of trade. Thus, the Qur'anic principles were interpreted to facilitate such trade.

Furthermore, consistent with the organizing principles of the Muslim state, an individual's status in dar al-Islam was dependent on his or her faith. To obtain status in the Muslim state, a non-Muslim from dar al-harb would have to either accept dhimma status or depart from the Muslim state on expiration of the grant of Aman, just like a modern-day visa.

The apparent irreconcilability of certain characteristics of traditional Islamic forms of protection and the modern context is, therefore, more obviously the result of a historical interpretation of Qur'anic and other underlying Islamic principles, in light of the contextual realities of that time, than a necessary result of the principles themselves.[44] Many scholars today agree that Islam prescribes no specific form of state;[45] it also does not prescribe a specific form of protection. Rather, any state must adhere to the more general and basic principles established in the Qur'an and prophetic traditions. This suggests the possibility and need for a renewed understanding and interpretation of underlying Islamic principles to address the modern context.

Looking beyond the medieval Islamic world as the historical context within which Islamic principles of protection must be interpreted but in keeping with the practical contextual approach adopted by jurists of that time, Islamic scholars of today and human rights advocates can seek a new understanding of the underlying Islamic principles as they relate to the modern context—a context where dar al-harb/dar al-Islam is no longer a mainstream paradigm, where there is no unitary Muslim state, and where the concept of *ummah* does not entitle one to free access to all Muslim countries.

Understanding the Islamic principles in the modern context may reveal that certain forms of protection previously underdeveloped because of the historical context may be commendable today or, possibly, obligatory on any Muslim state. For example, traditionally the obligation to provide protection was viewed as existing only when a person asked to hear about Islam. In other circumstances, the grant of protection was discretionary and generally was used for what was viewed as in the public interest, such as trade. The Qur'anic verse regarding protection of idolaters clearly addresses idolaters who left their homes specifically to fight the Muslims. Yet they were granted protection. Scholars then argued that if protection could be granted to such people, surely it could be granted (even if not required) where the person came in peace and would benefit the community.[46] Extending this reasoning further, one could argue that if both those categories of people were worthy of protection, surely someone both coming in peace and seeking refuge deserves protection. And surely, if the protection should be extended to non-Muslims, it also should be extended to Muslims.

International Islamic Human Rights Instruments

Muslim states have, in fact, recognized the commendablility of offering protection that is more expansive than the historical institutions of protection. In 1990, the Organization of the Islamic Conference, then consisting of forty-three Arab and non-Arab member states, issued the Cairo Declaration on Human Rights in Islam. Article 12 of the Declaration recognizes the right to seek asylum.[47] Specifically, it states,

> Every man shall have the right, within the framework of the shari'a [Islamic law] to free movement and to select his place of residence whether inside or outside his country and, if persecuted, is entitled to seek asylum in another country. The country of refuge shall ensure his protection until he reaches safety, unless asylum is motivated by an act which the Shari'a regards as a crime.[48]

Article 20 provides a supplementary form of protection. It prohibits the exile of an individual "without legitimate reason." In addition, it proscribes the use of physical or psychological torture or any form of humiliation, cruelty, or indignity. The prohibition on such treatment can be interpreted to include expulsion or return to a place where one's life would be threatened. The European Court of Human Rights has interpreted a similar provision in its Convention on Human Rights, which forbids torture or inhuman or degrading treatment or punishment, as preventing the return of an individual to a place where he or she may be exposed to such ill treatment.[49]

The Islamic Council of Europe, a nongovernmental organization, also adopted a Universal Islamic Declaration of Human Rights in which the right to seek asylum was recognized. Article 9 provides, "Anyone persecuted or oppressed has the right to seek refuge and asylum. This is guaranteed to every human being, irrespective of race, religion, color or sex."[50] As a declaration of a nongovernmental organization, however, it has no legal effect. The Cairo Declaration discussed previously is similarly not enforceable. No mechanism exists to ensure the implementation and protection of the rights guaranteed therein. Although the lack of legislation in the Arab and Muslim world relating to asylum leads one to consider the possibility of applying Islamic law of asylum, no Islamic body for enforcement and oversight exists. For example, the Islamic Conference could ideally provide an institutional framework, but it does not have any enforcement capacity. Furthermore, vast differences between Muslim states also present difficulty in creating a binding Islamic legal instrument relating to refugees. These impracticalities, just like the idealism of other regional human rights instruments, fail to capture the realistic approach of classical Islamic jurisprudence, which elaborated on institutions of protection that were consistent with the underlying Islamic principles while recognizing the evolving practical needs of the community in its particular place and time.

Of course, enforcement is a problem of international human rights law generally. If a state chooses to flout its obligations under an international treaty, the international community can only respond by condemning that state. Sovereign states can use diplomacy in an effort to compel compliance, but generally no international body can enforce compliance. International law is premised on the will of the member states to comply. As such, declarations issued by a supranational authority, such as various Muslim organizations or the League of Arab states, are of practical benefit only to the extent the national authorities choose to comply. This brings us back to an examination of domestic sources for the protection of refugees in the Middle East.

Domestic Sources

Constitutional Provisions The constitutions of the various Arab states offer some legal support for the right to seek asylum or the right not to be returned to a place where one would be persecuted. We identified three types of provisions that could be useful. First, most of the constitutions prohibit the extradition of political refugees. Second, a few constitutions explicitly recognize the right to seek asylum. Third, several of the constitutions prohibit torture or other such ill treatment.

Constitutional provisions can play an important role in upholding human rights in the absence of binding international obligations. For example, such provisions have been utilized in India, which is not a party to the 1951 Convention or the 1967 Protocol. The Supreme Court interpreted the right to protection of life and personal liberty in its constitution to impose an obligation on the state government to protect refugees of the Chakma tribe.[51] State authorities in Tripura and Assam were threatening these refugees with expulsion. The decision in *National Human Rights Commission v. State of Arunachal Pradesh* ordered the state government to protect the "life and liberty" of the Chakma refugees.[52]

Provisions prohibiting the extradition of political refugees are found in the following state constitutions: Bahrain (Art. 21),[53] Kuwait (Art. 46),[54] Jordan (Art. 21),[55] Libya (Art. 11),[56] Oman (Art. 36),[57] Syria (Art. 34),[58] and Yemen (Art. 45).[59] Although the language in these provisions could be used to prevent the return of refugees, two serious problems exist with this language. First, extradition occurs if state A requests state B to return a criminal originally from state A or who has committed a crime in state A. As such, this provision comes into effect only when there has been a request by the state of origin. Where the criminal is requested for political crimes, he or she can invoke the prohibition on return. This brings us to the second problem: the language is limited to political offenses. Individuals persecuted for race, nationality, or religion cannot invoke this provision unless they can show that the crime for which they are being sought is actually persecution disguised as prosecution and that persecution based on race or religion is tantamount to political persecution. In effect, this provision narrowly applies to situations where a state requests the return of a person and where that person is being sought for political offenses.

Second, several state constitutions recognize the right to seek asylum and, in some cases, to asylum itself, thus providing the clearest authority for enforcement. For example, Article 53 of Egypt's constitution provides that "the right to political asylum shall be granted by the State to every foreigner persecuted for defending the people's interests, human rights, peace or justice."[60] Article 34 of Iraq's constitution grants "the right of political asylum for all militants, persecuted in their country because of defending the liberal and human principles, which are assumed by the Iraqi people in this Constitution."[61] Article 42 of Saudi Arabia's Basic Law of Government stipulates that "the State grants political asylum when public interest requires it."[62] Finally, although not a direct source of authority, Yemen's constitution, under Article 118, lists granting political asylum as one of the president's responsibilities. These provisions, however, limit protection to political dissidents. Where a person is persecuted for his nationality or religion, it is not clear whether he can invoke one of the previously mentioned provisions.

Finally, provisions proscribing torture and other ill treatment can be found in several constitutions. For example, Article 31(2) of Kuwait's constitution provides that "no person shall be subjected to torture or degrading treatment." Article 22(a) of Iraq's constitution states, "The dignity of man is safeguarded. It is inadmissible to cause any physical or psychological harm." These provisions could be invoked to prevent refoulement. Such language could be interpreted as preventing the separation of a person to a place where her life would be threatened. The European Court of Human Rights has interpreted the prohibition on torture and inhuman treatment in its Convention on Human Rights in such a manner.

Domestic Asylum Law   Three countries in the Middle East—Iraq,[63] Lebanon,[64] and Yemen[65]—have passed domestic legislation regarding refugees. The law in Lebanon, however, has not yet been implemented,[66] and Yemen, as mentioned, is a party to the 1951 Convention and the 1967 Protocol. What is worth noting is the variety of the definitions of "refugee" under each domestic scheme, the rights and obligations of those recognized as refugees, and the conditions under which the host state can revoke protection.

Varied definitions of a refugee exist in domestic asylum law. For example, under the Political Refugee Act of 1971, Iraq defines a refugee as any person who seeks asylum in Iraq for political or military reasons.[67] Lebanon, on the other hand, defines a refugee as any foreigner who is a political offender or whose life or liberty is threatened for political reasons,[68] while Yemen, having signed the Refugee Convention, follows the definition therein.

As to the rights and obligations of a recognized refugee, the 1951 Convention accorded such a person an array of rights—the underlying principle being that he or she should be able to start a new life and assimilate. Iraq and Yemen offer refugees a generous range of rights accompanied by a series of obligations that reveal serious national concerns. Concerning economic and social rights, Iraq grants financial assistance, social services, and employment authorization to refugees. It also allows for family reunification. Under Article 11(1) of the Political Refugee Act, the Iraqi law states that a refugee recognized in Iraq shall enjoy the same rights of the Iraqi citizen with respect to social services, employment, land, and education. Civil and political rights are more circumscribed. There is limited freedom of movement and a prohibition on carrying firearms. Most important, unlike the 1951 Convention, the nonrefoulement provision is absolute. In Yemen, under a Ministerial Resolution Regarding the Organization of Refugees' Department, the refugee is not entitled to a set of rights. Rather, this resolution describes the duties and responsibilities of the Refugee Department from which we can infer what possible benefits a refugee may enjoy in Yemen. The Refugee Department must provide material assistance, shelter, employment opportunities, and social and medical care. Lebanon, in contrast, is less generous. Under its Law Regulating the Entry, Stay, and Exit of Foreigners in Lebanon of 1962, it forbids the refugee from engaging in any political activity, limits freedom of movement, and denies any judicial review of a negative asylum determination. However, the right to nonrefoulement is absolute.

There are, however, certain conditions that permit withdrawal of protection. Under the 1951 Refugee Convention, protection can be revoked in two circumstances. First, where the conditions that necessitated protection have ceased to exist, the host state can return the refugee to his country of origin.[69] Second, where the refugee commits a particularly serious crime in the host state or poses a threat to national security, the host state can revoke protection and return the refugee to his country of origin even if he or she would be threatened for one of the five enumerated grounds.[70]

Under Iraqi asylum law, nonrefoulement is absolute. Article 4 states, "Under no circumstances shall a refugee be handed over to his state." Iraqi law allows the revocation of protection where the refugee commits an offense affecting the security or political stakes of the state. This provision, however, is not listed as an exception to the nonreturn provision. As such, the nonreturn provision, in light of its strict language, arguably trumps the withdrawal of protection where a threat to the refugee's life persists. Therefore, where protection is revoked, a person can be expelled, but he or she absolutely cannot be returned to a place where a threat to his or her existence exists.

Yemen lists three circumstances under which protection can be withdrawn: first, when protection is no longer needed; second, when the refugee is a threat to national security or public order; and third, when the refugee violates objectives and principles of the United Nations or commits war crimes.

Under Lebanese law, protection can be canceled at any time. The same law states that nonrefoulement is absolute. However, the government may cancel protection and expel the individual consistent with the nonrefoulement provision if the expulsion is to another state where the refugee's life would not be threatened.

The three previously mentioned laws reveal that each state has drafted its domestic laws according to political and economic realities in their respective state. They provide a model for other states in the region that may resist the idea of adopting the 1951 Refugee Convention or the overly broad Declaration by the League of Arab States. In fact, UNHCR has recognized Iraq as a country that maintains a generous policy toward refugees in general and in particular to those who have sought asylum from neighboring countries.[71]

Refugee Protection on the Ground

In light of the previous analysis, several different legal bases can be identified for imposing an obligation to preserve the right to seek asylum. Yet the question persists: what is actually happening on the ground, particularly in those countries where relevant legal provisions are not enforceable? In most Arab states, UNHCR maintains a presence. Its legal authority derives from the Statute of the Office of the UNHCR, adopted by the UN General Assembly in its Resolution 428(v) of December 14, 1950.[72] The statute provides that "the High Commissioner shall assume the function of providing international protection, under the auspices of the United Nations, to refugees who fall within the scope of the Statute and of seeking permanent solutions for the problems of refugees by assisting governments and . . . private organizations to facilitate the voluntary repatriation of such refugees, or their assimilation within new national communities."[73]

Certain Arab states have concluded memorandums of understanding (MOUs) with UNHCR, giving UNHCR explicit permission to open an office and define UNHCR's role in that state.[74] For example, in the MOU with Kuwait, UNHCR's role includes not only international protection but also the organization and provision of humanitarian assistance to the refugees.[75] Similarly, the MOU with Jordan memorializes both parties' agreement to cooperate "in the field of international protection of and humanitarian assistance to refugees and other persons of concern to UNHCR."[76]

Even though these countries have not signed the 1951 Convention, they recognize the authority of UNHCR and its indispensable value in providing international protection to refugees. In particular, these states probably realize that UNHCR is far more adept at coordinating resettlement to third countries and humanitarian assistance for refugees than they are. Therefore, certain Arab states have formalized the presence of UNHCR within their jurisdiction. Finally, the League of Arab States and UNHCR have recently agreed to "cooperate in the humanitarian fields relating to the protection of refugee rights and assistance to refugees according to the Arab and the international instruments and legislations."[77]

Yet the absence of an MOU does not result in the absence of UNHCR. In Arab states that have not acceded to the 1951 Refugee Convention, do not have domestic asylum regimes, and have not signed MOUs with UNHCR, UNHCR is nonetheless permitted to establish a presence, particularly at borders at which refugees are arriving. In such cases, UNHCR assumes both a decision-making and a protective function. It first determines whether the forced migrant meets the definition of refugee as defined by its mandate, the 1951 Convention, and whether that individual is ineligible for protection. Typically, where a state has a functioning domestic asylum system, the determination process is carried out by domestic authorities. Where such internal mechanisms do not exist, UNHCR carries out the determination process.

Where the individual is found to be a Convention refugee, UNHCR gives that individual some form of identification card and humanitarian assistance. Again, such identification and assistance would normally be coordinated by state authorities. UNHCR also administers refugee camps and other shelter. In certain states, despite the existence of an asylum regime, economic realities are such that the host state simply cannot afford humanitarian assistance. In these circumstances, UNHCR fills the gap and supplies humanitarian assistance to needy cases. For example, Lebanon has passed but not implemented domestic asylum laws. UNHCR provides supplementary assistance, medical care, and educational grants with priority given to needy families and vulnerable cases. In Syria, a state that is not a party to the Convention and does not have a domestic asylum regime,[78] UNHCR gives assistance to Convention refugees in the form of monthly subsistence allowances, basic health care, and educational or vocational training.

Finally, UNHCR considers long-term durable solutions for the refugee, such as voluntary repatriation (if possible), integration into the host state, or resettlement to another state. For example, UNHCR organized the repatriation of 886 Eritreans and 152 Ethiopians in 1997 from Libya.[79] Similarly, UNHCR assisted 874 Somali refugees to repatriate to safe areas in their country of origin from Yemen. UNHCR also resettles refugees to third countries where options for repatriation or local integration do not exist. In Lebanon, for example, local integration is very difficult, and repatriation of most refugees residing in Lebanon is nearly impossible. UNHCR therefore resettled over 120 persons in 1997.

While the efforts and presence of UNHCR allow the principle of asylum to be upheld in the Middle East, refugee protection remains arbitrary, uncertain, and ad hoc. In addition, UNHCR itself faces resource constraints and external political concerns. It is subject to the vagaries of international politics. As such, significant reliance on UNHCR could be misplaced. The Arab states, in light of their experience with the Palestinian refugees, pursue a policy of keeping an international presence in the region through UN agencies so that the international community does not forget them. Yet such a strategy must be complemented by domestic involvement and domestic action. Leaving the refugees that arrive to UN-HCR's care is to abandon control over a matter intimately tied to state sovereignty: the entry and control of noncitizens. Practically speaking, it would be in the host state's interest to actively participate in the asylum regime that develops as forced migrants arrive.

Moreover, these states have recognized in one way or another the obligation of allowing a forced migrant to seek asylum: by signing the 1951 Convention, passing domestic asylum laws, or including a provision in their domestic constitutions related to asylum. There is a need, however, for developing national laws that actualize this obligation. National laws will set the foundation for a domestic asylum regime, which could help bring accountability, coherence, and security to asylum practices in the Middle East.

Conclusion

The previous discussion reveals several guidelines for advocates seeking the development of an effective asylum regime in the Middle East, which, because of its varying political landscapes and unpredictability, may not yet be ready to adopt a comprehensive asylum regime on a regional, multilateral basis. Therefore, advocates are likely to find the greatest success working at the state level. In so doing, they can adopt culturally sensitive approaches, thereby avoiding the obstacle that has faced arguments for acceding to the 1951 Refugee Convention. Furthermore, advocates can argue that strong refugee protection is commendable under basic Islamic principles and consistent with the spirit of Islamic history. They can also increase the likelihood that any asylum regime adopted will be effective by arguing for laws that are practical and sensitive to the state's historical experience with refugees and with the state's security concerns. Such an approach would greatly reduce the arbitrariness of refugee protection in each state and will also begin to relieve UNHCR.

Postscript on the Effect of Regional Human Rights Conditions on Asylum

As a postscript and to place the preceding discussion regarding asylum law into perspective, it is important to recognize that asylum law is only one

Table 4.2.   Asylum Flows to and from the Middle East[a]

Country of Origin	Number of Applications Submitted in 1999 Anywhere	Number Submitted in States of the Middle East (%)[b]	Number Submitted in the West —at least (%)
Middle East origin			
Egypt	1,390		1,110 (80%)
Iraq	49,240	12,720 (26%)	32,880 (67%)
Jordan	420		310 (73%)
Lebanon	2,170		1,910 (88%)
Libya	580		490 (84%)
Morocco	770		550 (71%)
Palestinians	470	130 in Yemen	Unknown
Sudan	13,330	7,790 (63%)	3,090 (23%)
Syria	4,710		4,160 (88%)
Tunisia	610		380 (62%)
Yemen	590		310 (53%)
Total	73,810 (excluding Palestine)		45,190 (61%) (73% excluding Iraq, Palestine, and Sudan)
Non–Middle East origin			
Ethiopia	12,280	510 (4.2%)	
Iran	19,560	560 (2.9%)	
Sierra Leone	11,500	110 (1%)	
Somalia	21,640	900 (4.2%)	

[a]Figures are based on 2001 UNHCR Statistical Overview of Refugees and Others of Concern to UNHCR. Because of reporting thresholds, the actual numbers are likely to be higher than reflected in this table.

[b]An empty cell means that no more than one hundred applications from refugees of the particular country were submitted in any state in the Middle East. In addition, for the applicants of non–Middle East origin listings, only four states are listed because no state in the Middle East received more than one hundred applications from refugees of any other single state.

aspect of an exceedingly complex human rights dilemma in the Middle East. Table 4.2 provides an approximate representation of the flow of asylum-seeking refugees to and from the Middle East in 1999.

A preliminary examination of these figures reveals several trends. For example, asylum seekers from the Middle East tend to seek asylum outside the Middle East. That trend is even more evident if excluding places of widespread unrest or deep instability (such as Iraq, Palestine, and Sudan). Furthermore, most of the asylum seekers apply for asylum in the West. Finally, very few people seek asylum in the Middle East, and the few who do are mostly from neighboring states with large-scale internal problems.

Refugees typically seek asylum in a country near their home state. Doing so is consistent with the hope of many refugees that they will be able to return to their homes. Furthermore, remaining close to home also reduces the shock of dislocation, as neighboring states are more likely to be culturally familiar and share similar languages. The trends in the Middle East, however, suggest that, except for massive disturbances that lead to large-scale flows where forced migrants need immediate physical security, most asylum seekers from the Middle East do not view application for asylum in another state in the region to be a viable option.

There are, undoubtedly, numerous factors that account for the reluctance to seek asylum in the Middle East, but one of the more important factors is likely the lack of any appreciable difference between the human rights situations in each of the states of the Middle East. To the extent that violence against minorities and government oppression are endemic problems in the Middle East, members of persecuted minority religious groups and political groups with opinions disfavored by the authoritarian governments are skeptical that they will be afforded any more protection in one Middle Eastern state than another.

Thus, no matter how sophisticated the multilateral and domestic asylum laws of the Middle East, asylum will remain a largely irrelevant institution as long as the human rights situation across the Middle East remains uniformly poor.

Notes

1. The European Court of Human Rights in its case law repeatedly emphasizes that states have the right, "as a matter of well-established international law and subject to their treaty obligations . . . to control the entry, residence and expulsion of aliens." *Cruz Varas and Others v. Sweden*, 201 Eur. Ct. H.R. (ser. A), at para. 70 (1991).

2. Convention Relating to the Status of Refugees, July 28, 1951, 189 U.N.T.S. 137 (hereinafter "1951 Convention").

3. Protocol Relating to the Status of Refugees, January 31, 1967, 606 U.N.T.S. 267 (hereinafter "1967 Protocol").

4. There are situations where a person can apply for asylum while he is still in his country of residence by applying at the embassy of a selected host state. But in life-threatening situations, there is no time for such measures. Furthermore, such an application process presupposes a high educational level and also certain financial conditions, neither of which is characteristic of most refugees.

5. Most states follow the definition of refugee set forth in Article 1(A)(2) of the 1951 Refugee Convention, which is any person who "owing to a well-founded fear of being persecuted for reasons of race, religion, nationality, membership of a particular social group or political opinion, is outside the country of his nationality and is unable or, owing to such fear, is unwilling to avail himself of the protection of that country." 1951 Refugee Convention, note 2 at Art. 1(A)(2).

6. Statute of the Office of the United Nations High Commissioner for Refugees, G.A. Res. 428, U.N. GAOR, 5th Sess., Supp. No. 20, at 48 (para. 8) U.N. Doc. A/1775 (1950) (hereinafter "UNHCR Statute").

7. 1951 Refugee Convention, note 2 at Art. 1(F).

8. 1951 Refugee Convention, at Art. 33(2).

9. Myron Weiner, "A Security Perspective on International Migration," *Fletcher Forum of World Affairs* 20 (1996): 17–33.

10. Weiner defines "security" as follows: "a social construct with different meanings in different societies. An ethnically homogeneous society, for example, may place higher value on preserving its ethnic character than does a heterogeneous society and may, therefore, regard a population influx as a threat to its security. Providing a haven for those who share one's values is important in some countries, but not in others. In some countries, therefore, an influx of 'freedom fighters' may not be regarded as a security threat. Moreover, even in a given country, what is highly valued may not be shared by elites and counterelites. One ethnic group may welcome migrants, while another is vehemently opposed to them." Weiner, "A Security Perspective on International Migration," 22.

11. Weiner, "A Security Perspective on International Migration," 28.

12. For example, states often penalize airlines or other carriers for failing to appropriately verify the legal status of a person boarding the plane. Detaining asylum seekers, returning them to "safe" countries through which they traveled, or simply designating certain countries as "safe" and thereby not recognizing asylum claims from nationals of these so-called safe countries are some restrictive policies that have been implemented. See Justice A. M. North and Nehal Bhuta, "The Future of Protection—The Role of the Judge," *Georgetown Immigration Law Journal* 15, no. 3 (2001): 479, 483. See also Andrew I. Schoenholtz, "Beyond the Supreme Court: A Modest Plea to Improve Our Asylum System," *Georgetown Immigration Law Journal* 14, no. 2 (2000): 541–42.

13. Article 1(A) states, "For the purposes of the present Convention, the term 'refugee' shall apply to any person who: As a result of events *occurring before 1 January 1951* and owing to well-founded fear of being persecuted for reasons of race, religion, nationality, membership of a particular social group or political opinion, is outside the country of his nationality and is unable or, owing to such fear, is un-

willing to avail himself of the protection of that country." 1951 Convention, note 2 at Art. 1(A)(2).

14. Khadija Elmadmad, "An Arab Convention on Forced Migration: Desirability and Possibilities," *International Journal Refugee Law* 3 (1991): 461, 473.

15. Ghassan Maarouf Arnaout, *Asylum in the Arab-Islamic Tradition* (Geneva: UNHCR, 1987), 45.

16. 1967 Protocol, January 31, 1967, 606 U.N.T.S. 267.

17. 1967 Protocol, January 31, 1967, 606 U.N.T.S. 267, at 268.

18. 1967 Protocol, January 31, 1967, 606 U.N.T.S. 267, at 268.

19. As a side note, the United States ratified and implemented the 1967 Protocol and not the 1951 Convention. Refugee Act of 1980, Pub. L. No. 96-212, 94 Stat. 102.

20. For example, the Preamble of the 1992 Cairo Declaration on the Protection of Refugees and Displaced Persons in the Arab World recalled the rights of the Palestinians, "[e]mphasizing the need for the effective Implementation of paragraph 11 of the General Assembly Resolution 194(III) of 11 December 1948, calling for the right of return or compensation for Palestinian refugees." UNHCR, Collection of International Instruments and Other Legal Texts concerning Refugees and Displaced Persons II (1995), 116.

21. Arab Convention on Refugees, March 26, 1994, Resolution No. 5389 (available only in Arabic).

22. Khadija Elmadmad, "Asylum in the Arab World: Some Recent Instruments," *Journal of Peace Studies*, January–February 1999, 25, 29.

23. Elmadmad, "Asylum in the Arab World," 29.

24. Cited in Elmadmad, "An Arab Convention on Forced Migration," 475.

25. OAU Convention Governing the Specific Aspects of Refugee Problems in Africa, September 10, 1969, Art. I(2), 1001 U.N.T.S., at 45, 47.

26. For example, in a leading asylum case in the United Kingdom, the British government sought to expel a prominent Sikh separatist lawfully residing in London on national security grounds. The government reasoned that his involvement in acts of civil disobedience and suspected participation in certain attacks on Indian leaders visiting the United Kingdom made him a threat to national security and therefore expellable. *Chalal v. United Kingdom*, Eur. Ct. H.R. Report of 27 June 1995, para. 98. Chahal's speech was clearly causing national security concern for the United Kingdom, which permitted it to proceed with deportation. Chahal brought a suit against the United Kingdom at the Court of Human Rights, which ruled against the United Kingdom on the grounds that Chahal's return would expose him to torture, which violated Article 3 of the European Convention on Human Rights. Under Article 3, no one shall be subjected to torture or

to inhuman or degrading treatment or punishment. The dispositive fact here was the clear threat to Chahal's life if returned to India, not the issue of his freedom of speech. Furthermore, Article 3 is nonderogable; as such, national security concerns are subordinate to the prohibition on proscribed ill treatment.

27. Mark A. Tessler, *A History of the Israeli-Palestinian Conflict* (Bloomington: Indiana University Press, 1994), 461–64; Speech to the United Nations General Assembly on October 18, 1982, in New York; Amine Gemayal, *Peace and Unity: Major Speeches 1982–1984* (Buckinghamshire: Colin Smythe, 1984), 16; Rashid Khalidi, *Under Siege: P.L.O. Decisionmaking during the 1982 War* (New York: Columbia University Press, 1986), 21.

28. Shortly after the Arab Convention on Refugees was released, the League of Arab States issued the Arab Charter on Human Rights. Article 23 recognizes the right to political asylum: "When faced with persecution, every citizen has the right to seek political asylum in another State. This right is not invoked in the case of a person condemned for the commission of a common crime." Arab Charter on Human Rights, September 10, 1994, reprinted in *Human Rights Law Journal* 18 (1997): 151. This charter, like the Arab Convention on Refugees, has not been ratified by any Arab state and has not yet entered into force.

29. See generally Karoline Kerber, "Temporary Protection in the European Union: A Chronology," *Georgetown Immigration Law Journal* 14, no. 1 (1999): 35.

30. See generally Susan Martin et al., "Temporary Protection: Towards a New Regional and Domestic Framework," *Georgetown Immigration Law Journal* 12, no. 4 (1998): 543.

31. See, for example, Qur'an 4:97–100; 8:74–75; 59:8–9.

32. See, for example, Astri Suhrke, "Refugees and Asylum in the Muslim World," in *The Cambridge Survey of World Migration*, ed. Robin Cohen (New York: Cambridge University Press, 1995), 457, 459 (stating that Muslims and non-Muslims "have a right to protection"), and Arnaout, *Asylum in the Arab-Islamic Tradition* ("In no case might the asylum-seeker be refused access or admission to the territory of the country where he has requested refuge" [21]).

33. See Qur'an 2:125 (*Ka'ba*); 3:97 (station of Ibrahim); 5:97 (precincts of the mosque surrounding the *Ka'ba*).

34. See Qur'an 4:97–100.

35. See, for example, Suhrke, "Refugees and Asylum in the Muslim World," 459; Martin et al., "Temporary Protection," 543; and Arnaout, *Asylum in the Arab-Islamic Tradition*, 18. Examples of verses of the Qur'an cited as implying an obligation to receive those who have made Hijra include 4:100, 8:74, and 59:8–9.

36. Sarakhsiy, *Sharh Al-Siyar Al-Kabir*, I, 189 quoted in Muhammad Hamidullah, *Muslim Conduct of State* (Lahore: Sh. Muhammad Ashraf, 1977), 209.

37. The Islamic concept of Aman was thus a continuation and expansion of the pre-Islamic practice of *ijara*, a form of tribal hospitality ensuring protection of any travelers or wayfarers. See Arnaout, *Asylum in the Arab-Islamic Tradition*, 14–16.

38. See Hamidullah, *Muslim Conduct of State*, 256. For a full discussion of the rules of granting Aman and the rights and obligations of a musta'min, see Hamidullah, *Muslim Conduct of State*, 209–11, 256–58; Majid Khadduri, *War and Peace in the Law of Islam* (Washington, D.C.: Middle East Institute, 1955), 162–69.

39. "Dhimma" literally means "a compact which the believer agrees to respect, the violation of which makes him liable to *dhamm* (blame)." Khadduri, *War and Peace in the Law of Islam*, 176–77. The rights and obligations of dhimmis differed from those of Muslims in several ways. For example, dhimmis had to pay the jizya and sometimes a land tax, the *kharaj*; Muslims did not. Muslims had to pay alms, or *zakat*; dhimmis did not. Fighting in *jihad* was a communal obligation for Muslims; dhimmis were not required to engage in fighting for any reason. The jizya was mainly in return for the protection received from the Muslims, though the tax was not required if the non-Muslims fought as allies with the Muslims. Majid Khadduri and Herbert J. Liebesny, *Law in the Middle East: Origin and Development of Islamic Law*, vol. 1 (New York: AMS Press, 1984), 363.

40. Article 34 of the 1951 Convention, however, urges state parties that have granted asylum to expedite the process of naturalization.

41. See Qur'an 4:97–100; Hamidullah, Qur'an, 110–11 ("[A]s soon as a Muslim migrates from his non-Muslim home and comes to Islamic territory, with the intention of residing there, he at once becomes a full-fledged citizen of the Muslim State; he has the same rights as other Muslim citizens and the same obligation as they.").

42. Hamidullah, *Muslim Conduct of State*, 129–30. Hamidullah also notes that there is little known about whether there was special treatment for Muslims traveling from one Muslim area to another after the Muslim world broke into more than one state.

43. Additional classifications that developed included *dar al-ahd* (abode of treaty) and *dar al-sulh* (abode of truce).

44. For a discussion of basic Islamic principles relevant to a discussion of asylum, see Arnaout, *Asylum in the Arab-Islamic Tradition*, 29–32. Other basic Islamic principles, for example, are those related to the commendability of assisting those who have made Hijra. On the inviolability of grants of protection, see Suhrke, "Refugees and Asylum in the Muslim World," 457, 459. On the notion of *ummah*, or community, see Sahih Bukhari, vol. 3, bk. 30, no. 94, 21:92, 49:10; on the pursuit of justice, even at detriment to self, see 4:135; and on the right of the needy in the wealth of Muslims, see 51:19.

45. See, for example, Hassan al-Turabi, "The Islamic State," in *Voices of Resurgent Islam*, ed. John L. Esposito (New York: Oxford University Press, 1983), 241–51, and Javid Iqbal, "Democracy and the Modern Islamic State," in Esposito, ed., 252–60.

46. See Hamidullah, *Muslim Conduct of State*, 256–57.

47. Cairo Declaration on Human Rights in Islam, August 9, 1990, available in UNHCR, *Collection of International Instruments and Other Legal Texts concerning Refugees and Displaced Persons*, vol. 2 (Geneva: UNCHR, 1995), 120.

48. UNHCR, *Collection of International Instruments*, 123.

49. See *Soering v. United Kingdom*, 161 Eur. Ct. H.R. (ser. A), paras. 98–99 (1989).

50. The Universal Islamic Declaration is available on the Islamic Council's website at www.alhewar.com/ISLAMDECL.html.

51. Speech at the Fourth Conference of the International Association of Refugee Law Judges on October 26, 2000, in Bern, Switzerland; Bellur N. Srikrishna, *The Indian Experience, citing National Human Rights Commission v. State of Arunachal Pradesh*, A.I.R. 1996 S.C.1 1234.

52. Speech at the Fourth Conference, 1234.

53. Constitution of Bahrain (1973).

54. Constitution of Kuwait (November 11, 1962).

55. Constitution of Jordan (November 1, 1952).

56. Constitutional Proclamation of Libya (December 11, 1969).

57. The Basic Law of the Sultanate of Oman, Royal Decree No. 101/96 (November 6, 1996).

58. Constitution of Syria (1973).

59. Constitution of the Republic of Yemen (September 29, 1994).

60. Constitution of the Arab Republic of Egypt (September 22, 1971).

61. Iraq Interim Constitution (1990).

62. Saudi Arabia Basic Law of Government (March 1, 1992).

63. Political Refugee Act, No. 51, Official Gazette No. 1985 (Aprril 10, 1971).

64. "Law Regulating the Entry, Stay and Exit of Foreigners in Lebanon," July 10, 1962, Official Journal No. 28-1962, at chap. 7 (hereinafter "Lebanon's Asylum Law").

65. Ministerial Resolution No. 10 regarding Organization of Refugees' Department (June 6, 1984).

66. Country Profile—Lebanon (available at www.unhcr.ch/world/mide/lebanon.htm; last updated April 1998).

67. Political Refugee Act, Article 1(3).

68. Lebanon's Asylum Law, Article 26.

69. 1951 Convention, Article 1(C).

70. 1951 Convention, Article 33(2).

71. UNHCR Country Profiles—Iraq (available at www.unhcr.ch/world/mide/iraq.htm; last updated September 1999).

72. UNHCR Statute.

73. UNHCR Statute. para. 8.

74. UNHCR has concluded MOUs with Egypt, Jordan, Kuwait, and Yemen. Of particular interest here are Jordan and Kuwait, neither of which has ratified the 1951 Convention. These MOUs are available on the UNHCR's Refworld website at www.unhcr.ch/refworld.

75. Cooperation and Office Agreement between the Office of the United Nations High Commissioner for Refugees and the Government of the State of Kuwait, April 8, 1996, Art. 4(a).

76. Agreement between the Government of the Hashemite Kingdom of Jordan and the United Nations High Commissioner for Refugees, July 30, 1997, Art. III.

77. Cooperation Agreement between the League of Arab States and the United Nations High Commissioner for Refugees, June 27, 2000, Art. 1.

78. Citizens of Arab countries may enter Syria without visas and seek and enjoy asylum. However, Iraqis and Somalis require security clearance from the Syrian authorities to facilitate their admission and residence.

79. UNHCR Country Profiles—Libya (available at www.unhcr.ch/world/afri/libya.htm; last updated July 1998).

Part Two
LEGAL REFORMS AND
THE IMPACT ON WOMEN

CHAPTER FIVE

INTERNATIONALIZING THE CONVERSATION ON WOMEN'S RIGHTS: ARAB COUNTRIES FACE THE CEDAW COMMITTEE

Ann Elizabeth Mayer

This chapter discusses how, when Arab countries elect to join the international human rights system, they are obliged to respond to public critiques of how their domestic laws and policies fall short by international standards. It offers analyses of selected excerpts from Arab governments' interactions with the committee that monitors compliance with the Women's Convention, the full title of which is Convention on the Elimination of All Forms of Discrimination Against Women, commonly known by the acronym CEDAW. This chapter probes how Arab countries have been placed on the defensive as they seek to justify their discriminatory treatment of women before the CEDAW Committee. When under scrutiny by this UN body, Arab countries effectively concede that discrimination against women is wrong and resort to a variety of tactics to make their policies look respectable, often seeking to portray them as compatible with women's international human rights even where they are fundamentally at odds with these rights. This chapter proposes that once the governments go on the record as supporting equality for women in their statements before international bodies, it becomes harder for these same governments to justify standing by discriminatory laws. Among other things, their responses to the CEDAW Committee are matters of public record, now accessible on Internet sites, where advocates of women's rights can harvest them for future use in challenges to discriminatory laws and policies, throwing the governments' own statements back at them and generating pressures for upgrading domestic laws to meet international standards.

Even as they resist reforming their laws to bring them into compliance with CEDAW, the fact that these countries work so hard to portray themselves as compliant with the principles of international human rights law signals that change is afoot. Arab countries may hope that calculated hypocrisy will enable them to stay members in good standing of the international community while they continue to treat women like second-class citizens on the home front. However, their formal acceptance of international human rights law sets in motion a dynamic that over time should lead to mounting pressures for actual compliance with human rights standards. Put another way, when Arab countries decide to speak to the CEDAW Committee *as if* they had already accepted the principle that women are entitled to equality, this serves as an indicator that their legal systems have moved into a transitional stage—even though the governments involved may not always appreciate this.

A clarification seems in order at the outset. In focusing on the difficulties that Arab countries have experienced as they adjust to international human rights law, this chapter does not intend to suggest that these difficulties are unique. Arab countries are far from being the only ones that are engaged in a tension-filled and complicated dialectic with the international human rights system. To appreciate how Arab countries' experience is part and parcel of a broader process of engagement in the international human rights system corroding barriers to equality within domestic legal systems, the U.S. experience will be briefly alluded to. Becoming integrated in the UN system highlighted nonconforming U.S. laws mandating racial discrimination and placed the supporters of such discrimination on the defensive. Long-standing tensions between the ideal of equality and the reality of racial discrimination became far more acute after the issuance of the 1948 Universal Declaration of Human Rights; racially discriminatory U.S. laws flagrantly violated the egalitarian principles of the declaration. In the 1950s, U.S. racial discrimination became more starkly exposed to the scrutiny and the opprobrium of the international community. Domestic laws and practices in the United States affecting nonwhites threatened to do fatal damage to U.S. prestige in the international arena and to thwart its efforts to win allies in the new UN system, where most members had populations that did not meet U.S. definitions of "white."[1] Among other things, many UN delegates and Washington embassy personnel learned firsthand about the ugly legacy of slavery and racism, be-

134

ing subjected to humiliating treatment by reason of their skin color. Meanwhile, African Americans were voicing their demands for full equality with new vigor, so that domestic pressures for reform complemented international pressures.

Although the need to dismantle racial discrimination seemed urgent, the executive and legislative branches were unwilling to confront the forces committed to preserving discrimination. It therefore fell to the judicial branch, more specifically to the U.S. Supreme Court, to cut the Gordian knot. There is reason to believe that the 1954 decision in *Brown v. Board of Education*, declaring racial segregation in primary schools unconstitutional, was prompted in large measure by the Court's concern about the grave harm that racist laws and practices were doing to the international image and the foreign policy of the United States.[2]

Like many Arab countries, the United States has continued to have difficulties adjusting to international human rights standards, in part because it, like them, remains reluctant to part with time-honored elements of its legal heritage, including a constitution that is the oldest constitution in the world still in force and that is bereft of modern human rights provisions.[3] While refusing to update its laws to meet international human rights standards, in international forums U.S. representatives try to depict U.S. laws and policies as if they meet or even exceed international criteria. They are not above dissimulating where there are embarrassing discrepancies. For example, with the proposed Equal Rights Amendment to the Constitution having been defeated in 1982, the United States lacks a constitutional guarantee of equality for women, a basic feature of modern constitutions that are informed by the philosophy of international human rights. This deficiency is something that the United States would like to suppress when discussing its laws on women's equality in international forums. As I have shown, in talking about how its domestic standards mesh with the International Covenant on Civil and Political Rights, the United States has deliberately endeavored to mislead the committee overseeing compliance with the Women's Convention by misrepresenting the constitutional protections afforded U.S. women.[4] One could say that the conversation between the United States and representatives of the international human rights system has become internationalized in the sense that in international forums the United States does not candidly discuss its nonconforming laws, preferring to speak as if it has already assimilated international human rights principles that it actually has still not digested.

Arab countries are finding themselves in a similar predicament. Being keenly aware of the prestige of international human rights, they seek to avoid being stigmatized for retaining nonconforming laws. The matter of women's international human rights is especially sensitive because Arab countries, in widely varying degrees, retain domestic laws and policies that violate these rights. Hoping to avoid condemnation by the international community, Arab countries may resort to hypocritical assertions and misleading statements about the status of their women citizens, often with some chance of confusing outsiders. The blatant discrimination affecting women in a country like Saudi Arabia is notorious, but the full scope of most Arab countries' discrimination against women is not obvious to the average outsider, who is unlikely to possess mastery of the details of Arab countries' domestic systems. Profiting from this lack of familiarity, in international forums, Arab countries may try to foster the impression that they are closer to complying with international human rights law than they actually are. Among other things, some Arab countries have tried to minimize the significance of the reservations that they entered to CEDAW at the time of ratification.[5] Via these reservations, they placed conditions on their adherence to CEDAW, indicating their determination to adhere to nonconforming domestic standards—often appealing to the need to respect Islamic law in this connection. Some reservations were worded in deliberately misleading ways in hopes of deflecting criticisms by other parties to the Women's Convention.[6] The full implications of the reservations were often obscure.[7]

Arab governments that are parties to the Women's Convention must submit required reports and defend their records before the CEDAW Committee, which exposes them to robust challenges that they are not always equipped to meet. They encounter many pitfalls as they seek to portray themselves as supporters of women's international human rights in the face of grilling by members—often called "experts"—of the CEDAW Committee. Probing questions from committee members about their reservations and other topics put them on the spot. For one thing, having put on the record reservations that indicate that they will uphold domestic norms in conflict with CEDAW, it becomes difficult for Arab countries to argue convincingly that their domestic laws *do* comply with

CEDAW. The most awkward questions often come from committee members who are women from Muslim countries. The latter are familiar with patterns of discrimination in Muslim countries and are prepared to challenge aggressively the notion that Islam requires discrimination against women and other rationales for discriminatory policies. CEDAW Committee members' store of information may be augmented by submissions offered by various feminist groups and human rights organizations, organizations that are subject to censorship inside Arab countries but that can freely report on and criticize governmental policies on women's rights in the context of UN-sponsored meetings in New York. For example, Algeria, which normally publishes the texts of ratified human rights conventions in the *Journal Officiel*, the official record of laws in force, had decided not to publish CEDAW in the journal, with the result that CEDAW was not treated as part of domestic law—hardly the way Algeria would have treated CEDAW had the government been sincerely committed to using the Women's Convention as an instrument of change. In a move that promised to embarrass Algeria, this crucial fact, which Algeria had deliberately omitted from its CEDAW report, was noted in a shadow report submitted to the CEDAW Committee by the FIDH, a French human rights nongovernmental organization.[8]

Why Arab countries that are determined to stand by discriminatory rules affecting women choose to ratify CEDAW and thereby expose themselves to public pummeling is open to speculation. It seems that CEDAW exerts a strong pull on Arab countries, rather like the sun's gravity, so that, even if they are philosophically as far away from CEDAW as the planet Neptune is from the sun, they nonetheless are attracted to move in its orbit. Despite having records that should make most of them wary of joining the CEDAW system, only a few have failed to ratify—Bahrain, Oman, Qatar, Sudan, Syria, and the United Arab Emirates. Knowing that they are reputed to treat women especially badly, Arab countries may calculate that ratifying CEDAW will by itself enhance their images.

A wish to polish a severely tarnished image may have prompted Saudi Arabia to ratify CEDAW on September 7, 2000, even though its official version of Islamic law calls for severe and pervasive discrimination against women, discrimination amounting to a kind of gender apartheid.[9] In 2000, the Saudi regime was bracing for compromises to its sovereignty that were needed for it to qualify for membership in the World Trade Organization.

It seems that it also embarked on a broad strategy of rehabilitating its poor image in the area of human rights, the need having become more urgent after the publication of a blistering report in the spring of 2000 by Amnesty International on the abysmal Saudi human rights record.[10] Saudi Arabia campaigned to win a position on the UN Commission on Human Rights, to which it was elected in May 2000. As surprising as the Saudi decision to become a party to CEDAW was, it was no more incongruous than Saudi Arabia taking a seat on this commission.

As would have been expected, when ratifying CEDAW, Saudi Arabia entered reservations to leave room for its continued noncompliance. Like the reservations of many other Arab countries, its reservations included an assertion that in case of conflicts, Islamic norms would override the Women's Convention. It stated, "1. In case of contradiction between any term of the Convention and the norms of Islamic law the Kingdom is not under obligation to observe the contradictory terms of the Convention." Those behind the reservation may have hoped that, shielded behind this reservation, the status quo could survive. Certainly Prince Nayef, the Interior Minister, did not want CEDAW ratification to be a prelude to any public debate on the status of women in Saudi Arabia, as is exemplified by his announcement on January 25, 2001, in response to a question about whether there would be such debate when he asserted that any discussion was "out of the question."[11] Despite this, Saudi Arabia's CEDAW ratification will open up whole new areas of contestation as CEDAW standards place the government's policies and its retrograde conception of Islam in a particularly unfavorable light. When one reviews the experience of some other Arab countries before the CEDAW Committee, one can predict that Saudi Arabia will be exposing itself to withering attacks from CEDAW experts, attacks that will at the very least force Saudi Arabia to start to reexamine and to reformulate its positions.

Another preview of what lies in store for Saudi Arabia can be found in the rough treatment that it received in January 2001 from the Committee on the Rights of the Child. In 1996, the kingdom had ratified the Convention on the Rights of the Child—with an Islamic reservation, asserting that it was entering "reservations with respect to all such articles as are in conflict with the provisions of Islamic law."[12] Saudi Arabia thereby opened itself to its first confrontation with a UN committee monitoring compliance with a human rights convention. The committee offered a harsh public indictment of Saudi policies as violative of human rights, an indictment that encompassed references to the kingdom's discriminatory treatment of girls and women. This may have surprised Saudi Arabia, which had submitted a detailed eighty-seven-page report that extolled the virtues of the Saudi system, boasted of its excellent human rights record and its extensive programs for children, and repeatedly referred to the Qur'an while skirting all discussion of problematic aspects of the actual treatment of children or the kingdom's stance on the Women's Convention.[13] The Saudi position was that its rules on children's welfare were derived from the divinely revealed teachings of Islam, "which are in harmony with and even surpass the provisions of the Convention."[14] Of course, this claim was paradoxical given Saudi Arabia's reservation to all Women's Convention articles that were "in conflict with the principles of Islamic law." This was not the only Saudi statement that was indecipherable. The report claimed that "reservations concerning all articles *conflicting* with the provisions of Islamic law" had accompanied ratification "because the Kingdom pays considerable attention to child welfare and aims to strengthen its international cooperation through the United Nations and because the provisions set forth in this Convention are *in conformity* with the teachings of Islamic law" (italics added).[15] Why it spoke of articles *conflicting* with Islamic law when it was simultaneously claiming that Women's Convention provisions were *in conformity* with Islamic law was not clarified. Saudi inability to formulate a coherent position on the relationship of Saudi domestic laws to international human rights law was manifest.

The committee dismissed the Saudi report, saying it was "essentially legalistic in nature and does not provide a self-critical evaluation of the prevailing situation of the exercise of children's rights in the country."[16] The committee rebuked Saudi Arabia for discriminating against women, harassing and assaulting youths who violated dress codes, and imposing "inhuman" punishments.[17] The committee also pointed its finger at "narrow interpretations of Islamic texts" by Saudi authorities, blaming these for Saudi violations of the Women's Convention.[18] That is, far from being deterred from criticizing rights violations that were attributed by

Saudi officialdom to the need to comply with Islamic law, the committee was ready to attack the legitimacy of official Saudi interpretations of the Islamic sources that correlated with such violations. In the course of the colloquy, the Saudi delegation boldly asserted that "women enjoy the same rights as men in Saudi Arabia," but the committee members noted that Saudi women were not allowed to drive a car, travel abroad, or visit a hospital without permission from a husband or other male relative.[19] These criticisms presaged trouble for Saudi Arabia in the CEDAW Committee.

The predicament of the Algerian representative on the occasion of the discussion of the 1999 Algerian CEDAW report illustrates how governments with records of denying women's human rights find, once they are in the CEDAW system, that it is no easy matter to justify the same discriminatory policies that they impose in their own countries without concern for women's reactions or for the harms that the policies may cause. Algeria was not the only Arab country to be unsettled when confronting Muslim women members of the CEDAW Committee who scathingly dismissed official rationales for discrimination against women. As will be shown, Algeria felt obliged to distance itself from its own laws, seeking to disavow any intent to discriminate against women—a position that strained credulity.

Since its 1962 victory in its war of liberation against French colonialism, Algeria has presented itself as a revolutionary socialist society. In reality, it has been governed by a corrupt and oppressive clique—known domestically as "le pouvoir"—that has proven unresponsive to the needs and wishes of its citizens.[20] Opposition forces among supporters of democratization, the Berber community, and powerful Islamist movements have wrested occasional concessions from Algeria's rulers but have been unable to open up the essentially dictatorial system.[21]

In 1984, the Algerian government enacted its Family Code, rejecting the progressive Tunisian model in favor of reinstatement of rules taken from medieval Islamic jurisprudence that effectively demoted Algerian women to the status of minors and wards of men. It was officially represented as resulting from the regime's commitment to respect true Islamic values.[22] This law was a top-down initiative imposed without consultation with women's organizations and with disregard for women's protests. Algeria's determination to stand by the discriminatory features of its Family

Code was demonstrated when it entered numerous reservations to CEDAW on ratification in 1996 that were designed to accommodate these features—as well as some discriminatory features of other laws.[23] However, as I have pointed out, unlike some other Arab governments, Algeria deliberately chose to avoid any mention of Islamic law as the justification for its reservations. I have attributed this tactic to Algeria's aspirations in the 1990s to win Western support for beating back the threat from Islamist movements, which had reacted violently when a brief, tentative democratic experiment was terminated in 1992.[24] Because it wanted to pose as the progressive, secular alternative to dangerous, terrorist Islamist forces, Algeria naturally preferred not to advertise in international forums that its own domestic policies on women were tied to retrograde readings of Islamic law.

When addressing the CEDAW Committee and presenting Algeria's report, Abdallah Baali, Algeria's permanent representative to the United Nations, did not acknowledge the government's responsibility for its laws affecting women. Instead, he spoke as if the government were fully in sympathy with the CEDAW philosophy of equality for women and as if external forces had obliged it to compromise its own commitment to modernity and universality. The problems in the way of women enjoying equality were represented as being attributable to centuries of backwardness, male domination exacerbated by illiteracy and ignorance, and terrorism (a coded reference to Algeria's Islamists) that threatened to take the country back to arbitrary darkness.[25] One saw the Algerian regime speaking as if it accepted CEDAW standards as normative and acting as if its own domestic laws deviating from CEDAW standards were an embarrassment that it needed to blame on other forces. To explain its failure to eliminate discrimination, Baali suggested that giving women full equality would only provoke a backlash, warning ominously against issuing "abrupt legal edicts that clashed so violently with social norms that they could not be enforced" because these "could lead to mistrust and conflict between the legislature and the citizenry, or even to open defiance of the public authorities, under the pretext of obedience to divine law."[26] This portrayal of the government as being concerned to respect the popular will and to avoid conflicts with the citizenry over questions of Islamic law would seem strange to anyone familiar with Algerian political realities. The undemocratic political system had long disregarded the popular will. There was certainly strong Islamist opposition to any reforms enhancing women's rights, but it was peculiar to speak as if, by itself, this would inhibit Algeria's ruling clique from ruthlessly pursuing its own priorities. After all, the government's actual record included decades of brutal suppression of dissent, including harsh repression of the Islamist opposition, which had burgeoned since the 1980s.

In speaking as if the government was to deal with conservative mentalities, Baali failed to acknowledge that there was an Algerian feminist community committed to women's equality, an omission that was most likely deliberate. To acknowledge the existence of Algerian supporters of women's rights would have been to reveal that, far from having to contend with a society that was uniformly backward and traditional or infected with fundamentalism, the government had faced a society divided on women's issues and had elected to side with foes of reform. However, the committee experts knew of Algerian feminist groups to whose opinions the government had turned a deaf ear. One expert who admonished Algeria to review its reservations and to consider the absence of reservations by other Muslim countries expressed a wish to know why some of the amendments to the Family Code proposed by Algerian women's non-governmental organizations had not been accepted by the government.[27] The fact that the Algerian Family Code was not keeping abreast of evolving social norms was not missed by one of the experts, who pointed to aspects of the code elements that placed women in an inferior position, asserting that these texts lagged behind the present situation in Algeria.[28]

When Baali invoked the specter of arousing fundamentalist ire, as if this excused the reservations that had accommodated retaining Islamic family law, one of the experts objected that in societies where the challenge of retrograde fundamentalist movements existed, women's equality needed to be in the forefront of political concerns. Another expert warned Algeria that a spotlight was turned on its performance as a regime confronting fundamentalism, admonishing,

Algeria was being watched by the world, and particularly by Muslim women, with some anxiety. . . . Religion and tradition should not be allowed to be used as an obstacle or excuse for limiting the Convention. The Government's responsibility was to ensure that its citizens were enlightened on the truly expansionist and compatible character of Islam with the needs and standards of modern times, especially as it concerned women's rights. Algeria was in a unique position to demonstrate its determination, commitment and energy to implement the Women's Convention without delay. That would not only ensure women's human rights, but also be a significant step towards liberating the Muslim religion from its place as hostage to the demands of deviant fundamentalists.[29]

As one can see from the comments of the CEDAW experts, they dismissed what Algeria envisaged would be good pretexts for its retaining discriminatory rules taken from medieval Islamic jurisprudence. Algeria spoke as if retaining these rules was necessary to avoid inciting fundamentalist passions, only to be criticized by CEDAW experts, likewise foes of fundamentalism, who insisted that moving ahead on Algeria's CEDAW commitments would be the sounder strategy in the war against fundamentalism.

Baali had trouble accounting for why a government as committed as his supposedly was to seeing the goals of the Women's Convention implemented would have entered such extensive reservations, as exemplified in his less-than-coherent statements to the CEDAW Committee, where he is reported as asserting that

> Algerian ratification of the Convention fell within the context of the gradual emancipation of women. Ratification had sparked discussion in the society, causing the Government to put forward some reservations to the Convention, none of which had really hampered the Convention. Algeria's reservations did not fly in the face of women fully enjoying their rights.[30]

He thereby took the stance that Algeria's discriminatory laws affecting women and the CEDAW reservations designed to accommodate these were not contrary to women's "fully enjoying their rights." The incoherence of Algeria's arguments did not escape the notice of the CEDAW Committee. Experts noted the inconsistency in the way Algeria represented its relationship to international law, speaking as if international law had primacy over domestic law, as one would expect, but then acting as though its domestic laws justified noncompliance with international law, as was the case when it insisted on standing by its reservations.[31] Experts expressed their concern about Algeria's reservations, especially the reservation to the central convention article, Article 2, which called for abolishing laws and customs discriminating against women. One expert pointed out that it was confusing to have Algeria enter reservations to Article 2 while it also asserted that it implemented the same article.[32]

Algeria's report asserted that in Algeria, as in all Arab–Muslim societies, the legal status of women presented a dichotomy.[33] According to the report, Algeria's constitutional principle of gender equality was scrupulously respected in the context of civil and political rights, where women enjoyed the status of full citizens. It conceded that in the area of personal status, women remained governed by the Family Code, which was based in part on the shari'a. Responding to this point, one expert noted that unless the reservations accommodating shari'a provisions were removed, Algerians would not be adhering to their own constitution.[34] Another expert argued that failure to recognize equality in the family impacted on the public life of women.[35]

In its report, Algeria acknowledged that certain provisions of the Family Code were seriously contested by human rights organizations, but it did not candidly discuss all the problematic provisions, acting as if it hoped to hide its more retrograde features. Problematic features mentioned in the report included a cursory reference to polygamy, a vague concession about there being some inequality in divorce law, and what it called "the formal nature of the daughter's obligation to seek permission for her first marriage"[36]—when, in reality, Algerian law required that a woman's marriage be contracted by a male marriage guardian in all cases. This was far from a complete listing of provisions to which human rights advocates had entered objections. In the sketchy list of discriminatory family law provisions, probably the most serious omission was the failure to acknowledge that Algerian law in Article 39[37] imposed on the wife a duty of obedience to her husband—a legal duty that all too clearly embodied the philosophy of Algeria's law, according to which wives were obligated to treat their husbands as their masters. Pursuant to this article, a woman could be prevented by her husband's whims from going out to work or to pursue an education—or even from leaving the house. That is, she could become a virtual prisoner.

Perhaps because of worries that even this sanitized version of Algeria's Family Code could make the country look backward, the report sought to minimize the significance of the code, proposing that its provisions needed to be regarded in the light of the extremely limited role of Islamic law in Algeria.[38] The report asserted that the role of religious law was diminishing in light of the sophistication of present-day problems, intercultural influences, and the secularizing trends under way in Algerian society. Only the Family Code made reference to the shari'a. The report sought to convince the committee that, despite its literal adherence to certain provisions of the shari'a, the Family Code could be seen both in its form and in certain rulings as an attempt to restrict the role of Islamic law.[39] How governmental imposition of discriminatory shari'a rules—rules that educated and progressive Algerians had denounced as unsuited for use in contemporary society—could be a way of *limiting* the scope of Islamic law was not explained. The report failed to offer a plausible explanation for why a government that had abandoned Islamic law in almost all areas would have elected to retain it in the area of family law, precisely where it would shore up traditional male prerogatives. Furthermore, the argument that the code sought to *limit* the scope of Islamic law could not be reconciled with Article 222 of the actual code, which specified that the shari'a was the residual source of law, allowing Family Code provisions to be amplified by references to any school of Islamic law or from the Qur'an and Sunna—thereby opening the door wide to the influence of precepts derived from Islamic law beyond those actually set forth in the text.

A Tunisian woman among the committee experts reacted with skepticism. She pointed out that women had not been consulted regarding Algeria's Family Code, which had been adopted by a conservative male parliament. She admonished that the Qur'an should be reinterpreted; it should no longer be used as an alibi to deny women their basic rights. Her own country, Tunisia, had abolished polygamy in 1956 and had restored women's rights. Indeed, the Qur'an could be a catalyst in ensuring acceptance of the proposed amendments to the Family Code in Algeria. It could also serve to change mind-sets and promote development. The issue was whether there was the political will to promote women's rights in Algeria.[40] That is, she shifted responsibility for the retention of discriminatory laws back onto the shoulders of Algeria's male rulers, implying that they lacked the will to promote women's rights.

Algeria also spoke as if the problems presented by the code might be temporary, claiming that the government was drafting amendments to the Family Code that would be submitted to the legislature.[41] However, over two years later, there was no sign that such amendments had been adopted, which suggests that the government may have been exaggerating its degree of commitment to undertaking family law reform. The reform proposals that have so far been tentatively put forward by the government are in any case too limited to satisfy CEDAW requirements.[42]

Algeria's failure to offer an accurate account of its domestic laws and policies may have seemed expedient in the short term. However, in the long term, the strategy of trying to disguise laws and policies that Algeria regards as too shameful to present candidly to the CEDAW Committee is not viable. There are too many forces at work to ensure that people inside and outside Algeria find out about the discrepancies between Algerian law and CEDAW provisions and the lack of correspondence between the way Algeria officially represents its positions to the CEDAW Committee and the reality of domestic government policies on women.

It is instructive to compare the presentations of Algeria and Morocco, the latter being a monarchy headed by a ruler who claims descent from the Prophet and who personally exercises authority over religious matters. Morocco did refer to Islamic law more than Algeria did when speaking to the committee, but it did not argue that the monarch had been entitled to impose Islamic law on his subjects.

Until his death in 1999, the autocratic King Hassan II insisted on remaining in charge of matters involving Islamic law and Moroccan personal status law. King Hassan allowed women to participate with men on an equal footing in many areas of life but rejected feminists' demands for major revisions in the personal status code, the *Mudawwana*. In large measure, the Mudawwana restated principles of medieval Maliki jurisprudence. In pronouncements aimed at the domestic audience, the king made it clear that he personally controlled such matters in his capacity as Commander of the Faithful and that he would not tolerate any personal status reforms that would contravene Islamic principles.[43] As a token of the regime's refusal to reform discriminatory features of the Mudawwana, when Morocco ratified CEDAW in 1993, it did so with reservations to Articles 2 and 16 (providing equal rights in the family), invoking Islamic law and the idea of complementary gender roles as the reasons.

Facing mounting protests by feminists, Hassan II allowed a few modest reforms in 1993.[44] His successor, Muhammad VI, showed greater openness to the idea of reforming the personal status code than his father had done, but tentative proposals for reforms in 2000, which included raising the minimum age for marriage for women to eighteen and abolishing polygamy, prompted mass protest demonstrations in Casablanca by Moroccan conservatives and Islamists in addition to smaller demonstrations in support by those in favor of reforms. Obliged to cope with daunting economic woes and social problems, the new monarch may not be prepared to carry through reforms in women's status that threaten to provoke a major backlash at a time when there are so many other causes of popular discontent.

Speaking to the CEDAW Committee in 1997, when King Hassan was still on the throne, Morocco's representative, Ahmed Snoussi, struggled to defend Morocco's record on women's rights and its CEDAW reservations. Revealing a mentality at odds with the CEDAW philosophy of equality, he tried to deploy the complementarity thesis, according to which unequal treatment of men and women was actually equitable because men and women were by nature so different that they needed to be treated in ways that were specifically suited to them. He spoke of a need to maintain the dignity of women and to preserve them from anything contrary to the rules of morality. Thus, Islam allowed women to work only within a framework of respect for morality, keeping them from work that might damage society; prevent them from fulfilling their other obligations to their husbands, children, and homes; or demand of them more than they are able to give in accordance with the teachings of the Islamic shari'a. That is, he spoke as if both natural differences between women and men as well as Islamic law were related rationales justifying deviations from CEDAW.[45]

Snoussi had to deal with sharp criticisms from the committee, whose members charged that Morocco's reservations were striking at the very heart of the convention. They raised repeated objections to Morocco's reservations to CEDAW Articles 2 and 16. Unconvinced by Morocco's appeal to Islam, one expert warned that the Qur'an could not be used as a pretext for not implementing the Women's Convention, noting that other Muslim countries had made more progress than Morocco had in achieving equality between men and women. Another asserted that, coming from a Muslim country, she was well aware that there was nothing in Islamic teachings that stood in the way of fully implementing women's human rights. It was proposed that the Moroccan monarch had a special standing in the Islamic world and that a compilation of women's rights in Islamic law under his aegis could do a great deal to help save the next generation from a misinterpretation of the Qur'an.[46] That is, Morocco's appeals to Islam as the justification for its discriminatory treatment of women did not impress the committee's members, who insisted that Islam did not require such discrimination and called for Morocco to reverse course and undertake a leadership role in promoting an enlightened understanding of the Qur'an.

In at least one area, Morocco's strategy turned out to be similar to Algeria's, involving the government's disavowal of responsibility for its own discriminatory laws. Not acknowledging how King Hassan had boldly asserted his personal control over the Mudawwana when speaking to Moroccans, Snoussi deliberately sought to obscure the reality that Morocco's discriminatory personal status code rested on the fiat of an autocratic monarch. Seeking to absolve the Moroccan government from responsibility for the plight of Morocco's women, he presented the government as being constrained by social, cultural, and political factors that stood in the way of repealing discriminatory laws. He maintained that religious practice represented a lifestyle and integral part of Morocco's culture and traditions. It was also a rampart against fundamentalism and terrorism at a time when Morocco was seeing a rise in fundamentalism in other countries. A basic concern of Morocco was religious fundamentalism. The government was not trying to avoid its obligations to implement the Women's Convention, but it could not make a decision based solely on ideological considerations. Morocco was a developing country with limited resources, and it had to confront certain attitudes.[47] That is, the government was portrayed as being constrained by its limited resources, popular resistance to change, and the menace of Islamic fundamentalism and by having to deal with circumstances where reforms unsettling the traditional culture would remove a bulwark against fundamentalism. One of the experts' responses was that religious fundamentalism was not restricted to Muslim countries.[48] Via this observation, Morocco was put on notice that problems of coping with fundamentalism would not serve as an excuse for noncompliance with CEDAW.

Snoussi also sought to absolve the government of responsibility for the reservations that Morocco had entered. According to Snoussi, Morocco's reservations were the result of a national consensus and were not simply a decision of the government. Pressure on the government would therefore not change that situation.[49] Unimpressed, one of the experts asked how "a national consensus" could be reached on the reservations when women did not participate fully in society and their illiteracy rate was so high.[50] For this as for some other critical questions, Snoussi had no answer. Dissatisfied with some of Snoussi's responses, Salama Khan of Bangladesh, the chairperson, noted his failure to reply to all the questions and comments of the experts.[51]

Obviously, Morocco had little success defending its discriminatory laws and CEDAW reservations before the CEDAW Committee and was unable to convince the members that it had legitimate reasons for failing to grant Moroccan women their rights under CEDAW. Unless Muhammad VI succeeds in enacting reforms to improve women's rights, Morocco will continue to be placed on the defensive in its dealings with the committee.

Libya's government has little in common with Morocco's, the country having been ruled by Mu'ammar al-Qadhafi's eccentric military dictatorship since 1969. The regime tries to pose as a leader of progressive causes. Aspiring to be regarded as a great revolutionary figure along the lines of Chairman Mao Tse-tung, Qadhafi has promoted his own ideology, which is set forth in his *Green Book*, in the tenets of which all Libyans are indoctrinated. Women's treatment reflects Qadhafi's idiosyncratic blend of revolutionary style—he often appears in public flanked by a coterie of gun-toting women bodyguards—and his own prejudices and crude gender stereotypes, which are articulated at length in the third part of his *Green Book*. From the *Green Book*, one gathers that Qadhafi believes in separate, complementary roles for men and women, imagining that these are an inevitable outcome of profound biological differences and the fact that childbearing and menstruation are incapacitating experiences. The *Green Book* instructs Libyans that there are innate characteristics that "form differences because of which man and woman cannot be equal," these being realities that "assign to each of them a different role or function in life."[52] "A woman is but a female," *The Green Book* advises.[53] Maternity is woman's "natural role in life."[54] "To demand equality between them [men and women] in any dirty work, which stains her beauty and detracts from her femininity is unjust and cruel," as is education that leads to work unsuitable for woman's nature.[55] Men are created to be strong and tough, whereas women are created to be "beautiful and gentle."[56]

Women are "exactly like blossoms which are created to attract pollen and to produce seeds."[57] "If a woman carries out man's work, she will be transformed into a man abandoning her role and beauty."[58] Men and women differ in "the psyche, mood, nerves and physical appearance. A woman is tender. A woman is pretty. A woman weeps easily. A woman is easily frightened."[59] Mixing the different roles of men and women is "absolutely uncivilized."[60]

Not surprisingly, under Qadhafi, Libya has emphasized women's maternal role and has been unwilling to adjust to the egalitarian model proposed in CEDAW. Far from advocating the strengthening of women's international human rights, in international forums like the Beijing + 5[61] meeting held in 2000, Libya figured among the countries most reluctant to accept advances in women's human rights, ranking with countries such as Algeria, Iran, Pakistan, and Sudan in that regard.[62]

Libya's first CEDAW report was considered in 1994.[63] Significantly, Libyan officialdom grasped that discussing *Green Book* teachings on how women's maternal function and innate characteristics precluded their having equality with men could only encumber its efforts to defend its policies. In the colloquy with the CEDAW Committee, Qadhafi's promotion of gender stereotypes was not mentioned. In introducing Libya's CEDAW report, the Libyan representative, Ibrahim Abdelaziz Omar, asserted that in his country there were no laws that were in any way discriminatory against women. Libyan legislation contained the principle of equality of women and men. The shari'a equally emphasized the importance of women in society.[64] Women were considered as the cornerstone of the society. They were equal to men before the law.[65] This was a remarkable statement to make given that Libya's official ideology expressly precluded women having equality. Libya's representative claimed that any laws that discriminated against women had been abolished.[66] According to him, the Islamic religion was designed to emancipate men and women from all forms of slavery by prohibiting injustice, making the promotion of women a precondition for the road to paradise and calling for equality among all human beings.[67]

Regarding CEDAW Article 2, Libya's representative claimed that the principle of gender equality was clearly spelled out in Libya's constitution and in the Great Green Charter of Human Rights.[68] In so doing, he provided an example of how the need to make a country's legal system look respectable by international standards may prompt its representatives to engage in outright lies; Libya has no constitution in force and has, a fortiori, no constitutional principle of gender equality. Instead, it has the 1977 Declaration of People's Power, which superseded the 1969 constitution and does not guarantee women equality but does affirm that the Qur'an is the source of legislation and the shari'a of Libyan society.[69] Qadhafi's 1988 Great Green Charter of Human Rights does contain a statement in Article 21 that men and women are equal in *humanity* and that discrimination against them is an injustice—but it provides no guarantee of equality in *rights*.[70] Given other provisions in the charter, such as the Article 20 requirement that mothers breast-feed and care for their children at home and the fact that various forms of de jure discrimination against women persisted in the era after the charter was issued, in Libya "discrimination" was obviously not being defined the way it was in CEDAW.

Because Libya has retained discriminatory features of Islamic law in the area of personal status, it was not surprising that on ratifying CEDAW in 1989, Libya made a reservation announcing that its accession was "subject to the general reservation that such accession cannot conflict with the laws on personal status derived from the Islamic Shariah."[71] It thereby indicated that it would be standing by Islamic laws in the area of personal status that conflicted with CEDAW, which was proof that Libya conceived of Islamic law as being at odds with provisions in the Women's Convention. Like other Arab countries that have entered Islamic reservations to CEDAW but that nonetheless insist that their Islamic laws do *not* discriminate against women, Libya was hard-pressed to come up with a logical explanation for its self-contradictory stances. Members of the CEDAW Committee expressed serious concern about Libya's reservation and about the fact that the reservation was not at all touched on in Libya's report. Members asked whether the government had not taken into consideration the objections to the reservation that had been raised by other parties. Bearing in mind that the shari'a had given equality to women, as was asserted in Libya's report, it did not seem clear why the reservation was still maintained, particularly as it constrained the government's ability to comply with Article 2, the central article of the Women's Convention.[72]

The experts admonished that reservations that were incompatible with the goals of the Women's Convention were not acceptable. They opined that the Libyan reservation was very much related to the question of interpreting the shari'a, indicating their disagreement with the proposition that Islamic law provided a basis for CEDAW reservations.[73] Committee experts from Bangladesh, Egypt, and Tunisia lectured Libya about Islamic law, maintaining that it granted women full equality.[74] However, it had come into force 1,500 years ago and was not immutable. The shari'a itself gave equality to women; the problem that had to be overcome was that of interpretation. Religions should evolve over time, but the interpretation of the shari'a had come to a standstill centuries ago.[75] Since the Qur'an permitted *ijtihad* for the interpretation of the Islamic religion, efforts should be made to proceed to an interpretation of the shari'a that did not block the advancement of women.[76]

The experts called for Islamic laws to be properly interpreted so as not to derogate from women's rights, maintaining that these laws were not immutable and must be adopted within the context of the Women's Convention. The interpretation of the Qur'an had to be reviewed in the light of the provisions of the convention and in the light of the current social environment.[77] That is, they flatly rejected Libya's rationale for discrimination and indicated that since the Woman's Convention was consonant with a sound contemporary understanding of Islam, Libya's Islamic laws should be rethought to conform to the convention.

They also pointed out that in some countries the shari'a had been interpreted in a more progressive way as a result of the political will of the government.[78] The Libyan government was urged to take a leading role in its interpretation of the shari'a as a model for other Islamic countries.[79] Here the committee touched on a sensitive issue for the Libyan government, which prides itself on its revolutionary character; Qadhafi would be discomfited by suggestions that his regime had shown itself less committed to advancing women's rights than some of its neighbors.

In replying, the Libyan representative flailed about in an attempted defense of the CEDAW reservations that it had entered, insisting that Islamic law did *not* discriminate against women but without finding any way to reconcile this claim with the fact that Libya's reservation indicated that Islamic law *was* in conflict with CEDAW. He made the puzzling assertion that reservations were entered by Islamic countries in order to avoid embarrassment in view of the literal meaning of legal texts.[80] He offered no specific account of what the "legal texts" were whose "literal meanings" caused "embarrassment" or what the nature of this "embarrassment" would be.

Committee members also objected that it was not possible to speak of equal rights of women and yet to maintain gender differentiation and sexual stereotypes, such as insisting on the role of women as housekeepers.[81] Picking up on the fact that Libya relied on gender stereotypes, the members requested clarification of the concept of "women's natural tasks," as referred to in the report.[82] The members also noted with concern the contradiction in Libya's claim to be introducing revolutionary measures for the emancipation of women on the one hand while on the other hand it was emphasizing their role as mothers and housewives, thus reinforcing what was already stiff cultural resistance to substantial change.[83] The Libyan representative claimed that any gender difference, if considered objectively, did not constitute discrimination based on sex.[84] Thus, like Morocco's representative, he seemed to be endorsing the popular complementarity thesis, according to which it is not discriminatory to afford women different rights because of the natural differences between women and men—a stance that, in the light of the general incoherence of its presentation, the Libyan government may not realize is at odds with the CEDAW philosophy.

The committee members did not hesitate to comment on the incoherence of Libya's position, remarking that they were still unclear about the reasons for the country's maintenance of its reservation to the Women's Convention. Members advised that the implementation of an antidiscrimination policy required that policies be coherent even though they touched on religious and ideological issues. True gender equality did not allow for varying interpretations of obligations under international legal norms depending on internal religious rules, traditions, and customs.[85]

In Libya's case, criticisms of its original reservation ultimately prompted an attempt at obfuscation. Apparently worried about criticism that could be leveled at it in the context of the 1995 Beijing Conference, in that period Libya reformulated its first CEDAW reservation to eliminate any language indicating that Libya's Islamic laws conflicted with CEDAW. Instead, the wording of the second reservation implied that

CEDAW threatened to dilute the *superior* rights that Libyan women enjoyed, asserting with regard to subparagraphs c and d of Article 16 (guaranteeing women equal rights in marriage and divorce and equal rights as parents) that their implementation "shall be without prejudice to any of the rights guaranteed to women by the Islamic Shariah."[86] Although the second reservation on its face looks less objectionable than the first, Libya will likely be disappointed if it hopes by this sleight of hand to conceal over the long term its failure to upgrade its laws to meet CEDAW standards. The changed wording was not accompanied by reforms in laws affecting women. Meanwhile, the embarrassment that Libya had experienced at the hands of the CEDAW experts might lead to some rethinking in official quarters regarding its policies on women.

Conclusion

These assessments of selected excerpts from some colloquies involving Arab countries and members of the CEDAW Committee reveal the dilemma that Arab governments create for themselves when they decide to ratify CEDAW without undertaking the reforms needed to afford women equality. They do not quarrel with the principle of equality for women, and they want to maintain the pretense that they are in substantial compliance with the Women's Convention. However, when they address the skeptical members of the committee, they find themselves unable to defend their actual policies on women and must resort to twisted logic, obfuscations, and misrepresentations in their attempts to dodge criticisms. They struggle futilely to reconcile their endorsements of equality for women with the reservations that they have entered to CEDAW. At moments, they imply that Islamic law conflicts with the convention, but, heedless of logic, they also try to maintain that, even while sticking by Islamic law, they adhere to the convention. As all these reports and colloquies are documented, the inconsistent positions taken by Arab governments could later come back to haunt them when domestic or international critics try to hold them to account.

In the way that the Saudis sought to present their human rights practices relating to children before the Committee on the Rights of the Child, one had a preview of how relatively poorly prepared the Saudis were to deal with independent critics in U.S. organs who were well informed about the scope of their rights violations, critics whom they did not have the power to censor or intimidate. Presaging troubles that they may face when dealing with the CEDAW Committee, when facing the Committee on the Rights of Child, the Saudis seriously miscalculated, imagining that simply reiterating their own propaganda about their impeccable human rights performance along with a plethora of references to the Qur'an would suffice. Instead, they met with a critical reaction that probably prompted some apprehension and anxiety about whether the kingdom was equipped to handle challenges from the CEDAW Committee.

A more sophisticated approach, adopted by some Arab countries as they faced the CEDAW Committee, was to make limited concessions to the effect that their laws might not be perfectly congruent with CEDAW but to rationalize the deviations, as happened when they invoked the need to take into account women's natural differences, or to place the blame for the deviations on forces beyond the control of governments, such as popular devotion to upholding rules of Islamic law or the menace of Islamic fundamentalism. Governments' efforts to exonerate themselves from blame for their own laws involved considerably hypocrisy, but, unlike the Saudi approach, these efforts did betoken the onset of critical self-awareness. Even though countries like Algeria, Libya, and Morocco had not made the reforms needed to comply with CEDAW, they were at least aware of the shortcomings in their laws, an awareness that prompted their attempts at dissimulation and rationalization. In the ways that these governments represented their positions before the committee, one also saw a realization that the lines that these same governments espoused domestically were unsuited for use in the international arena. For example, it was noteworthy that Morocco did not tell the CEDAW Committee that the king, as Commander of the Faithful, was entitled to dictate to Moroccans what Islamic law entailed and that Libya, whose citizens are all indoctrinated with *Green Book* gender stereotypes, did not lecture the women on the committee that they were designed by nature to be tender and pretty or that they were unsuited for the hard tasks naturally assigned to men since they wept easily and were easily frightened.

The shifts from their domestic stances on women's rights to ones that they could hope would have more credibility in the CEDAW Committee were emblematic of the adjustments that Arab countries were obliged to make as they embarked on the painful process of rethinking their traditionally discriminatory treatment of women in relation to international human rights law, a law the normative character of which they effectively conceded in their conversations with CEDAW experts. Even as they sought to explain away their retention of nonconforming domestic standards, they were engaged in a dialectic that was corroding the legitimacy of their discriminatory domestic laws and that was likely to augment pressures for reforms in the direction of affording women equality.

Notes

1. The severity of the damage caused to the international image of the United States by the notoriety of its domestic policies on race in the Cold War era is discussed in Mary L. Dudziak, *Cold War Civil Rights: Race and the Image of American Democracy* (Princeton, N.J.: Princeton University Press, 2000).

2. See Dudziak, *Cold War Civil Rights*, 91–110.

3. The U.S. estrangement from international human rights is evinced, among other things, by its long delay in ratifying many human rights conventions, its insistence on imposing reservations to qualify its adherence to those human rights conventions that it does ratify, and its refusal to ratify important conventions like the International Covenant on Economic, Social, and Cultural Rights; the Convention on the Rights of the Child; and the Women's Convention.

4. It has relied in part on the intricacies of U.S. equal protection jurisprudence as a smokescreen to cloak the deficiencies of U.S. law. See Ann Elizabeth Mayer, "Reflections on the Proposed United States Reservations to CEDAW: Should the Constitution Be an Obstacle to Human Rights?," *Hastings Constitutional Law Quarterly* 23, no. 3 (spring 1996): 789–92. One of the U.S representatives even stooped to proffering a bald-faced lie, falsely asserting that the U.S. Constitution "explicitly guarantees men and women equality" (794).

5. Texts of the reservations and objections to these can be found at http://untreaty.un.org/ENGLISH/bible/englishinternetbible/part1/chapterIV/treaty9/asp (accessed February 3, 2001).

6. See the discussion in Ann Elizabeth Mayer, "Rhetorical Strategies and Official Policies on Women's Rights: The Merits and Drawbacks of the New World Hypocrisy," in *Faith and Freedom: Women's Human Rights in the Muslim World*, ed. Mahnaz Afkhami (New York: I. B. Tauris, 1995), 105–19.

7. On the difficulties of deciphering these reservations, see Ann Elizabeth Mayer, "Religious Reservations to the Convention on the Elimination of All

Forms of Discrimination against Women: What Do They Really Mean?," in *Religious Fundamentalisms and the Human Rights of Women*, ed. Courtney W. Howland (New York: St. Martin's Press, 1999), 105–16.

8. See Rapport Alternatif de la FIDH au Rapport initial Presente par l'Algerie au Comite sur l'Elimination de la Discrimination a l'Egard des Femmes 19eme Session (January 19–February 5, 1999).

9. See my discussion of why the Saudi treatment of women amounts to gender apartheid in Ann Elizabeth Mayer, "A 'Benign' Apartheid: How Gender Apartheid Has Been Rationalized," *UCLA Journal of International Law and Foreign Affairs* 5 (fall/winter 2000–2001): 252–56.

10. See Amnesty International, *Saudi Arabia: A Secret State of Suffering*, report, March 28, 2000.

11. See "UN Report Blasts Saudi Record on Children's Rights," Agence France Presse, January 26, 2001, available in LEXIS, World Affairs Stories.

12. See the discussion in Ann Elizabeth Mayer, "Islamic Reservations to Human Rights Conventions," *RIMO* 15 (1998): 39–40.

13. See "Consideration of Reports Submitted by States Parties under Article 33 of the Convention," *Initial Report of Saudi Arabia due in 1998*, CRC/C/61/Add.2 March 29, 2000.

14. "Consideration of Reports," 8.

15. "Consideration of Reports," 15.

16. "UN Report Blasts Saudi Record on Children's Rights." For a sanitized official version of the exchange, see "Issues, Final Conclusions and Recommendations on Reports of Latvia, Liechtenstein, Ethiopia, Egypt, Lithuania, Lesotho, Saudi Arabia, Palau and the Dominican Republic," UN press release, CRC 26th Session, January 26, 2001, Round-Up.

17. "Saudi Arabia: News in Brief," *Facts on File World News Digest*, January 26, 2001, available in LEXIS, World Library, ALLWLD file.

18. "U.N. Panel Says Strict Saudi Laws Violate Rights," *New York Times*, January 27, 2001, A3.

19. "In First, Saudis Defend Protection of Women's Rights before UN," Agence France Presse, January 24, 2001, available in LEXIS, World Affairs Stories.

20. Jason Burke, "Algeria Tries to Forget Its Dark, Tortured Past: France's Former North African Colony Is Racked by Violence, Brutality and Poverty. But Some Believe Its Long Nightmare Could Soon End. Jason Burke Reports from Algiers," *The Observer*, August 12, 2001, 18.

21. Giles Tremlett, "Death and Dissent as Algeria Goes to Polls: After a Decade of Bloodshed, Few Bother Voting and Power Remains in Hands of a Shadowy Clique," *The Guardian*, May 31, 2002, 15.

22. See Mary Jane C. Parmentier, "Secularisation and Islamisation in Morocco and Algeria," *Journal of North African Studies* 4 (winter 1999): 44.

23. See the discussion in Mayer, "Islamic Reservations to Human Rights Conventions," 33–34.

24. Mayer, "Islamic Reservations to Human Rights Conventions," 33–34.

25. "Algeria to Adopt Progressive Approach to Women's Rights," *Africa News*, January 22, 1999, available in LEXIS, World Library, ALLWLD file.

26. "Algeria to Adopt Progressive Approach to Women's Rights."

27. "Algeria to Adopt Progressive Approach to Women's Rights."

28. "Algeria to Adopt Progressive Approach to Women's Rights."

29. "Algeria to Adopt Progressive Approach to Women's Rights."

30. "Algeria to Adopt Progressive Approach to Women's Rights."

31. See "Rapport Alternatif."

32. "Progress for Women Is Linked to Question of Democracy," *Africa News*, January 22, 1999, available in LEXIS, World Library, ALLWLD file.

33. See "Algeria to Adopt Progressive Approach to Women's Rights."

34. "Algeria to Adopt Progressive Approach to Women's Rights."

35. "Progress for Women Is Linked to Question of Democracy."

36. "Algeria to Adopt Progressive Approach to Women's Rights."

37. Article 39 states that the wife is to obey her husband and to defer to him in his capacity as head of the family.

38. Article 39.

39. Article 39.

40. "Progress for Women Is Linked to Question of Democracy."

41. "Progress for Women Is Linked to Question of Democracy."

42. See the discussion in "Rapport Alternatif."

43. See Ann Elizabeth Mayer, "Moroccans—Citizens or Subjects? A People at the Crossroads," *New York University Journal of International Law and Politics* 26 (1993): 63–105.

44. These meant that husbands lost their right to unilateral extrajudicial repudiation and had henceforth to go to court to terminate their marriages, wives were given the right to terminate their marriages if their husbands took second wives, and the requirement that brides consent to their marriages was reinforced. Ann Elizabeth Mayer, "Reform of Personal Status Laws in North Africa: A Problem of Islamic or Mediterranean Laws?" *Middle East Journal* 49 (summer 1995): 439.

45. "UN Committee on Elimination of Discrimination against Women Concludes Consideration of Morocco's Report," M2 Presswire, January 22, 1997, available in LEXIS, World Library, ALLWLD file.

46. "UN Committee."

47. "UN Committee."
48. "UN Committee."
49. "UN Committee."
50. "UN Committee."
51. "UN Committee."
52. *The Green Book: Part Three*, 28–29, available at www.greenbook.cjb.net (accessed February 10, 2001). The pagination at the Internet site corresponds to the pagination of the original hard-copy version of the book.
53. *Green Book*, 35.
54. *Green Book*, 39.
55. *Green Book*, 35.
56. *Green Book*, 36.
57. *Green Book*, 39.
58. *Green Book*, 40.
59. *Green Book*, 40.
60. *Green Book*, 40.
61. Beijing + 5 is an abbreviation for the session of the UN General Assembly "Women 2000: Gender Equality, Development and Peace for the 21st Century," New York, June 5–10, 2000.
62. See Barbara Crossette, "Rights Gains Are Preserved at U.N. Forum on Women," *New York Times*, June 11, 2000.
63. See "Report of the Committee on the Elimination of Discrimination Against Women, Thirteenth Session, General Assembly, Official Records—Forty-Ninth Session, Supplement No. 38 (A/49/38) Libyan Arab Jamahiriya" (hereinafter "Report of the Committee on Libya"). The material on Libya appears in paragraphs 126–85 of the report, and paragraph numbers will be used in the following references.
64. "Report of the Committee on Libya," para. 127.
65. "Report of the Committee on Libya," para. 129.
66. "Report of the Committee on Libya," para. 141.
67. "Report of the Committee on Libya," para. 131.
68. "Report of the Committee on Libya," para. 140.
69. See the discussion in Ann Elizabeth Mayer, "In Search of a Sacred Law: The Meandering Course of Qadhafi's Legal Policy," in *Qadhafi's Libya 1969–1994*, ed. Dirk Vanderwalle (New York: St. Martin's Press, 1995), 115, 126.
70. Mayer, "In Search of a Sacred Law," 126.
71. Mayer, "Islamic Reservations to Human Rights Conventions," 31.
72. "Report of the Committee on Libya," para. 130.
73. "Report of the Committee on Libya," para. 131.

74. "Friday Highlights," Federal News Service, January 24, 1994, available in LEXIS, World Library, ALLWLD file.

75. "Report of the Committee on Libya," para. 131.

76. "Report of the Committee on Libya," para. 131.

77. "Friday Highlights."

78. "Report of the Committee on Libya," para. 131.

79. "Report of the Committee on Libya," para. 132.

80. "Report of the Committee on Libya," para. 131.

81. "Report of the Committee on Libya," para. 130.

82. "Report of the Committee on Libya," para. 135.

83. "Report of the Committee on Libya," para. 180.

84. "Report of the Committee on Libya," para. 131.

85. "Report of the Committee on Libya," para. 135.

86. See my discussion in Mayer, "Islamic Reservations to Human Rights Conventions," 32.

CHAPTER SIX
TAHLIL MARRIAGE IN SHARI'A, LEGAL CODES, AND THE CONTEMPORARY *FATWA* LITERATURE

Barbara Freyer Stowasser and Zeinab Abul-Magd

*T*ahlil is a legal notion that has to do with a couple's right to (re)marriage in a case in which the husband has (irrevocably) divorced his wife three times. The traditional legal conditions stipulated consequent to the husband's pronouncement of the triple-divorce formula are that the wife has to observe the prescribed waiting period, marry another man, and consummate the marriage with him. She is then to be divorced by the second husband and complete the waiting period after the divorce before it becomes legal for her to remarry her former husband. Tahlil is legislated in the Qur'an (Sura 2:230). In the classical legal texts, tahlil also refers to the more specific and more problematic practice of marriage with intent to divorce as strategy to render the woman legally fit to remarry her (first) husband.

Islamic law developed within a number of paradigmatic blueprints that were later ascribed to the "founders" of "law schools" (*madhahib*, sing. *madhhab*), of which eventually there were four in the Sunni tradition. The "founders" belonged either to the "first generation" of scripturalist experts who worked within a century and a half after the Prophet Muhammad's death (Abu Hanifa, d. 767; Malik ibn Anas, d. 795) or to the "second generation" that succeeded them (al-Shafi'i, d. 820; Ahmad ibn Hanbal, d. 855).[1]

Speaking mainly in the language of traditions, medieval scholars of jurisprudence (*fiqh*) formulated legal rules variably based on communal consensus. Many of the rules remained embedded in "examples," Hadith-reported case studies, and/or Qur'anic exegesis, while elaboration of the underlying principles formed an essential part of the developing legal tradition. The fact that neither rules nor rulings were codified provided the system with an inherent flexibility, enabling judges and juriconsults to develop the law over a period of eleven or twelve centuries. The first section of this chapter is a study of the ways in which the four classical Sunni law schools dealt with the concept of tahlil marriage and how their formulation of this legal notion represents an example of discrete principles and doctrines that were operative in the four legal traditions.[2] The second section is a study of how tahlil marriage has fared in some modern Arab personal status codes and the contemporary *fatwa* literature (an answer to a question, a formal legal opinion, a considered opinion embodying an interpretation of the shariʻa; pl. *fatawa*).[3]

During the late nineteenth and early twentieth centuries, socioeconomic changes in the Arab world provoked the emergence of two new paradigms in the area of Islamic marriage law (even though they were in some unequal measure based on the preceding four). On the one hand, modernization policies as formulated and implemented by colonial bureaucracies and local elites produced a sizable number of national status codes that "patched" (*talfiq*, "patching") legal notions derived from the classical Sunni tradition together with European concepts of family and the family's role in society. Given the social and economic importance attributed to nuclear family stability and permanence in the European legal tradition, the Arab personal status codes largely refused to deal directly with the Islamic concept of tahlil marriage. By contrast, scholars of shariʻa law, especially after many of them lost their positions as judges with their countries' abolishment of shariʻa courts, have struggled to retain authority in the area of issuing fatwas as spokesmen of an alternate, more authentic legal tradition. Their fatwas, however, tend to reflect a unified position of categorical rejection of tahlil marriage, which is itself an innovation.

Variances on Tahlil among the Four Madhahib

Tahlil means "to expiate an oath, to sanction, to make lawful," and in this case it is the second husband, the *muhallil*, who provides the woman with tahlil, that is, makes her lawful for marriage with the first husband who had thrice divorced her and who is therefore called *al-muhallal lahu*. In all four madhahib, this legal item rests more or less uneasily on three sacred texts: first, the Qur'anic text of Sura 2:230, mentioned previously;[4] second, a *hadith* that stipulates that "the man and the woman must taste the sweet honey of sexual pleasure" during the tahlil marriage (referred to in what follows as hadith A);[5] and, third, a hadith in which both "the muhallil and the muhallal lahu are cursed" (referred to in what follows as hadith B).[6]

Islamic scholars past and present have worked on listings of *ikhtilafat* (differences, disagreements) between classical law schools (and/or legal experts). Interest in and information on ikhtilafat go back to early medieval times, to which many fiqh books devoted special chapters.[7] The following discussion of variances on tahlil marriage is based on a modern comparative textbook on fiqh published in 1938 by Abd al-Rahman al-Jaziri, a shaykh of the Azhar, under the title *Kitab al-Fiqh 'ala al-Madhahib al-Arba'a.*[8] The Azhari *shaykh* prefaces his chapter on tahlil with a terse paragraph on the fact that this is a contested issue. This is then followed by an exposition of the teachings of the four madhahib on the issue in question. The main points in a tahlil marriage are, first, the marriage contract; second, the issues of intercourse; and, third, the question of whether the second husband may charge a fee for his service.

Variances in Legal Principles among the Four Madhahib

The Hanafi text lays emphasis on the validity of the tahlil contract as a formal (abstract) entity, without consideration of the intentions of the muhallil or any other of the partners who conclude it. To stipulate a fee is reprehensible because it defies the hadith-based legal norm that "stud services (of billy goats, donkeys, and other male animals) are free," but it does not invalidate the marriage contract; for some Hanafi jurists, the conditions are valid, while for the majority the conditions are void but the contract itself remains valid. The contract creates and represents its own legal category whence consummation of the marriage is lawful even if occurring in situations where the woman would otherwise be ritually "off limits," such as menstruating, in a state of postpartem bleeding, or in the state of ritual consecration (*ihram*). In addition, the Hanafi text focuses on establishing categories concerning what sort of males and what sort of sexual activities fulfill the conditions of effective tahlil. In this context, much of the speculation about physical incapacity (in the man) and limits of consciousness (in either

163

of the two partners) represents a mode of legal argumentation that proceeds by *qiyas* (analogy). After the effective legal instruments of tahlil (a valid marriage contract and consummation of the marriage) are established as the jurisprudential *'illa* (effective cause), all other potential variations to the formula are subsumed under the rubrics of valid or invalid by processes of analogy.[9]

For the Malikis, the primary condition for the validity of the tahlil marriage contract is that the muhallil be free of the stated or unstated intention to divorce the woman; in addition, purpose of action, consent to action, and awareness of action, as well as public acknowledgment of action, must all be part of this legal construct. Consummation of the marriage must occur within the boundaries of "lawful sex," that is, when the woman is ritually lawful for intercourse (by any standards). Among the four madhahib, the Malikis stand out by paying attention to the mental (not just physical) involvement of the woman in the tahlil situation.[10]

The Shafi'i school's conditions fall between Hanafi and Maliki schools in its requirements for validity of contract between muhallil and the woman. If he stipulates in the contract that he intends to divorce her, the contract is null and void; if such is his unexpressed intention, then (though this represents reprehensible behavior on his part) the contract is valid. Unlike the Hanafi, the Shafi'i stance progresses beyond the legal notion of contract to ethical and psychological considerations regarding the tahlil experience with the intent to emphasize its loathsome qualities (including for the female partner); this reflects Prophetic hadiths such as that "God hates divorce."[11] This position underlies, for example, the school's verdict that sexual pleasure is not a condition of legally valid tahlil and that intercourse must be effected by the muhallil even with prepubescent girls, "as a device that makes divorce loathsome." In addition, the Shafi'i blueprint includes some criticism regarding the doctrines of earlier schools, such as the Hanafi, as well as the practice of law among the "common/secular folk" (*al-a'wamm*),[12] who lack awareness of the true Sunna.[13]

For the Hanbalis, the whole category of tahlil marriage is suspect and fraught with danger, and thus they try to limit its validity. Primary in the argumentation are the prophetic hadiths transmitted by Ibn Maja (and others) according to which the Prophet likened the muhallil to the billy goat (that one borrows for stud services) and put a curse on both the muhallil and the *muhallal lahu* (hadith B) as well as multiple traditions originating with the Prophet and also the second caliph Umar ibn al-Khattab that forbid "temporary marriage" (*mut'a*).[14] Only a valid marriage contract on the part of the second husband will (possibly) fulfill the conditions of tahlil, but for this to happen, the second husband may not marry the woman with the stated purpose of divorcing her, nor can he do so on the basis of an agreement that he will divorce her, nor can he harbor the private intention that he will divorce her because in all of these cases the marriage contract is void. Even though the woman is due her dower and the legitimacy of any potential offspring is legally established, her reputation is tarnished, and the union, based as it was on an invalid contract, does not effectively render her *halal* (lawful) for marriage with her former husband.[15]

What Goes (or Went) into a Legal Paradigm?

With one Qur'an and one holy Sunna of the Prophet, why are there four Sunni law schools and not just one? Or why are there not more than four (which at one point in history there were)? And what exactly is it that sets them apart? The eminent Yemeni judge and scholar Isma'il al-Akwa' replied to this question that "it is a matter of traditions."[16] The traditions were functions of Islamic legal argumentation from the beginning. The "founders" of the law schools and their followers all used traditions as their primary mode of argumentation within different social and cultural settings. The Hadith thus helped Islamicize local custom, which was essentially based on *'urf* (legal convention, customary law) while also profoundly influencing early Qur'anic exegesis. The "founders" performed their scripture-based *ijtihad* (independent analysis or interpretation of sacred texts)[17] in a world of oral transmission where an authority on law and theology would not produce a ready "handbook" to bequeath to posterity but where sometimes sons and/or immediate students and sometimes students of students several generations later would put the orally transmitted texts into some written form whose larger paradigmatic focus would then also be ascribed to the first authority. Therefore, it is more correct to speak in this context of Malikis instead of Malik, Hanafis instead of Abu Hanifa, and Hanbalis instead of Ahmad ibn Hanbal. This is even true of al-Shafi'i, at least some of whose works were also compiled by his students and their students, with ample additions on their part. Following the convention to "personalize" the paradigms of the four law schools by ascribing them to their "founders," the issue of tahlil as presented by al-Jaziri helps identify some of their differences, which can in part be ascribed to differences in time, place, and context. Malik's paradigm was Medinan in origin and context, where the Hijazi (and still largely Arabian) traditional environment of the Prophet's city may have had to do with the importance that the Malikis placed on the notion of "intention" in faith, devotion, and especially contracts. For Abu Hanifa and his followers in intercultural Iraq with its new boomtown places like Kufa and Basra, a contract was valid per se if it was formally correct, that is, concluded according to objective and abstract requirements that defined validity of contracts. For al-Shafi'i, the positions of these two predecessors often de facto served as parameters of his own paradigm, while theoretical interests and ambitions underlay his efforts to design a more unified system of law finding. Insisting on the superiority of the prophetic Hadith over doctrines derived from local tradition and precedent, al-Shafi'i's school was in some measure anti-Maliki, while by rejecting formalistic qiyas (analogy) unless verified by scripture-based proof, it was anti-Hanafi. For Ahmad ibn Hanbal, prophetic traditions, traditions related from and about the righteous forefathers as well as the "consulta" (fatawa) of the Companions and their later successors, presented a massive reservoir of available data that he felt free to "interpret" from the vantage point of doing so almost two hundred years later but within a paradigm that attempted to preserve what he saw as "the original spirit" of Islamic tradition. For this reason, his arguments were often more literalist and more moralistic than those of his predecessors. Ibn Hanbal's school, including such later followers as Ibn Taymiyya (d. 1328), Ibn Qayyim al-Jawziyya (d. 1350), and Muhammad ibn Abd al-Wahhab (d. 1792), largely understood the model of the righteous forefathers in ritualistic and ethical terms, whence derives both the emphasis that Hanbalism places on "intention" and also its moral scrupulousness that requires avoidance of "dubious things" that lie between the permitted and the forbidden, such as may be suspected in the tahlil situation.

Tahlil and Choice

Neither of the four classical schools wholeheartedly supported tahlil marriage. Obliged to deal with the issue because it was based on a clear

Qur'anic text (Sura 2:230) but also clearly aware of social customs that to their mind pushed its limits to the detriment of "regular" shari'a marriage law, Islamic jurists largely subsumed the question of "legality" of tahlil marriage under other, more mainstream rubrics of lawyerly construction, such as validity of contracts.

There is presently no literature available to these writers that would give indication of the frequency of tahlil marriages in premodern Muslim societies. Anecdotes and rumors past and present appear to suggest that they have occurred fairly frequently. Even if called on in only a small number of cases, as the legal literature hopefully surmises, tahlil law provided irrevocably divorced couples with access to madhhab-specific variations among the four schools of law. Before the legal reforms that began in the nineteenth century in most parts of the Arab world, to be discussed in what follows, men and women of the Muslim community usually had access to courts and judges, juriconsults, and lawyers of several madhahib simultaneously. This provided individuals in search of tahlil with a choice based on their knowledge of each school's position on the issue.

The Modern Concept of "Family," Legal Reform, and National Status Law Codes

The term "family" (*usra*, or *'a'ila*) that appears prominently in today's legal literature signifies a brand-new concept in Muslim culture without precedent in Qur'an, Sunna, or classical fiqh. Scholars of the four classical Sunni schools did not combine legal rules concerning wives and husbands with rules regarding their offspring (*al-nasl*) into one category. Rather, shari'a law dealt with marriage, divorce, child custody, and the like under various separate titles.[18] In addition, shari'a law defined the marriage contract as a fairly flexible instrument that the spouses could enter and exit within reasonable regulations. Both legal treatises and court records of the premodern period indicate that, in juridic understanding, the marriage contract represented but one example of the wider category of contractual law. An eighteenth-century comparative textbook on the four legal schools compiled by the Syrian legal authority Husayn ibn Muhammad al-Mahalli al-Shafi'i (d. 1757), for example, reports consensus among the prominent members of the four Sunni schools that marriage is a legal contract available to any person wishing to satisfy his or her sexual desires in a lawful manner. Al-Mahalli indicates that according to many authorities a valid marriage contract requires a written form (*sigha*), two spouses, a guardian, two witnesses, and a dowry (*sadaq*), but he adds that there is disagreement among the Sunni schools regarding these requirements.[19] Nowhere, however, does he indicate that marriage as an institution was, is, or should be based on permanence. Premodern Arab court records in Egypt and Jordan reflect the same position. In terms of legal practice before codification, the Hanafi school was the official madhhab of Ottoman state courts, but litigants also had the choice to plead their cases in Shafi'i and Maliki courts.[20] The same holds true for Syria and Palestine; especially when shari'a courts in seventeenth- and eighteenth-century Syria and Palestine enjoyed greater autonomy because of a measure of decentralization in the Ottoman legal system, their records on civil transactions indicate that the institution of marriage was not at all rigidly defined and that various divorce practices, including *khul'* (woman-instigated divorce), were liberally used.[21]

The new notion of "family" first appeared in the Arab–Islamic discourse on marriage and divorce during the second half of the nineteenth century. Its initiators were mainly Egyptian reformist and/or nationalist intellectuals, such as Rifa'a al-Tahtawi (d. 1873),[22] Muhammad Abduh (d. 1905),[23] Qasim Amin (d. 1908),[24] and Malak Hifni Nasif (d. 1918),[25] who had encountered European culture and adopted Western (French or British) definitions of family and the family's role in the modern nation-state. The European model emphasized "family stability" and limited divorce rights, largely on the basis of Christian doctrine, in order to solidify citizen relations for the ultimate purpose of state control and planning in the political and economic realms.[26] While their advocacy for adopting the Western formula in an Arab context was based on motives ranging from the desire for religious reform to that of rebuilding the Arab nation and/or reflected a nascent Egyptian nationalism or feminism,[27] these and many other nineteenth-century voices were important in the processes that eventually resulted in the promulgation of Egypt's first personal status codes in 1920 and 1929.

In the nineteenth century, European pressure for reform by the Ottoman state led to the codification of shari'a law and the creation of personal status codes that established new categories of gender relations, embraced the new notion of the family, and also largely ended the flexibility of the Ottoman legal system.[28] The Ottoman laws on marriage, divorce, and other social transactions (*mu'amalat*) were codified in 1867–1877 as *Majallat al-Ahkam al-'Adliyya* (Turkish, *Mecelle*). This Ottoman civil code, put together by a committee of legal experts, adopted "the preferred" (*al-rajih*) among existing Hanafi opinions and practices that were arranged according to modern categories.[29] In addition, modern European codes, especially the French and Belgian, left their mark on this and the later Ottoman legislative efforts of 1916 and 1917, when European notions of marriage and family were "patched together" with inherited shari'a law provisions derived from more than one school. After the fall of the Ottoman Empire, most of the Arab states based their personal status codes on the Ottoman civil code of 1867–1877 and the Ottoman "Law of Family Rights" of 1917.[30] Because of its long history of modernization under a nascent nation-state and colonial administration, Egypt was the leading force in the trend toward Western-oriented legal modernization in the Arab world. While on the whole privileging the Hanafi school,[31] the early Egyptian codes of 1920 and 1929 also showed the influence of selected doctrines and opinions of the other schools.[32] Legal reforms in other Arab countries largely followed the Egyptian model, and the civil codes of Syria, Jordan, Palestine, and Iraq still bear similarities to the Egyptian code regardless of national differences in the dominant madhhab in each country.[33] Traditional judges in Egypt as elsewhere resisted the onset of legal reform, which they correctly understood as a harbinger of a gradual decline in their authority. The Azhar-educated *'ulama* as a whole contested the validity of the new legal codes by objecting to the novel methodology of "patching." In Egypt it was at first mainly the Maliki and Shafi'i 'ulama who felt threatened since the new legal system somewhat privileged the Hanafi school.[34] Eventually all Egyptian traditional judges lost their official authority when the shari'a courts were abolished in 1956, and the traditional jurists were replaced by graduates of modern law schools teaching both European and shari'a law.

Tahlil Marriage in Arab Personal Status Codes

Arab legal codes largely exclude the issue of tahlil marriage. Even though the various national codes are said to rely heavily on one school of fiqh or another, they commonly ignore the opinion on Tahlil of the school that they claim as their basis and instead focus on the (novel) principles of permanence of marriage contract and family stability.[35] In this manner, the modern law codes have squeezed out the tahlil situation between the now code-driven definition of marriage as a lasting contract and the prohibition of any kind of "temporary" marital arrangement. Issues of validity or invalidity of the tahlil contract, which were the main focus of classical law finding on this item and usually reflected each school's more general definition of the relationship between action and intention, are now dealt with by nationally issued fatawa for the recourse of judges and other legal practitioners.

Egypt

The Egyptian personal status code, recently amended as Law No. 1 of 2000, assumes the permanence of the marriage contract by stipulating that "the expressions in the contract should indicate permanence. This is required in view of the fact that the objectives of the contract are to make cohabitation lawful on a stable basis, to establish family and to produce and raise children."[36] Any contract that would impose conditions on the duration of the marriage is invalid under Egyptian law.[37] This leaves a gray area where the old paradigm (validity of tahlil contract) and the new (marriage permanence) collide and do not seem to mesh. Nevertheless, tahlil marriages still do occur. In such cases, the Egyptian courts as well as the Association of Marriage and Divorce Registrars (*Jam'iyyat al-Ma'dhunin al-Shar'iyyin*) are to rely on official fatawa issued by the *Dar al-Ifta' al-Misriyya* (The Egyptian Fatwa Bureaucracy), which applies the Hanafi opinion. The Association of Registrars uses fatwa materials that indicate that in cases of temporary and tahlil contracts, the registrar should validate the contract but not the condition of time limitation, if any are spelled out.[38] In terms of court decisions, Egyptian judges are required to follow the Hanafi school in validating a written marriage contract of tahlil as long as it does not include any stipulations on the duration of the marriage; the judge, therefore, does not take the parties' intent into consideration.[39]

Jordan

The notion of family permanence and stability is likewise essential in the Jordanian personal status code. Based on the 1917 Ottoman Code of

Family Law,[40] Jordan's Law No. 61 of 1976 now stipulates in Article 2 that marriage is "a contract between a man and a woman who is lawful to him with the objective of the forming of a family and producing children."[41] To be valid, the marriage contract must be free of any conditions regarding duration. Article 34(b) states that "marriage shall be irregular in the following cases: . . . mut'a marriage and temporary marriage."[42] Article 100 specifically mentions tahlil marriage by stating that "absolute irrevocability [of divorce] shall be negated by the marriage of the irrevocably divorced woman who has completed the waiting period to another husband, without the intention of tahlil. This shall be on the condition that the marriage is consummated, and after she is divorced from the second husband and has completed the waiting period she shall be lawful to the first husband."[43] It is noteworthy that by categorically denying permissibility of "intention" in a manner well beyond the classical Hanafi paradigm (on which it is supposedly constructed), the Jordanian law squeezes tahlil marriage into the accepted rubric of marriage-in-general.

Syria

Like the Egyptian code from which it was essentially copied, Syrian law considers marriage the pillar of the family and the family the main building block of society.[44] The Syrian family code, Law No. 34 of 1975, was primarily based on the Hanafi school, but the opinions of other schools were on occasion included by way of "patching."[45] Article No. 1 of this code defines marriage as "a contract between a man and a woman who is lawfully permitted to him, the aim of which contract is to establish a bond for shared life and procreation."[46] The authoritative Syrian lawyer Mustafa al-Siba'i (d. 1964) interpreted this article to mean that the marriage contract should be permanent (*mu'abbad*) and not temporary, in accordance with the opinion of most scholars (*jumhur al-'ulama*) that temporality nullifies the marriage contract and that mut'a marriage is therefore invalid.[47] More surprising in this context is al-Siba'i's insistence that in contracts—again, according to the majority of 'ulama (*al-jumhur*)—it is the meaning that has to be taken into consideration rather than the wording (*al-'ibra fi al-'uqud lil-ma'ani la lil-alfaz*); therefore, even if the contract of a temporary marriage does not include a stipulation on the duration of the marriage, the "meaning" of the contract tilts toward mut'a marriage, which is forbidden.[48] This legal stance is clearly based on the Maliki school, even though al-Siba'i offered it in Hanafi Syria by way of his authoritative interpretation of the Syrian personal status code during the 1960s. Articles 47 and 48 of the Syrian code differentiate between two types of marriage contracts: invalid (*batil*) and irregular (*fasid*). Prime example of the first category is the marriage of a Muslim woman to a non-Muslim man. The second category includes "any marriage in which the basic principles (of the contract) are completed, by offer and acceptance, but in which some conditions are breached."[49] The tahlil contract falls under the second type, fasid. Al-Siba'i affirms that the two spouses in an irregular marriage should be immediately separated.[50] However, it is still possible to authenticate irregular contracts by canceling the invalid conditions included; therefore, it is still possible to validate a tahlil contract by transforming it into a "permanent" marriage contract.[51]

Yemen

Before codification of its personal status law in 1992, Yemen had applied the legal opinions of Zaydi Shi'ism and the (Sunni) Shafi'i school, mainly according to regional differences in the majority religious profile of the inhabitants of its provinces. The prominent premodern Yemeni Zaydi scholar Muhammad ibn Ali al-Shawkani (d. 1839) endorsed the tahlil institution as a valid instrument for restoring the irrevocably divorced wife to her former husband on condition that sexual intercourse (sexual pleasure, hadith A) occurred during this tahlil marriage; all other considerations, such as whether "intent" to divorce was stipulated in the contract or merely present in the [second] husband's mind, did not affect validity of the tahlil marriage contract.[52]

The Yemeni Unification Constitution (adopted in May 1991 and amended in September 1994) in Article 26 stated that "the family is the basis of society and its pillars are religion, custom and love of homeland."[53] Yemen's personal status code, issued as Law No. 20 of 1992, was based on "patched" opinions selected from the Zaydi Shi'ite tradition as well as all Sunni madhahib, that is, quite beyond the Shafi'i.[54] The new Yemeni code neither raises the issue of "temporary" (mut'a) marriage nor contains provisions on tahlil; according to Article 6 of Law No. 20 of 1992, "marriage is the joining of two spouses by a lawful pact which makes the woman lawful to the man, and whose object is the founding of a family based on the community of husband and wife."[55] These definitions of the nature of family in Yemen's most recent foundational texts, the constitution and the Personal Status Code, clearly privilege the Sunni over the Zaydi (Shi'i) tradition; they also bear witness that Arab state-sponsored reforms in the area of family law tend to enforce patriarchal structures while generating increased state involvement in personal matters.[56] In addition, given the historical volume and weight of sectarian divergence on the nation's cultural and religious map, Yemen's decisions on how to deal with, especially, such issues as mut'a or tahlil marriages have special paradigmatic import.

After the codification of the family law in 1992, the Yemeni Ministry of Justice approved two prominent books in Islamic fiqh as basic reference works for the nation's jurists and lawyers. The first, *Sharh al-Azhar*, written by the Zaydi authority Ahmad ibn Yahya al-Murtada (d. 1437), is a comparative textbook that includes the opinions of all major schools of fiqh, Shi'a as well as Sunna. The author states that any "temporary" marriage is generically allowed by those who do not forbid mut'a marriage (the Shi'a), but not the Sunni schools. For the latter, he maintains validity and legal efficacy of the tahlil contract even if the second husband enters into it with the intent of divorce, as long as intercourse takes place and the intention of divorce is not written into the contract as a precondition.[57] The second highly popular reference work is *Ahkam al-Ahwal al-Shakhsiyya* by the contemporary Yemeni legal expert of Zaydi background Muhammad ibn Yahya ibn al-Mutahhar. While this book is also laid out as a comparative study, the author nevertheless professes to emphasize the Zaydi and Shafi'i traditions as the privileged schools.[58] In the end, he does neither. Reflecting a modern focus on social stability and national cohesion, Ibn al-Mutahhar places the purpose of marriage well beyond all classical definitions ("lawful fulfillment of the spouses' sexual desires") into the realm of nation building where each marriage represents one of the small entities bent on "permanence and stability" of which the (nation's) greater family is comprised.[59] All marriage contracts that include a written time clause are invalid; but even when a contract is written with the husband's (unstated) "intention" to terminate the marriage at a later date, the contract is invalid; this position agrees with the Maliki school rather than the Zaydi or Shafi'i. Ibn al-Mutahhar consequently classifies tahlil marriage as a sort of "temporary" marriage and declares that it is invalid.[60]

Morocco

In 1957 and 1958, Moroccan personal status law was codified in six books that together make up the *Mudawwana*. The law was based on the "preferred"/most appropriate Maliki practices and opinions;[61] just as in Egypt and elsewhere, however, French law also had considerable influence on both the process of codification and the body of the law, the latter especially as it concerned nature and role of the family in society. Article 1 of book 1 defines marriage as "a legal pact of association and solidarity which is meant to last. Its objective is chastity, wedlock, and multiplying the nation through the founding of family, under the patronage of the husband, on solid ground."[62] For the purpose of family stability, modern Moroccan law has also substantially limited the right to initiate divorce.[63] All temporary marriages were outlawed.[64] But the issue of tahlil lingered on. According to Article 71 of book 2 of the Mudawwana, tahlil marriage is "required, to restitute an irrevocably divorced wife to her former husband but must be concluded without intent of time limitation, and must be consummated."[65] This clause in the Moroccan civil code clearly derives from the Maliki school (historically, Morocco's own). By contrast, Article 38 of book 1 of the Mudawwana ("if a condition is attached to the contract which conflicts with its lawful essence or its aims, the condition shall be void and the contract valid")[66] is clearly based on the Hanafi madhhab. In the Moroccan national code, as in many others, some twentieth-century "patchings" of discrete elements taken from different premodern Islamic schools of legal theory and practice have been meshed with European law. Regardless of whether tahlil contracts in Moroccan law, however, are now governed by residual legal principles of the Maliki or Hanafi school, tahlil by any definition belongs in a different universe from the (nineteenth-century, French-inspired) twentieth-century Moroccan view of marriage as "chastity, wedlock, and multiplying the nation through the founding of family, under the patronage of the husband, on solid ground."[67] In Morocco as elsewhere, the French concept of family introduced a "new form of patriarchy" into Arab family law that also came with increased state involvement in personal matters.[68] Against this modern backdrop, the gray area of tahlil marriage (lying as it does between "ordinary marriage" and "not-so-ordinary marriage") presents an example of the "bad fit" that can occur when the old paradigm runs into the new.

Contemporary Fatawa and Tahlil Marriage

In its traditional format, a fatwa usually presented the opinion of the legal school of which the issuer (*mufti*) was a member. Some fatawa included the opinions of all four schools but usually did so by referencing the other three to the mufti's own, which then acted as the standard. Even if a mufti did not state which madhhab he followed, his name (and also the gist of his fatwa) would make identification quite easy. Since fatwas were grave affairs by being interpretations of the shari'a, their texts frequently included citations of madhhab-specific sources. Perhaps the reason for this "footnoting" was partly to legitimate specific fatwas by way of school consensus, but surely the desire to solidify the school's paradigm in the general realm of "responsa" also played a role.

With the beginning of the processes of legal reform that eventually led to the promulgation of national personal status codes in the Arab world, traditional scholars of shari'a law registered their objections to the reformers' methodology of "mixing" (or "patching") opinions of the four schools of shari'a law.[69] During and after many decades of large-scale 'ulama disempowerment and marginalization, especially in countries that had abolished shari'a courts by the middle of the twentieth century, legal specialists of traditional educational backgrounds regrouped to work in the area of ifta', the granting of fatwas that they presented as expressions of an alternative and more authentically Islamic position compared to that of the modern civil codes. These contemporary fatwas, however, have also been new creatures. For one, the Sunni mufti himself now (ironically) also "patches together" the opinions of the four madhahib without stating his own background or indicating which of his opinions is or was derived from which school. Second, the contemporary thrust in fatwa issuance has been toward advocation of the most restrictive stance among the four schools, perhaps on the basis of equating greater authenticity with greater strictness; in the present case (the controversial issue of tahlil marriage), this has been the Hanbali. Third, the Hanafi stance (which presently underlies most

Arab-world personal status codes) is consistently downplayed in this fatwa literature. Finally, the muftis themselves have adopted the "modern" concept of family by calling it *al-usra al-muslima* (the Muslim family), which must be protected against Western colonialist or neocolonialist attack; consequently, their fatwas paradigmatically resemble the modern national personal status codes in emphasizing that the Islamic marriage is built on permanence.

Mahmud Shaltut, rector of al-Azhar University in the late 1950s and early 1960s who had served as a symbol of Egyptian reformism and legal modernization, relied on Hanbali sources such as Ibn Taymiyya, Ibn al-Jawzi, and Ibn Qayyim al-Jawziyya to build a case that deemed tahlil marriage illegal in twentieth-century Egypt.[70] Forty years later, his present-day successor as the rector of al-Azhar, Sayyid Tantawi, is publishing similar fatwas, likewise based on the Hanbali opinion of Ibn Taymiyya and others.[71] Such has also been the position of the internationally renowned Egyptian shari'a jurist and mufti Yusuf al-Qaradawi. The young Yusuf al-Qaradawi was a member of the Muslim Brotherhood in Egypt in the 1950s, when he enrolled for study and later graduated from al-Azhar University in Cairo. After his move to Qatar in the 1960s, he founded and directed the Faculty of Shari'a at the University of Qatar as well as the Qatar Center of Sira and Sunna Research. At present he chairs a multi-million-viewer weekly Al-Jazeera Satellite Channel shari'a law show (*al-Shari'a wal-Hayat*, "Shari'a and Life"), and he has also been instrumental in the recent creation of the Qatar-based Internet site "Islamonline," which hosts a database of his and other scholars' fatwas on modern Muslim life questions. Regarding family matters, the common tenor in al-Qaradawi's opinions has been the modernist affirmation that marriage in Islam is based on stability, that God and his Prophet condemn divorce, and that the husband should keep the wife even if he hates to do so.

On tahlil, al-Qaradawi's *responsa* have been consistently negative. He considers tahlil marriage a form of adultery in which both (male) partners are cursed (hadith B); this is because, according to shari'a law, marriages must be concluded with the intent of permanence. Al-Qaradawi therefore frequently urges his petitioners to investigate whether the triple, irrevocable divorce of the wife by the first husband was, indeed, fully valid, that is, whether tahlil is truly required in their situation. While adopting the strictest opinion on the issue of tahlil (the Hanbali), al-Qaradawi neither declares his own madhhab nor quotes the opinions of past or present scholars of any of the four schools; this represents a reduction of the law to a single interpretation that is then advanced as equivalent to the law as a whole.[72] Traditional scholars in other Arab countries are taking similar positions in both the methodology and the substance of their legal opinions. The president of the Ifta' committee at the Islamic University in Gaza, Yunus Muhyi al-Din al-Astal, for example, received a question about a wife who annoyed her second husband so that he would divorce her, which would enable her to return to her first husband, who had divorced her three times. The mufti replied that the Prophet forbids tahlil marriage; therefore, this wife committed two sins, one by disobeying her second husband and the other by agreeing with her first husband to annoy the second.[73]

In the contemporary fatwa literature, it no longer matters which school the mufti follows; what matters is the protection of the whole body of shari'a law by way of comprehensive use of the four legal traditions. Whether affiliated with the state or in opposition to it, the modern mufti presents his legal opinions from a self-perceived position of religious correctness and authenticity. Nevertheless, in the area of family law, the modern national personal status codes and the modern fatwas penned by traditionalist muftis have much in common. The main reason for the resemblance may lie in the fact that the 'ulama, that fatwa-wielding corps of shari'a specialists, have over many decades adopted (and modified) the modernist position of twentieth-century Arab state legislatures that the family is the cornerstone of society. In this new legal universe, any internal or external attack on the existing personal status codes calls forth the defense of traditionalist forces that include the very 'ulama, who otherwise deem the modern legal codes as Western inspired and therefore inauthentic.

Notes

1. By contrast, six Hadith experts of the "third and fourth generation" (Muslim ibn Hajjaj, d. 875; al-Bukhari, d. 870; al-Tirmidhi, d. 892?; Abu Da'ud, d. 888; Ibn Maja, d. 886; and al-Nasa'i, d. 915) came to be recognized in more general terms as compilers of the six canonical collections of Sound (*Sahih*) Hadith but not as founders of law schools.

2. An earlier version of this section was published by Barbara Freyer Stowasser under the title "What Goes into a Paradigm? Some Reflections on Gender-Issue 'Differences' between Sunni Law Schools, and the Problematic of Their Historical Attribution," *Islam and Christian-Muslim Relations* 9, no. 3 (1998): 269–83 (on the relationship of early fiqh with the Hadith, see 269–72, 278–81).

3. John L. Esposito, ed., *The Oxford Encyclopedia of the Modern Islamic World*, vol. 2 (New York: Oxford University Press, 1995), 10.

4. "That a woman may not return to the husband from whom she was divorced three times before she has had connection with a second husband" is also exemplified in traditions recorded by al-Bukhari, Muslim, Abu Da'ud, al-Tirmidhi, al-Nasa'i, Ibn Maja, al-Darimi, Malik ibn Anas, Ibn Sa'd, Ahmad ibn Hanbal, and al-Tayalisi; see A. J. Wensinck, *A Handbook of Early Muhammadan Tradition* (Leiden: E. J. Brill, 1926), 56.

5. This hadith is quoted, for example, by Malik ibn Anas, *Al-Muwatta of Imam Malik ibn Anas: The First Formulation of Islamic Law*, trans. Aisha Abdurrahman Bewley (Granada: Madina Press, 1992), 212–13, and by al-Shafi'i, *Kitab al-Umm*, vol. 5, ed. Muhammad Zuhri al-Najjar (Beirut: Dar al-Ma'rifa, 1973), 79–80, 248–50.

6. Curse on the practice of tahlil is found in traditions recorded by Abu Da'ud, al-Tirmidhi, al-Nasa'i, Ibn Maja, al-Darimi, and especially Ibn Hanbal; see Wensinck, *A Handbook of Early Muhammadan Tradition*, 56.

7. See, for example, Susan A. Spectorsky, *Chapters on Marriage and Divorce: Responses of Ibn Hanbal and Ibn Rawah* (Austin: University of Texas Press, 1993), 4. Even in one of the "six books" (of Sahih tradition), the *Jami'* by al-Tirmidhi, each tradition quoted is followed by a list of points of difference between the law schools concerning the tradition.

8. Abd al-Rahman al-Jaziri, *Kitab al-Fiqh 'ala al-Madhahib al-Arba'a, vol. 4, Qism al-Ahwal al-Shakhsiyya* (Cairo: Matba'at Dar al-Ma'mun, 1938).

9. Al-Jaziri, *Kitab*, 77–80.

10. Al-Jaziri, *Kitab*, 81–82.

11. Reported by Abu Da'ud and Ibn Maja; see Wensinck, *A Handbook of Early Muhammadan Tradition*, 56.

12. On the concept of *a'wamm*, see *The Encyclopedia of Islam, New Edition* (Leiden: E. J. Brill, 1995), 185.

13. Al-Jaziri, *Kitab*, 82–84.

14. See Wensinck, *A Handbook of Early Muhammadan Tradition*, 145.

15. Al-Jaziri, *Kitab*, 84.

16. Interview with Barbara Stowasser in San'aa, December 21, 1997.

17. See Fazlur Rahman, "Concepts Sunnah, Ijtihad, and Ijma' in the Early Period," in *Islamic Methodology in History* (Karachi: Central Institute of Islamic Research, 1965), 1–26. Rahman defines ijtihad as "fresh thinking" (149).

18. Such as "rules on women" (*ahkam al-nisa'*), "rules on marriage" (*ahkam al-nikah*), "rules on divorce" (*ahkam al-talaq*), "rules on breast-feeding" (*ahkam al-rida'*), "rules on child custody" (*ahkam al-hadana*), and so on.

19. Husayn ibn Muhammad al-Mahalli al-Shafi'i, *Al-Ifsah 'an 'Aqd al-Nikah 'ala al-Madhahib al-Arba'a*, ed. Ali Muhammad Mu'awwad and Adil Ahmad Abd al-Jawwad (Aleppo: Dar al-Qalam al-Arabi, 1995), 24–29.

20. Abdal-Rehim Abdal-Rahman Abdal-Rehim, "The Family and Gender Laws in Egypt during the Ottoman Period," in *Women, the Family, and Divorce Laws in Islamic History*, ed. Amira El Azhari Sonbol (Syracuse, N.Y.: Syracuse University Press, 1996), 97; Amira El-Azhary Sonbol, *Women of Jordan: Islam, Labor, and the Law* (Syracuse, N.Y.: Syracuse University Press, 2003), 34.

21. Judith Tucker, *In the House of the Law: Gender and Islamic Law in Ottoman Syria and Palestine* (Berkeley: University of California Press, 1998), 37–112.

22. Rifa'a Rafi' al-Tahtawi, *Al-A'mal al-Kamila*, vol. 2, ed. Muhammad Imarah (Beirut: Al-Mu'assasa al-'Arabiyya lil-Dirasat wal-Nashr, 1973), 563–645.

23. Muhammad Abduh, *Al-A'mal al-Kamila*, vol. 2, ed. Muhammad Imarah (Beirut: Al-Mu'assasa al-'Arabiyya lil-Dirasat wal-Nashr, 1972), 116–29.

24. Qasim Amin, *Tahrir al-Mar'a wa-l-Mar'a al-Jadida* (Cairo: Al-Markaz al-'Arabi lil-Bahth wal-Nashr, 1984), 110–55.

25. Bahithat al-Badiya, *Al-Nisa'iyyat* (Cairo: Dar al-Huda lil-Tab' wal-Nashr, n.d.), 55–66.

26. Mary Lyndon Shanley, *Feminism, Marriage and the Law in Victorian England* (Princeton, N.J.: Princeton University Press, 1989), 3–21; Sayyid Abd Allah Ali Hasan, *Al-Muqaranat al-Tashri'iyya Bayna al-Qawanin al-Wad'iyya wal-Tashri' al-Islami* (Cairo: Dar al-Salam, 2001), 154–55.

27. See Omnia Shakry, "Schooled Mothers and Structured Play: Child Rearing in Turn-of-Century Egypt," in *Remaking Women: Feminism and Modernity in the Middle East*, ed. Lila Abu-Lughod (Princeton, N.J.: Princeton University Press, 1998), 126–70.

28. Amira El Azhary Sonbol, "Law and Gender Violence in Ottoman and Modern Egypt," in Sonbol, *Women, the Family, and Divorce Laws in Islamic History*, 277–80.

29. See Sonbol, *Women of Jordan*, 20, 36–38.

30. Dawoud Sudqi El Alami and Doreen Hinchcliffe, *Islamic Marriage and Divorce Laws of the Arab World* (London: Kluwer Law International, 1996),

36–37; George N. Sfeir, *Modernization of the Law in Arab States* (San Francisco: Austin and Winfield, 1998), 27–28; Sonbol, *Women of Jordan*, 36–38.

31. El Alami and Hinchcliffe, *Islamic Marriage*, 51.

32. El Alami and Hinchcliffe, *Islamic Marriage*, 51. See Ron Shaham, *Family and the Courts in Modern Egypt: A Study Based on Decisions by the Shari'a Courts 1900–1955* (Leiden: E. J. Brill, 1997), 11–15.

33. Sonbol, *Women of Jordan*, 20.

34. Latifa Salim, *Al-Nizam al-Qada'i al-Misri al-Hadith*, vol. 2 (Cairo: Markaz al-Dirasat al-Siyasiyya wal-Istratijiyya, 1984–1986), 494, 528–30.

35. The Egyptian legal scholar Hasan al-Fakahani, for example, defines "marriage" (in new Islamic language) as "the pillar of a stable family which receives its rights and responsibilities by religious sacredness . . . marriage is the first pillar for the family and family is the first unit in building society . . . a strong society consists of strong families" (Hasan al-Fakahani, *Mawsu'at al-Qada' wal-Fiqh lil-Duwal al-'Arabiyya*, vol. 3 [Cairo: Al-Dar al-'Arabiyya lil-Mawsu'at al-Qanuniyya, 1975–1976], 17–19).

36. Dawoud Sudqi El Alami, *The Marriage Contract in Islamic Law: The Shari'ah and Personal Status Laws of Egypt and Morocco* (London: Graham and Trotman, 1992), 24.

37. Al-Fakahani, *Mawsu'at*, 34–36.

38. Muhammad Tahir Kharashi, *Ahkam Qada'iyya fi Fiqh al-Ma'dhuniyya* (Cairo: Jam'iyyat al-Ma'dhunin al-Shar'iyyin, 1985), 49–51.

39. Communication with Egyptian attorney Ali Abul-Magd Ali in Aswan, February 3, 2003.

40. Sonbol, *Women of Jordan*, 20.

41. El Alami and Hinchcliffe, *Islamic Marriage*, 80.

42. El Alami and Hinchcliffe, *Islamic Marriage*, 87–88.

43. El Alami and Hinchcliffe, *Islamic Marriage*, 100.

44. Al-Fakahani, *Mawsu'at*, 62–63.

45. Al-Fakahani, *Mawsu'at*, 215.

46. Al-Fakahani, *Mawsu'at*, 215.

47. Mustafa al-Siba'i, *Sharh Qanun al-Ahwal al-Shakhsiyya*, vol. 1 (Damascus: Matba'at Jami'at Dimashq, 1962), 80–81.

48. Al-Siba'i, *Sharh Qanun*, 88–89.

49. El Alami and Hinchcliffe, *Islamic Marriage*, 223.

50. Al-Siba'i, *Sharh Qanun*, 200.

51. Najat Qassab Hasan, *Qanun al-Ahwal al-Shakhsiyya ma'a al-Ta'dilat al-Sadira fi 31/12/1975* (Damascus: Manshurat al-Muwatin wal-Qanun, 1976), 46–47.

52. Muhammad ibn Ali al-Shawkani, *Al-Darari al-Mudiyya: Sharh al-Durar al-Bahiyya*, vol. 1 (Cairo: Maktabat al-Turath al-Islami, 1986), 275.

53. www.law.emory.edu/IFL/legal/yemen.htm.

54. El Alami and Hinchcliffe, *Islamic Marriage*, 249.

55. Eugene Cotran, "Women's Rights in Yemen Today," in *Yearbook of Islamic and Middle Eastern Law*, vol. 6 (London: Kluwer Law International, 1999–2000), 83; El Alami and Hinchcliffe, *Islamic Marriage*, 250.

56. Sonbol, *Women of Jordan*, 38–39.

57. Ahmad ibn Yahya al-Murtada, *Sharh al-Azhar*, vol. 2 (San'aa: n, 1980), 238–39, 460–61.

58. Muhammad ibn Yahya ibn al-Mutahhar, *Ahkam al-Ahwal al-Shakhsiyya min Fiqh al-Shari'a al-Islamiyya* (Cairo: Dar al-Kutub al-Islamiyya, 1985), 18.

59. Ibn al-Mutahhar, *Ahkam al-Ahwal al-Shakhsiyya*, 22–23.

60. Ibn al-Mutahhar, *Ahkam al-Ahwal al-Shakhsiyya*, 140–41.

61. El Alami and Hinchcliffe, *Islamic Marriage*, 197.

62. El Alami, *The Marriage Contract in Islamic Law*, 11–12.

63. Al-Fakahani, *Mawsu'at*, 56.

64. Al-Fakahani, *Mawsu'at*, 88.

65. Al-Fakahani, *Mawsu'at*, 78–79; el Alami, *The Marriage Contract in Islamic Law*, 26.

66. El Alami and Hinchcliffe, *Islamic Marriage*, 205.

67. Article 1 of book 1 of the *Mudawwana*; see el Alami, *The Marriage Contract in Islamic Law*, 11–12.

68. Sonbol, *Women of Jordan*, 38–39.

69. The principle underlying 'ulama objection was phrased in terms of an interschool consensus on the illegality of "patching": *Al-Talfiq Batil bil-Ijma' wa-fihi Ta'addin 'ala al-Shar' wa-Ifsad lil-Ahkam al-Shar'iyya* (Latifa Salim, *Al-Nizam al-Qada'i al-Misri al-Hadith*, vol. 2 [Cairo: Markaz al-Dirasat al-Siyasiyya wal-Stratijiyya, 1984–1986], 494).

70. Mahmud Shaltut, *Al-Fatawa* (Cairo: Dar al-Shuruq, 1986), 316–17.

71. See, for example, *Al-Liwa' al-Islami*, July 25, 2002.

72. Yusuf al-Qaradawi, *Hadi al-Islam: Fatawa Mu'asira* (Cairo: Dar Afaq al-Ghad, 1991), 462–63 (www.islamonline.net/fatwa/arabic/FatwaDisplay.asp?hFatwaID=1413).

73. www.islamonline.net/fatwa/arabic/FatwaDisplay.asp?hFatwaID=18600.

CHAPTER SEVEN
EGYPTIAN FEMINISM: TRAPPED IN THE IDENTITY DEBATE

Lama Abu-Odeh

⌣

T his chapter argues that if we wish to account for the limited gains in reform of family law in Egypt throughout the twentieth century, it is crucial for us to relate the debate on family law with another debate, the one revolving around the identity of the Egyptian legal system. Whereas the debate on reforming family law forced decisions on gender and the family, the debate on identity centered around the ongoing and agonized struggle by Egyptians to define the nature of their country's contemporary cultural identity. The "character" of Egypt's law was one of the more important ways in which the question of identity was posed, and contenders in this debate had to stake a position on the question, Should law in Egypt be reconstructed to reacquire its lost Islamic identity, or should it remain European/secular? That the debate on the nature of Egypt's cultural identity would hinge on law,[1] specifically the question of the origin of the law, is due to the fact that the transplantation of the (secular) European civil law system into Egypt, over the course of a century and a half, had the effect of displacing Egypt's historic (religious) legal system based on Islamic law. The only exception to this phenomenon of transplantation was family law (though it was formally codified in a Western legal fashion), the substantive rules of which preserved their Islamic origins. This had the effect of rendering the Egyptian legal system into a secular system for the most part with the exception of family law, understood to be derived from religious law. This historic process of the displacement of the local (the Islamic) by the outsider (the European) in the field of law came to symbolize, in a condensed form, the process of a more generalized form of cultural "displacement" that Egypt[2] experienced with the rise of European modernity and colonial advancement.

Specifically, I argue here that mainstream Egyptian feminists' attempt to reform family law (incorporating such concepts as consent, autonomy, and formal equality between the genders) was to a large degree undercut by the constraints created by the debate on the identity of the legal system. Liberal feminism was consistently compromised so that the relative autonomy of religious law manifest in family law could be preserved, and so, equally important, the secular nature of the rest of the legal system could also be preserved. This position, in which liberal feminism was compromised to create an intricately balanced secular/religious space in the legal system, was forced on the feminists by the allies they had sought to help pass certain microreforms in family law throughout the twentieth century. Those allies included the liberal enlightened 'ulama (religious scholars) of Egypt and the secular nationalist elites controlling the legislature and the judiciary. The adversary of this alliance was the conservative 'ulama and the religious right.

I conclude by arguing that there are signs of a new alliance emerging in the attempt to avoid the trap of the previously mentioned compromise. Instead of sacrificing liberal feminism for the sake of preserving a secular legal space, the new alliance argues for a full-fledged liberal feminism, one that is located in Islamic text(s), in conjunction with an agenda of Islamicizing the rest of the legal system (albeit in a liberal fashion). This emergent alliance consists of a new strand within Egyptian feminism as well as a group of liberal modernizing Islamicizing male elites. In the new alliance, secularism is sacrificed for liberal feminism.

The first section of this chapter, "Gender and Identity: The Family Drama," lays out a map of the competing positions on the debates of gender and identity of the legal system. I hope to communicate to the reader the level of ideological complexity and degree of entanglement that exists between the two debates. The second section, "Egyptian Feminism: Trapped in the Identity Debate," shows the specific ways in which Egyptian feminists, debaters in family law reform, find themselves trapped in and hostage to the way the debate on identity has been pitched in Egypt. The third section, "An Unholy Alliance?," lays out the terms of the compromise on the question of women that the entanglement between the two debates has produced and the nature of the alliance involved in this compromise. The fourth section, "The New Alliance," begins by offering a description of an emergent alliance that advocates liberal reform in family law in Egypt but that also advocates the Islamicization of the rest of the legal system. The goal of this new alliance in pitching its reform agenda in this combined manner is to avoid being undercut by the debate on identity, as has historically happened in Egypt. I conclude this chapter by providing my critique of this new alliance.

Gender and Identity: The Family Drama

I begin by providing a map of the contenders in the twin debates taking place over the past one hundred years of Egypt's history: the one on gender and the other on the identity of the Egyptian legal system. These debates have occupied Egyptian elites and intelligentsia for the past hundred years or so, dividing them into several social and political forces. Mainstream Egyptian feminism is one of those various social forces, and its destiny has been intricately related to the way these struggles have unfolded.

On the issue of gender, the questions requiring responses are, What kind of gendered relationship in the family should law regulate, and should the law conceive of men and women as equal meaning the same, equal but different, or unequal because different? On the issue of identity, the question is, Should the ruling laws in Egypt be Islamically derived, or is secular, European-derived legislation (as is the case in most of the post-colonial Islamic world) acceptable in a country like Egypt that identifies itself as Muslim?

Since the contemporary legal system in Egypt is a European transplant, the answer to the second question seems to be conceptually related to the following subquestion, namely, How should we conceive of the relationship of the West to the Muslim East? Is it one of (fundamental) difference, incorporation (of the West), or resistance (to the power of the West)?

It is important to note that each of these questions (concerning gender and identity) divides the participants along a political spectrum of left, center, and right. One may occupy a certain political position on one issue and a diametrically opposite one on the other. For instance, to be a centrist on the question of family legal reform by no means implies that you are a centrist on the question of the identity of the legal system as well.

Mapping the Siblings

On the question of reform of family law, one may describe the contenders as divided in the following manner:

1. The rightist position is that transactional reciprocity in the family is the ideal. The normative position that rightists advocate on the question of the family can be reduced essentially to the "maxim" of what I call "transactional reciprocity": husbands maintain, and wives obey. This maxim has its origins in medieval Islamic jurisprudence, and it had been passed on to the various family codes in the Islamic world in different formulations. These formulations vary in their more specific content along a political spectrum of liberal to conservative depending on how the specific code defines the duty of obedience on the part of the wife (the less "obedience" it involves, the more liberal the code) and the duty of maintenance on the part of the husband (the more financial obligations it involves, the more liberal the code). The 'ulama and the conservative religious intelligentsia in Egypt typically hold this position and advocate an understanding of the maxim that is more conservative than liberal:

> [There is] a difference between women's freedom and women's liberation. Islam gives women many rights, and more freedom and respect. But it does not recognize the wave of liberation, which some ladies are calling for. Islam protects the Muslim woman who is decent and who respects her home, her husband and children. Islam does not give rights to the woman who rebels and who is *nashiz* [one who leaves her husband's house and refuses to return].[3]

Also included in this category is "Islamist feminism," the strand of feminism that seems to uphold transactional reciprocity (husbands maintain, and wives obey) as the basis of healthy gender relations, provided that men pursue both their powers over women and their responsibilities toward them conscientiously and according to God's commands. The danger according to this strand lies not in the formal inequality structure implicit in this arrangement, as liberal mainstream Egyptian feminism claims, but both in the abuse by men of these religiously based powers and responsibilities and also and equally important by women trying to "cross over" to the men's world to assume powers and responsibilities that are rightly men's:

> In the opinion of Islamist feminists, women are oppressed precisely be- cause they try to be "equal" to men and are therefore being placed in un- natural settings and unfair situations, which denigrate them and take away their integrity and dignity as women. For example, women are "forced" to go out and compete in the labor market—a task which means that women may come into contact with men (as in public transport, for example) in a humiliating and inappropriate way.[4]

2. The centrist position on the question of family law reform is di- vided into two subpositions adopted by two different social/political forces in Egypt. The first advocates were splitting the difference between the de- mands of the religious right (discussed previously) and those of main- stream feminists demanding equality. The national secular male elites of Egypt have historically pursued this strategy both in legislation and in ad- judication. The Supreme Constitutional Court of Egypt in particular is committed to this strategy. Examples of such "splitting" in the decisions of the Court include narrowly restricting polygamy (rather than abolishing it), banning the veil while affirming modesty, restricting no-fault divorce by men rather than giving an equal right to women, and so on.[5] The sec- ond is promoted by liberal feminism based on adopting a particular arrangement of legal concepts (equality, autonomy, and consent) that are unique to liberal feminism as such feminism is understood in the West. Egyptian feminism over the past seventy years or so has been committed to this discursive structure.[6]

3. The leftist position is liberal feminism. As far as I can tell, there is no "radical feminism" in Egypt (understood as a radical critique of the tenets of "equality," "consent," and "autonomy" implicit in liberal femi- nism). There is, however, a feminism *of* the left. It is a liberal feminism that relies heavily on the *secular* discourse of *"rights"* both as constitution based and as derived from the UN Charter on Human Rights.

Secular feminists firmly believe in grounding their discourse outside the realm of any religions, whether Muslim or Christian, and placing them instead within *international human rights discourse*. They do not "waste their time" attempting to harmonize religious discourses with the concept and declarations pertinent to human rights. To them, religion is respected as a private matter for each individual, but it is totally rejected as a basis from which to formulate any agenda on women's emancipation.[7]

In this sense, the leftist and the centrist positions on the question of gender are indistinguishable. Sometimes what distinguishes the liberal feminism of the left from that of the center is the insistence by leftist women that women's struggle is inseparable from other struggles in society. The New Women Research Center, an organization in Egypt established in 1984, describes its mission in the following way: "The Center seeks to articulate an Arab and feminist vision of the social causes in general and of women's causes in particular."[8]

The closest to a "radical feminism" I have been able to identify in Egypt is the position of the famous feminist Nawal Saadawi. I describe her as a radical feminist because she posits the thesis that *sexual* oppression of women is at the heart of Arab patriarchy (symbolized by the cultural obsession with women's virginity): "Arab society still considers that the fine membrane which covers the aperture of the external genital organs is the most cherished and most important part of a girl's body, and is much more valuable than one of her eyes, or an arm, or a lower limb."[9] Saadawi has been more daring than anyone else in promoting an agenda of sexual liberation in the Arab world. She shares with other forces of the left the idea that women's oppression functions and could only be addressed in conjunction with other forms of oppression.

That is why I firmly believe that the reasons for the lower status of women in our societies and the lack of opportunities for progress afforded to them are not due to Islam but rather to certain economic and political forces, namely, those of foreign imperialism operating mainly from the outside and of the reactionary classes operating from the inside. These two forces cooperate closely and are making a concerted attempt to misinterpret religion and to utilize it as an instrument of fear, oppression, and exploitation.[10] However, when it comes to actual positions on reform of family law, Saadawi adopts feminist views that are typical of the center (liberal feminism).[11]

On the question of the identity of the legal system in Egypt as a whole (that is, "should it be Islamic or not?"),[12] the positions have also varied between the rightists, the centrists, and the leftists. For the rightists, all laws should be Islamic. They argue that Islamic law is different from Western law. The upholders of this position contend that the adoption, historically, by the Egyptian political elites of the Western legal system has alienated the Muslims of Egypt from their authentic traditions based on Islamic law. According to them, what is secular about the legal system today should be reconstructed and reconceived to become Islamic.

Even the nonreligious (Muslims) can appreciate the need for laws that reflect the convictions of the people and engage their support. Islamic jurisprudence (*fiqh*) is one of the greatest achievements of Islamic civilization, and many believe that Muslims may retain it and still find their own way in the modern world. They can adopt from the West what is useful, but not at the cost of their cultural identity.[13]

This view, which has been adopted by the 'ulama and the conservative religious intelligentsia,[14] holds that there is a radical cultural difference between the Muslim "East" and the non-Muslim "West." For example, the West is Christian (while we are Muslim), it is materialist (while we are spiritual), its family has disintegrated and its sexual prohibitions have collapsed (while our family is tight and our women have honor), and so on.

The rightist position has produced a variety of stances and subpositions on the question of identity according to the preferred methodology of reconstruction of Islamic law. For some, Islamic law should be ideally based on the historic system of *Taqlid* law, injected now and then with the use of *Usul al-Fiqh* to come up with new rules whenever the need arises. Taqlid law is a reference to the legal doctrine that was produced by Muslims in the premodern era and during the reign of the various Islamic caliphates. Taqlid, meaning "conformism" in Arabic, is a reference to the historic legal era, spanning from the tenth century to the nineteenth century, during which Muslim jurists and judges were understood to have abandoned the religiolegal project of coming up with new rules of law directly inspired by the sources of the religion (*ijtihad*, that is, exerting one's effort to find out God's law on a particular matter). Rather than pursuing the project of legal innovation, the jurists/judges of the taqlid era concentrated their legal activity on consolidating the legal doctrine of the school of law to which they affiliated. Taqlid, one might say, is the era during which the doctrines of the various schools displaced and overshadowed the Qur'an and prophetic traditions as the sources of the law. One followed ("conformed to") the doctrine of one's school rather than attempt a fresh reading of the word of God to come up with new rule.[15] Usul al-fiqh, on the other hand, is a reference to the legal era of usul al-fiqh, meaning the "sources of jurisprudence," the title given to the "legal theory" first innovated by the famous Muslim jurist Shafi'i in the ninth century.[16] The era of usul was one in which the schools of law started to innovate rules inspired directly by the sources of the religion, that is, the Qur'an and Hadith.[17]

The specific proposed reconstructive methodology of Islamic law that I refer to here advocates respect for the doctrine of taqlid as an expression of Islamic civilization while allowing for microchanges in taqlid law through the return by Muslim jurists to the original sources of the religion whenever the need for change in the law is pressing. This methodology mimics or is nostalgic for the legal era that preceded westernization of the legal system in Egypt. This position has been historically adopted by the 'ulama of Egypt's oldest center of religious learning, al-Azhar.

The second method proposed by the culturalist right advocates reconstructing Islamic law through the use first of a legal realist critique of usul that would "deconstruct" *qiyas* (analogy), the principal source of law (after the text of the Qur'an and Hadith), as "incoherent" and that would then proceed to reconstruct Islamic law through the use of the category of *maslaha* (public good or welfare) as the alternative privileged source of the law. Rashid Rida, the disciple of Mohammad Abduh, is known to have advocated this position. Rida looked to the concept of *maslaha* as a source of law. Because the Qur'an and the *Sunnah* (the words and deeds of the Prophet Mohammad, as recorded in the Hadith, or reports), two primary sources of Islamic law, have fallen short of providing all the answers to problems related to civil transactions (as opposed to those questions related to worship and belief), it is necessary to consider worldly interests (*masalih dunyawiyya*) to deal with such problems. In addition, Abduh advocated the methodology of *supra-madhhab*. This particular method consisted of adopting rules from the doctrinal pools of the various Islamic schools of law (madhhab) through a pick-and-choose legislative activity. It is a supra-madhhab method of legislation in the sense that the legislature is understood to be without loyalty to a specific school/madhhab (as was the case in the premodern era of Islamic history) but is approaching the task with a sense of "floating" loyalty to all the schools, picking the most "eligible" rule wherever it may be found (thereby expressing a modern legislative sensibility).[18]

The third method proposed by the cultural right argues that Islamic law should be reconstructed through a realist analysis of the medieval taqlid law (as opposed to usul, as the methodology explicated earlier proposes), which is then treated as the "raw material" to be reconceived against the grain of the main religious sources of the Qur'an and the prophetic tradition. According to this methodology, the modern scholar approaches medieval taqlid law trying to find "various rational explanations for [its] rules,"[19] only to discover that whereas there was a "number of intelligible principles that do appear to animate the law,"[20] in fact none of these principles seems to "explain all results."[21] The modern scholar is then forced to concede that, "as in many areas of law in any legal system, outcomes do not follow from any single policy, but from many which, by competition and cooperation, seem to give law its final shape."[22] This realization should then "liberate" the modern scholar and allow her to come up with new doctrines that combine the medieval with a new reading of the original sources.

The fourth method proposed by the cultural right argues that Islamic law should be reconstructed through a reinterpretation of the Qur'an and Hadith that attempts to "strike a balance between authoritativeness and authoritarianism." Khaled Abou El-Fadl, the advocate of this position, argues that

> [because] religion, as doctrine and belief, must rely on human agency for its mundane existence, one runs the risk that those human agents will either render it entirely subjectively determined, or render it rigid and inflexible. In either case one risks that the Divine will be made subservient to human comprehension and human will. [What needs to be explored is] the inevitable negotiation that must occur between the author, text, and the reader.[23]

Another attempt has been promoted by the Lebanese American Aziza al-Hibri. This proposed method of reconstruction is based on a feminist agenda. The proponents of this method argue that Islamic law should be first reconstructed through a critique of the medieval taqlid law as patriarchal (premodern Muslim jurists who interpreted the sources of the religion were all really sexist) and then reconceived afresh on the basis of new interpretations of the Qur'an and prophetic traditions on gender. This position specifically argues that a serious reading of these sources reveals that God and his prophet have always really supported a vision of gendered equality. Thus, Aziza al-Hibri advocates the idea that traditional jurists, who believed in the patriarchal model, actively worked to make this model a universal reality by passing conservative laws that were highly restrictive and harmful for women. Relying on prevailing stereotypes about gender roles, they used their legal power to assert the automatic *qiwamah* (guardianship over women) of all men. According to al-Hibri, this defeated both the intention of Qur'anic verses that sought to limit the scope of qiwamah as well as the Equality Principle laid out in various verses of the Qur'an. Al-Hibri argues that "thoughtful Muslims should no longer accept that interpretation; and Muslim women must rediscover the truth of the Qur'anic Equality Principle in order to achieve liberation and freedom without guilt." To achieve this goal, Muslim women must formulate a strategy for change that includes a dramatic increase in the number of women seeking legal and religious education.[24]

I include Azizah al-Hibri in my typology although she is not Egyptian because al-Hibri sees herself as involved in the project of reform of Muslim family law in the Arab world, including Egypt. There are several echoes to her project in Egypt, but she seems to be one of the most articulate on this brand of Islamic reconstruction. It is noteworthy that her project places her easily in the camp of "liberal feminism," as the thrust of her reconstructive argument seems to be "to do away" through reinterpretation with all those Islamic textual references to formal inequality between the genders and to argue that formal equality, with its implicit advocacy of choice, consent, and autonomy for women, is the defining message of the Qur'an on men and women.

The centrist position on the question of the identity of the legal system as a whole is based on the implicit advocacy of legal hybridity. This position argues that the contemporary identity of Egypt is hybrid, embracing not only Islam but other sources of identity as well, such as Arabness (conceived in modern times as a form of nationalist identity that covers the Arabic-speaking world) and Egyptianness (conceived in modern times as a form of local nationalist identity peculiar to the Egyptians themselves). The dominating concern of those who hold this position seems to be "modernity" rather than "authenticity," and if the concern for the former has driven modern Egyptian elites to transplant Western law in Egypt in order to modernize the legal system, so be it. According to the contenders of this position, modern strategies of legal reform by local elites should be treated as sources of modern identity that are at par with the medieval Islamic law. The reconstructive methodology this position supports includes the possibility of combining rules derived from Western law with those derived from the historic legal system of Muslim taqlid law, an approach that they do not regard as jeopardizing the identity of an "authentic cultural self" as those of the right tend to think.[25]

The advocates of this position seem to me to be wrought with deep ambivalence on the question of the relationship between the Muslim "East" and the non-Muslim "West." The West is both good and bad. It is a source of identification but also injury. It is good because it is the site of liberal humanism and legal liberalism, more specifically democracy and human rights. It is bad because it is biased in relation to Islam and is guilty of hostile and arrogant misrepresentation thereof; moreover, it does not appear to appreciate the "greatness" of the Muslim Orient and its civilization.[26]

Instances of the centrist position on the question of identity include the historic compromise struck between the secular nationalist male elites of Egypt and the religious 'ulama based on Islamicizing family law and Europeanizing the rest of the legal system is an instance of this centrist position. Describing the historic process during which this compromise was struck, Daniel Crecelius notes that the modern leaders of Egypt found it impossible to impose reform on the 'ulama and therefore created "entirely new institutions to duplicate the functions of the religious ones still under the control of the conservatives."[27] For instance, secular laws were passed to coexist with shari'a law, and the number of secular courts was increased. It was through this slow process of indirect change and subversion that the system was slowly changed. Over the course of the nineteenth century, these new secular institutions "gradually expanded their functions at the expense of traditional institutions until the scope of the Sharia was reduced to personal status law . . . and the *kuttab-madrasa* (religious schools) system had fallen to a secondary status behind the secular system of primary, secondary and university schools developed by the state and the non-Muslim minorities."[28]

Abd El-Razzak Sanhuri's reconstructive methodology,[29] with its reliance on comparative law and various mediation strategies, also injects the Western-transplanted law with taqlid law. For instance, the committee charged with drafting the first Civil Code in postcolonial Egypt, which was presided over by Sanhuri himself, considered for inspiration not only the experience of the Egyptian judiciary since the changes of the nineteenth century, as well as modern codes in place in other civil law countries (of Europe), but also Islamic law, or shari'a.[30]

A third example is the test developed by the Supreme Constitutional Court of Egypt in its exercise of judicial review. This could also be seen as exemplifying this hybridity position. This test was developed by the Court in order to determine the Islamicity of various pieces of contemporary legislation on the request of (religious) litigants who demanded that the Court strike down certain laws as un-Islamic and therefore in violation of Article 2 of the constitution.[31] The Court's test asserted that legislation that went "against the grain" of what the determinate rules included in the Qur'an and the Hadith would be treated as unconstitutional (because un-Islamic); however, when there was no evidence that such determinate rules were being violated by the modern legislation, such legislation would be deemed constitutional even if its origins were secular or European.[32] In other words, the Court's test seeks to preserve the contemporary hybrid quality of the Egyptian legal system.

The leftist position on the question of the identity of the legal system is not entirely clear. In general, the leftist position seems to be based on the background political idea that the problem with the West is not really its difference but its power. The West is colonialist, imperialist, orientalist, disciplinary, and patriarchal.[33] What puzzles, however, is that while the left tends to treat the historic event of the introduction of the Western legal system into Egypt as an instance of power (either in the mode of the exercise of Western power over the Muslim East, in the adoption by local Eastern elites of Western styles of power and discipline through law and regulation, or in the form of collaboration between Western power and local patriarchy), the left, nevertheless, does not seem to have a position on the question of the identity of the legal system that could be understood as analytically related to its "power" theory.

An emerging strand in Middle East historiography located in American academia would, to my mind, represent an instance of the leftist position on this issue. In describing the attempt to pass European-style criminal codes in Egypt in the early part of the nineteenth century, Khaled Fahmi used the Foucauldian concepts of discipline and power to describe this new form of legality. He argued that the goal of the move from the "rituals" of public punishment to the "routines" of a criminal legal code was to represent the Pasha (ruler) in his absence, using the law as a powerful symbol of his wishes and desires. According to Fahmi,

> By defining offenses, fixing scales of punishments, identifying who in the bureaucratic-legal hierarchy is to execute the punishment, the legal code instills in the minds of people the feeling of the inevitability of punishment and its link to the crime being performed. Laws, civilian or military, owing to their abstract codification of crimes and their corresponding punishments, and to their association of the possible benefits of crime with the greater disadvantages of punishment, function as an effective deterrent to crime, *and thus as a powerful means to impose discipline.*[34] (emphasis added)

The new historiography on women in the Islamic world with its view that the codified reforms in family law carried out by the secular nationalist elites of the post-Ottoman era amounted to a form of state patriarchy that these elites needed to enact as part of their alliance with European imperial powers, combined with these historians' assertion that women in the Ottoman era did indeed enjoy quite a bit of freedom, choice, and autonomy if only the researcher looked hard enough, seems to me to be an instance of this leftist position of "the West is power."

El Azhary Sonbol is an example of those promoting such a stance. She argues that as modern nation-states in the Islamic world began to make and arbitrate laws, their legal jurisdiction was extended to include discourse on social issues. States thus become a major determinant of patriarchal relations, which were molded along the lines of the discourse of the ruling elites. El Azhary Sonbol refers to this phenomenon as "state patriarchy," which differed from early forms of patriarchy in that instead of the head of the family arbitrating power, as dictated by *'urf* (tradition), the state became the "creator" of culture in addition to the drafter of laws that were enforced by a central government. El Azhary Sonbol further argues that the new states and rulers, as the direct or indirect creations and allies of imperial European powers, could not depend on traditional legitimacy alone to defend their hegemonic rule. Thus, they led attempts at modernization that included the education of women as well as their integration into the workforce. These modernizing efforts did not, however, involve a change in prevailing cultural norms that defined gender roles.[35]

Because of the left's tendency to represent the modern/European as bad (colonial, disciplinary), it seems open to and willing to accommodate cultural reconstructive projects of Islamic law proposed by the right.

Egyptian Feminism: Trapped in the Identity Debate

When debating reform of family law throughout the twentieth century, mainstream Egyptian feminist activists have often had to contend with the fact that, quickly and without much ado, the discussion on the reform always turned into an argument with their adversaries about Islamic law. More often than not, the interlocutor adversary, resistant to the feminist reform, hurled back in the direction of those feminists a Qur'anic verse or a prophetic tradition that feminist reformist goals were *un-Islamic*.[36] Naturally, some of the feminists involved in the debate found themselves drawn into the hermeneutic path as a response: reinterpret the verse and the tradition to show that the reformist project was religiously based.[37] Adding to that the argument that most rules on the family were actually conjured up in the past by jurists living in and influenced by a patriarchal medieval culture often proved useful.[38] Other feminists, those of more secular leaning, resorted to arguments of social science hoping that the religious adversary would be impressed by numbers and statistics about broken marriages and impoverished children of divorce.[39] The interlocutor's argument, challenging the Islamicity of the feminists' reforms, was a normative success, effectively locking the feminists *into* a discussion about "Islam" as well as locking them *out* of a discussion on patriarchy.

The normative power of the adversary should not be underestimated. Not only was it often experienced by those feminists as silencing, but, more important, it seems to have historically succeeded in inhibiting the

development of an elaborate cultural critique of the institution of patriarchy in the family forcing mainstream Egyptian feminists to be content
with microlegal reforms that can pass the "Islamic" muster. As a result,
much of the Egyptian feminists' critique of family law throughout the
twentieth century could in retrospect be characterized as moderate: most
feminists did not challenge the notion of the family predicated on the dis-
tribution of what some scholars call complementary rights and responsibilities to women and men (that is, transactional reciprocity). In essence,
they seem to have accepted the notion of different gender roles in the family while insisting on equality in difference, adhering thereby to the mainstream cultural view that women's and men's family roles and relations
were ordained by religion. Indeed, much of their attention was focused on
the abuse by Muslim men of what is recognized, according to the traditional interpretations of Islam by the scholars and jurists of al-Azhar, as
their *lawful* rights and responsibilities.[40] In this respect, the difference between the position adopted by those mainstream Egyptian feminists on
the question of gender roles within the family and that of what I have described in this chapter as "Islamist feminism" is that for the former the advocacy of "equality in difference" seems to be tactical and nonideological,
whereas for the latter "equality in difference" represents the normative
ideal that expresses the proper structure of gender relations. It is for this
reason that mainstream feminists have always engaged in and supported
their tactical agenda of reform advocacy with an elaborate discourse on
liberal feminism.

While its normative power is undeniable, there is nevertheless something odd about the Islamic argument in that it is taking place against the
background of an Egyptian legal system that has undergone, over the past
130 years, a serious and radical rupture from its Islamic legal past.
Throughout this period, the political elites of Egypt have for various political reasons progressively dismantled the Islamic legal system: they abolished its rule structure, dismantled its courts, and disenfranchised both its
qadis (judges) and its 'ulama.[41] No longer was the Egyptian state, though
identifying itself constitutionally as Islamic, organized around the idea
that it derives its legitimacy from overseeing the application of God's law
(the shari'a), as had been the case in the Islamic world for centuries before. Indeed, everywhere in the contemporary Egyptian legal system, applied laws have European origins, courts are secular, and judges are trained

in secular law schools and appointed by the centralized powers of the state to interpret and implement laws in ways familiar to European civilian lawyers.[42] Long gone are the days when the Islamic rulers were dependent on the ʿulama for legitimacy.[43]

Moreover, the claim of the un-Islamicity of these feminists' demands was, typically, neatly and conveniently packaged by the same religious adversary with another equally powerful claim, namely, that feminists were agents of the West. The frequency and consistency of this twin package of critique suggests that the two charges are often experienced by the proponents of the critique, as implicit in each other.[44] Mainstream feminists may be charged with advocacy of Western culture, of sexual promiscuity that is uniquely Western, or of a Western style of feminist male hating, or they may be charged with an intent to destroy the Muslim family just as happened in the West, a blindness to the actual difference of the religious East from the materialist West, or, paradoxically, an attempt to impose the norms of the Christian West on those of the Muslim East.

Even more complexly, many Egyptian feminists, since the birth of the Egyptian feminist movement in the early part of the twentieth century until the present, invariably found themselves engaged in the project of defending Islam against its Western detractors. As the position of women in Islam has been the privileged site of interrogation and critique for both the anti-Islamic West and the reformist local feminists agitating for reform of family law, the latter have from time to time found themselves in "bed" with what they experienced as unattractive bedfellows.[45] Western detractors of Islam often appeared to these feminists to be in "bad faith" in their critique, using such critique to assert cultural superiority and to rationalize projects of unwanted intervention in the Islamic world.[46]

Finally, legal concepts like equality, autonomy, and consent have historically performed such a crucial role in the discourse of mainstream Egyptian feminism in its response to patriarchy as to make it strongly reminiscent of American feminism of the nineteenth century as the latter struggled against the Blackstonian patriarchal legal regime.[47] Egyptian feminists have historically identified a number of legal institutions as both premodern and bastions of male power that as such were the focus of their political activism. These institutions included marriage of minors, no-fault divorce for men, polygamy, the doctrine of obedience, improving the financial well-being of divorced women, increasing the age of custody, and so on. Liberal feminism, as such feminism is known in the West, remains to this day the most powerful ideological engine that informs and shapes the nature of Egyptian feminist demands for reform of family law.[48]

Islam, the West, and patriarchy represent the defining ends of the triangle within which Egyptian feminism finds itself trapped today. Toward each, it has developed a response. In relation to the first (Islam), it is modernizing (when its interlocutor is a religious adversary). In relation to the second (the West), it is an apologist (when its interlocutor is Western). In relation to the third (patriarchy), it is liberal.

In fact, on a closer look, liberal feminism seems not only to inform the response to patriarchy but also the response of modernization and apology. The modernizing of Islam, combined with apologizing for Islam, per the arguments, relies strongly on the notion that a true reading of Islamic texts, a liberal feminist Islam is to be discovered.

An Unholy Alliance?

Historically, mainstream Egyptian feminism has had to rely on its allies (mainly the national secular male elites and some modernizing 'ulama)[49] to wage its struggles for family law reform against those opposing such reforms (the conservative ulema).[50] According to my typology of positions in the first section of this chapter, the feminists' allies were those (mostly men) who adopted the centrist position both on the question of identity and on the question of gender. Their adversaries, on the other hand, were those (also mostly men) who adopted a combination of a rightist position on the question of identity and an equally rightist position on the question of gender.

But mainstream Egyptian feminism has also had to suffer repeated defeats because of its allies' compromising legal and judicial position. The centrist secular male elites of Egypt control the legislature and the courts and have consistently pursued the strategy of splitting the difference between the demands of mainstream feminism and that of the rightist conservative ulema.[51] An example of such a splitting would be for the mainstream Egyptian feminists to demand that polygamy be abolished on the one hand, while the conservative 'ulama argue that polygamy is a God-given right. The secular courts then intervene by positing that polygamy, though a God-given right, is nevertheless one that is of a restricted nature. Polygamy per se is not harmful to women, although women are allowed to prove in court that in certain instances polygamy was indeed harmful to them. It is then up to the court to determine whether, in this particular instance, this was in fact the case. The compromise was neither abolishing polygamy nor treating it as an absolute right but rather simply recognizing that it is a right to be exercised by men, albeit in a restricted manner.

Splitting the difference on the substantive level, however, was not the only compromising strategy that the feminists' centrist secular allies have pursued. As a matter of fact, this strategy came at the heels of yet another historic compromise that these same secular elites struck with the religious rightist 'ulama. In this case, the nature of the Egyptian legal system itself was split, its very identity bifurcated: most Egyptian laws in place were of European origin (understood to be secular), displacing the historic Islamic legal system, with the exception of family law. The rules of the latter were derived from Islamic medieval jurisprudence (understood to be religious).

It is in fact due to this compromising strategy of double splitting, I would argue—first of the substantive doctrine on the family and then of the identity of the legal system as a whole—that mainstream Egyptian feminism came to be squeezed or, rather, trapped in this unyielding triangle of Islam, the West, and patriarchy. The strategy of splitting the difference on the doctrinal level perpetuated these feminists' longing for liberal feminism: complete, uncompromised, unsplit, and unadulterated equality, autonomy, and consent.

In the meantime, the splitting of the identity of the legal system exposed these mainstream feminists to the relentless attacks by the religious 'ulama every time they called for reform; as such, reforms were experienced by these 'ulama as pushing that which was religious to become secular/European. For these 'ulama, the historic compromise of splitting the identity of the legal system was being destabilized by the feminists' calls for reform.

The New Alliance

Historically, while Egyptian feminism advocated liberal feminism as a response to the particular taqlid-based organization of the family, it had to rely on its alliance with the secular male elites controlling the state to promote its agenda. However, because of those elites' pursuit of the strategy of splitting the difference, *liberal feminism* has been a continuously frustrated project. It is for this reason perhaps that no internal critique of liberal feminism seems to have been developed in Egypt. Concepts such as equality, autonomy, and consent still have, seventy years or so after their initial inception, such normative power for these feminists that they are marshaled repeatedly, as if they had determinate and clear content.

The search for an alliance that will free liberal feminism from the compromises imposed on it by the secular allies has brought certain mainstream Egyptian feminists to consider a shift in strategy. The coming together of historians writing a new historiography on Muslim women in area studies, mainstream Egyptian feminists, and those advocating the project of cultural identity in the Islamic world at a conference titled "The Islamic Marriage Contract"[52] may very well represent this shift.

A perusal of the literature presented at this conference[53] indicates that liberal feminism has now become the call to arms of certain strands of the religious intelligentsia who are rightist on the question of identity (advocating the radical difference of Islam from the West and the project of Islamicizing law), thereby strongly distinguishing themselves from the conservative religious right, with whom they share the rightist agenda on the question of identity. Contrary to the latter, these religious culturalists see themselves as centrist (liberal) on the question of gender. For the most part, they seem to be pursuing projects of reconstruction of Islamic law to arrive at a liberal feminist account of the law on the family.

What is attractive about these new modernizing religious culturalists is that their advocacy of liberal feminism comes as part of a larger package of Islamicizing the legal system. Many of these factions are involved in the reconstruction of Islamic law as an alternative to the contemporary secular legal system that is in place in Egypt today. Therefore, they seem to be offering mainstream Egyptian feminists an attractive deal: no need for splitting the difference, the price that the secular centrist male allies extracted from the feminists. These modernizing reconstructivists of Islamic law carry the stamp of legitimacy in the eyes of the conservative religious right (the conservative 'ulama) because of their antisecular culturalist project. Such a position would seem to spare them having to pursue an agenda of splitting the difference in the manner pursued by the centrist secularists, the historic allies of mainstream Egyptian feminism. Therefore, they may very well be better situated to push the agenda of liberal feminism so dearly desired by Egyptian feminist activists. Certain factions of Egyptian feminism may now decide that it is far more profitable and effective for them to enter into an alliance with a liberal feminist, culturalist rightist, religious intelligentsia that is on the rise.

The shift may be represented in the following manner: in the old alliance with the secular centrist male elites controlling the legislative and the judiciary, liberal feminism had to be sacrificed through splitting so that a secular legislative space could be preserved. The conservative 'ulama, having been deprived of their historical domain of taqlid law and forced to be content with family law as the remaining area of jurisdiction, experienced every reform of family law as an attack on a God-given right. Incremental reform that preserved transactional reciprocity on the family but attempted to eliminate its most brutal institutions seemed to be the only possible path to follow.

In the new alliance, the feminists' allies promote an Islamicizing project and present themselves as hostile to secular legislation. Splitting as a compromise/sacrifice of liberal feminism does not, therefore, seem necessary. As long as it comes garbed with Islamic legal discourse, the new allies promise it should be fine. The new feminists, in order to achieve the goals of liberal feminism, seem to be willing to sacrifice secular legislative space.

Critique of the New Alliance

Implicit in the new alliance is a twofold danger for mainstream Egyptian feminists. First, the sacrifice of secular space in exchange for liberal feminism may be problematic. Women need secularism in the long run. Any reforms that are pitched as God-ordained, even though they are liberal feminist reforms, may prove hard to critique after a while. As we have learned from the modern history of feminism in the Islamic world, anything accepted as God-ordained is resistant to change. Were the liberal feminists to achieve their agenda, thereby facing public criticism for shortcomings of their program (as happened in the American feminist movement), the restrictive nature of their position could become problematic.

Second, liberal feminist reforms in the context of Islamic family law have been interpreted by their advocates as requiring a major trade-off for women: instead of the current transactional reciprocity in the family (husbands maintain and wives obey) as incorporated in contemporary Islamic family codes, the liberal feminist argues that women should be released from the duty of obedience in exchange for taking on the legal duty of participating equally with the husband in the maintenance of the family. Through such reform, the liberal feminist argues, women would begin to achieve formal equality with men in the family. In other words, women earn equality by participation in the workforce.

Tunisian family law presents an opportunity to exemplify this situation. The incorporation of liberal feminist demands in the Tunisian Personal Status *Majallah* of 1956 represents for many Egyptian feminists (and many other feminists in the Islamic world) the ideal that needs to be pursued. However, there is a serious danger implicit in the liberal feminist trade-off adopted by the Tunisian *Majallah*.

In 1993, the Tunisians amended Article 23 of their Personal Status *Majallah* of 1956. The amendment seems like a radical departure from its predecessor, a serious liberalizing move on the part of the Tunisian legislature. What it signals is an elaborate effort to abolish the legal command of obedience typical of the taqlid legal system, a desire for equality between the spouses. The earlier version of Article 23 reads as follows:

> The husband has to treat his wife well and avoid inflicting any harm on her. He also has to maintain her and the children according to his ability and her social status in all things included under his duty of maintenance.
> The wife may contribute to the family's maintenance if she has any money.
> The wife must care for the husband as the head of the family and obey him in all those matters that are considered his rights as such.
> The wife carries out her spousal duties according to custom.

The amended version of Article 23 reads as follows:

> No spouse should inflict any harm on the other and each spouse must treat the other well.
> Both spouses should carry out their spousal duties according to custom.
> Both spouses cooperate in conducting the affairs of the family and in raising the children well. They also cooperate in managing the

affairs of the children including their education, travel, and financial affairs.

The husband, as head of the family, has to maintain the wife and children according to his ability and their social status in all things included under his duty of maintenance.

The wife must contribute to the family's maintenance if she has money.

The particular social/legal transaction required of Muslim women who want to be part of a legal regime based on the formal equality of liberal feminism, one that uses terms in its dicta such as "no spouse" or "both spouses," is clear. Participate in maintaining the family if you no longer want to obey the husband.[54] If your desire is to be equal to your husband, your money will no longer be immune from his demands and those of the children. This seems to be the way Tunisians have conceived of the legal pathway to equality for women, when such equality is conceived of as requiring an intervention in the taqlid legal conception of the family. The Tunisian path to liberal feminism, by exposing women's purses to family demands in exchange for equality, typifies the way liberal feminism has come to be articulated as demand and goal not only by Egyptian feminists but also by most Arab feminists demanding reform of their local Muslim laws.[55]

The political strategy adopted by these feminists is hostage to and accepts uncritically the transactional logic explicit in the contemporary codified legal regulation of the relationship between the spouses, itself the legacy of the taqlid legal system. According to this transactional logic, the wife owes her husband obedience by virtue of his offer to her of wifely maintenance. Take one, and the other must go.

Proposing this particular form of trade-off as the liberal feminist response to transactional reciprocity looks on its face to be ignoring a very important social and economic fact in the Islamic world. Women in fact "earn" their maintenance in a way that is not recognized by the particular transactional legal formulation of Islamic jurisprudence (obedience for maintenance). Women do housework, and in the vast majority of cases, women undertake the arduous task of child care unaided by their spouses. Submitting to the logic of the taqlid transaction in one's political strategy to reform it, in this manner, risks reinforcing the invisibility of this fact. It is a formalist way of reforming that, if pursued, not only threatens to give little gain to women but also exposes them to loss of their property and earnings. It is unfortunate that the Tunisian formulation in its amended form still insists that spouses have to do their spousal duties according to custom. While exposing their money to the family's maintenance needs in exchange for no-obedience, the law still requires them to carry out their "spousal duty according to custom," which, let us make clear, for women means doing housework and taking care of children.

This interpretation is hard to avoid if one keeps in mind that the waged employment rate for women in the Arab world is no more than, in the best of cases, 12 percent of the population.[56] Most women are simply housewives or work as peasants, who also in this economy are expected to do housework.

The social critique of the household division of labor between the spouses does not seem to exist in a powerful way anywhere in the Islamic world. This is not the case even among the elite or the intelligentsia. There is no escaping the fact, it seems, that it is women who will be doing housework in Tunisia and that even under the amended law they will not be compensated for it.

Substantive equality (as opposed to formal equality) should be the self-conscious goal of feminist reform in the Islamic world. Substantive equality in this sense would be preoccupied with improving the daily bargaining power of women vis-à-vis their spouses rather than be invested in simply granting women the same powers and responsibilities understood as the sole path to equality. It may very well be that sometimes the "sameness" of powers and responsibilities is indeed the way to improve women's bargaining position. But this is not necessarily the case, and it is a position that has to be interrogated by the feminists' interlocutors in a manner that resists the magic and temptations of the discourse of sameness as equality. One of the possible formulations to be pursued in legal reform and that seeks to achieve substantive equality between the spouses would have to be that men maintain and women do not obey. A way of getting away with such a formulation may be by preserving the legal transactional logic of "maintenance for obedience" but proceeding to define the obligation of maintenance in a way that expands such an obligation on the part of the husband. Such an expansive definition would seek to incorporate the idea that men are compensating women for house labor. In the same manner, the reform would redefine the duty of obedience on the part of the wife in a way that severely limits the requirements of "obedience" so as to render the concept practically meaningless. Of course, other rules would also have to change to allow this approach of substantive equality to be effective, particularly those regulating inheritance as well as those regulating divorce and its financial consequences for women.

Notes

1. As was/is the case with the rest of the Islamic world.

2. As was/is the case with the rest of the Islamic world.

3. Nadia Hijab, *Womanpower: The Arab Debate on Women at Work* (Cambridge: Cambridge University Press, 1988), 33.

4. Azza Karam, *Women, Islamisms, and the State* (New York: St. Martin's Press, 1998), 10.

5. Lama Abu-Odeh, "Modernizing Muslim Family Law: The Case of Egypt," unpublished manuscript.

6. See Margot Badran, *Feminists, Islam, and Nation: Gender and the Making of Modern Egypt* (Princeton, N.J.: Princeton University Press, 1995), 124–64.

7. What I call "the liberal feminism of the left," which is both self-consciously secular but also espouses an agenda of women's rights that is reminiscent of the liberal feminism of the center, Azza Karam calls "secular feminism"; see Karam, *Women, Islamisms, and the State*, 13.

8. See cover of the new journal issued by the New Woman Research Center titled *Feminism and Identity*, January 2002.

9. Nawal El Saadawi, *The Hidden Face of Eve*, trans. and ed. Sherif Hetata (London: Zed Press, 1980), 26.

10. El Saadawi, *The Hidden Face of Eve*, 41.

11. "Many verses of the Quran refer to the fact that all people are equal before Allah, and that he created males and females so that there could be mercy and love between them. 'He it is who created out of you couples, so that you may live together, and have mercy and love for one another' (Sura 30:21). This verse is interpreted as bestowing upon a woman the right to choose her husband, and to be separated from him if she no longer wishes to live with him, since love, mercy and cohabitation presuppose free choice rather than compulsion. On the basis of this verse Muhammad gave women the right to choose their husbands, as well as the right to be separated

from them. However, women were stripped of these rights at a later stage through the statutes and laws promulgated on the basis of so-called Islamic jurisprudence." *The Nawal El Saadawi Reader* (London: New York: Zed Books, 1997), 82.

12. As opposed to the current bifurcation in the system today between Islamic rules on the family and secular rules on almost everything else.

13. See Frank Vogel, *Islamic Law and Finance: Religion, Risk, and Return* (Boston: Kluwer Law International, 1998), 20.

14. For an account of who in contemporary Egypt occupy this position, see Tamir Moustafa, "Conflict and Cooperation between the State and Religious Institutions in Contemporary Egypt," *International Journal of Middle East Studies* 32 (2001): 3–22.

15. Sherman A. Jackson, *Islamic Law and the State: The Constitutional Jurisprudence of Shihab al-Din al-Qarafi* (Leiden: E. J. Brill, 1996), 69–184.

16. Shafi'i's theory was a powerful intervention in the legal culture of the time, so much so that the era spanning the seventh to the tenth century came to be named after the title of his theory.

17. See Majid Khadduri, *Islamic Jurisprudence: Al-Shafii's Risala* (Baltimore: Johns Hopkins University Press, 1961); N. J. Coulson, *A History of Islamic Law* (Edinburgh: Edinburgh University Press, 1971), 61; and Joseph Schacht, *An Introduction to Islamic Law* (Oxford: Clarendon Press, 1964), 57–68.

18. See Norman Anderson, *Law Reform in the Muslim World* (London: Athlone Press, 1976), 35–85. For an elaborate discussion of Abduh's methodology, see *Biography of Mohammad Abduh*, by Muhammad 'Imarah (in Arabic).

19. See, in general, Frank Vogel, *Islamic Law and Finance*, 19–69.

20. Vogel, *Islamic Law and Finance*, 78.

21. Vogel, *Islamic Law and Finance*, 78.

22. Vogel, *Islamic Law and Finance*, 78.

23. Khaled Abou El-Fadl, *And God Knows the Soldiers* (Lanham, Md.: University Press of America, 2001), 34.

24. Aziza al-Hibri, "Islam, Law and Custom: Redefining Muslim Women's Rights," *American University Journal of International Law and Policy* 12, no. 1 (1997): 34.

25. Enid Hill, "Islamic Law as a Source for the Development of a Comparative Jurisprudence," in *Islamic Law: Social and Historical Contexts*, ed. Aziz Al-Azmeh (London: Routledge, 1988).

26. Hill, "Islamic Law."

27. See Daniel Crecelius, "The Course of Secularization in Modern Egypt," in *Religion and Political Modernization*, ed. Donald E. Smith (New Haven, Conn.: Yale University Press, 1974), 79.

28. Crecelius, "The Course of Secularization in Modern Egypt," 79.

29. Abd El-Razzak Sanhuri was the drafter of the Egyptian Civil Code of 1949.

30. Hill, "Islamic Law."

31. Article 2 of the Egyptian constitution was amended to read "Islamic law is the primary source of legislation" in Egypt.

32. The Court's test proceeds like this: First, the Court searches for determinate rules in the Qur'an and sometimes in the prophetic traditions that might allow a reading of the legislation under its purview to be in violation thereof. The Court often finds that no such rules exist. It then proceeds to assert that whatever rules do in fact exist are jurist made and themselves the subject of controversy among the various medieval schools of jurisprudence. This being the case, the Court then takes one of two alternative steps. Either the Court asserts the right of the legislative to legislate outside the domain of the determinate rules taking public welfare into account, or the Court reads into the various determinate but ambiguous rules a general principle that the legislation does not necessarily violate and declares it constitutional as a result. The overall apparent looseness of this test expresses, to my mind, the Court's commitment to the preservation of the secular legislative domain as it exists today and to its desire to deliver it from the encroaching reach of the interpretive arm of God's law. See "Modernizing Family Law: The Case of Egypt" (unpublished manuscript with author). For another view of the Court's test, see Clark Benner Lombardi, "Islamic Law as a Source of Constitutional Law in Egypt: The Constitutionalization of the Sharia in a Modern Arab State," *Columbia Journal of Transnational Law* 81 (1998): 99–100.

33. Leila Ahmed, *Women and Gender in Islam* (New Haven, Conn.: Yale University Press, 1992), 151.

34. Khaled Fahmi, *All the Pasha's Men* (New York: Cambridge University Press, 1997), 133–34.

35. El Azhary Sonbol, *Women, the Family, and Divorce Laws in Islamic History* (Syracuse, N.Y.: Syracuse University Press, 1996), 8–9.

36. An example of the verses of the Qur'an that figure prominently in debates surrounding family law is Sura Al Nisa 34 (figures in discussions on the doctrine of "wife's obedience"): "Men shall take full care of women with the bounties which God has bestowed more abundantly on the former than on the latter, and with what they may spend out of their possessions. And the righteous women are the truly devout ones, who guard the intimacy which God has [ordained to be] guarded. And as for those women whose ill-will you have reason to fear, admonish them [first]; then leave them alone in bed; then beat them; and if thereupon

they pay you heed, do not seek to harm them. Behold, God is indeed most high, great." *The Message of the Quran,* translated and explained by Muhammad Asad (Gibraltar: Dar al-Andalus, 1984). For an account of the arguments and counterarguments that are typically used in debating reform of family law in Egypt, along with the various religious textual references that both sides of the debate have historically used, see Badran, *Feminists, Islam, and Nation,* 124–64.

37. An example of such reinterpretation would be to consistently insist, as the Tunisians have historically asserted and reflected in their own legal system, that the Qur'anic verse permitting polygamy (up to four wives) has also made this practice *conditional* on doing justice to these wives, such justice, according to the reinterpretation of the verse, being impossible to achieve: Sura Al Nisa 3: "And if you have reason to fear that you might not act equitably towards orphans, then marry from among [other] women such as are lawful to you—[even] two, or three, or four: *but if you have reason to fear that you might not be able to treat them with equal fairness, then [only] one*—or [from among] those whom you rightfully possess. This will make it more likely that you will not deviate from the right course. See Asad, *The Message of the Quran.*

38. For an example of both "moves"—the reinterpretive one and the cultural one—see al-Hibri, "Islam, Law and Custom," 1–44. Although al-Hibri is a Muslim American, her argumentative tropes are familiar and have historically been used by Egyptian feminists as fully illustrated in Badran, *Feminists, Islam, and Nation.*

39. Badran, *Feminists, Islam, and Nation,* 131; Ghada Hashem Talhami, *The Mobilization of Muslim Women in Egypt* (Gainsville: University Press of Florida, 1996), 113.

40. Badran, *Feminists, Islam, and Nation,* 125. Limiting feminist critique to the idea that men simply "abused" their religiously ordained rights and responsibilities seems to me to be by definition a limited attempt at critiquing patriarchy. The fact that those rights were understood on a mass level as "religiously" ordained made the possibility of an elaborate critique difficult, if not altogether impossible. This, I would argue, remains the case today.

41. For a full account of the transformation in the nature/identity of the legal system in Egypt, see Herbert J. Liebesny, *The Law of the Near and Middle East* (Albany: State University of New York Press, 1975), 258–67.

42. See Farhat J. Ziadeh, *Lawyers, the Rule of Law and Liberalism in Modern Egypt* (Stanford, Calif.: Hoover Institution on War, Revolution, and Peace, 1968), 99–147.

43. For an account of the process of the disenfranchisement of the 'ulama in Egypt, see, in general, Crecelius, "The Course of Secularization in Modern Egypt."

44. This twin charge of un-Islamicity and West identification often propped these feminists up into a reactive position of both assertion and dissociation. Yes, they are Muslim, and, God forbid no, they are neither male hating nor West identified. They are *modernizing* Muslims proposing a real and authentic reading of the original Islamic religious texts and critics of the legal rules inherited from the medieval patriarchal culture of the Muslim jurists. Talhami, *Mobilization*, 115.

45. Badran, *Feminists, Islam, and Nation*, 25.

46. See Leila Ahmed, *Women and Gender in Islam*, 149, 151–52. While the Ahmed text refers to European colonialism as the discourse that combines "concern" for Muslim women and advocacy of intervention via colonialism, see "Is It Possible to Produce a Film on Female Circumcision That Is Engaging while Being Neither Condescending nor Sensationalist? Mariz Tadros Views the Latest Release" (http://web1.ahram.org.eg/weekly/1999/428/feat3.htm [accessed May 25, 2000], which provides an account of how Egyptians today think of international human rights movement as the new discourse that combines "concern" for women and advocacy of intervention.

47. The majority of American feminists of the nineteenth century insisted that all legal and social institutions that reinforced the power of men over women and privileged the former over the latter should be removed, even as they for the most part believed that women and men had different roles to play in the family context. Their liberal feminism resides in their insistence on the removal of the hurdles of formal inequality. See James Cooper and Sheila McIsaac, *The Roots of American Feminist Thought* (Boston: Allyn and Bacon, 1973). For a historical account of the American liberal feminism of the nineteenth century, see Reva B. Siegel, "Home as Work," *Yale Law Journal* 103 (1994): 1073–217. See also Reva B. Siegel, "The Modernization of Marital Status Law: Adjudicating Wives' Rights to Earnings, 1860–1930," *Georgetown Law Journal* 82 (1994): 2127–211.

48. See Badran, *Feminists, Islam, and Nation*, 127–35. Implicit in the previously described activist agenda is faith in the triple liberal concepts of equality (women should be able to divorce too), consent (there should be a minimum age for marriage to ensure women's consent as adults), and autonomy (the doctrine of obedience should be abolished).

49. The most prominent example of such enlightened 'ulama would be Muhammad Abduh, who was one of the proponents of the reform of family law in Egypt.

50. For the latest of such political "rounds," see the debate on legislating *Khul'* (no-fault divorce for women) in Egypt, in *Al-Ahram Weekly*, January 13–19, 2000; February 3–9, 2000; March 1–7, 2000; April 25–31, 2000; June 22–28, 2000.

51. See my "Modernizing Muslim Family Law: The Case of Egypt" (unpublished manuscript with the author) for a list of compromises adopted by the (sec-

ular) Supreme Constitutional Court in Egypt on the question of women. The current 1985 law amending 1923 and 1929 laws on the family is itself a compromise on Jihan's law of 1979, after the Court had struck down the latter as unconstitutional.

52. The conference was sponsored by the Islamic Legal Studies Program at Harvard Law School in January 1999.

53. See the Islamic Legal Studies Program of Harvard Law School's newsletter, January 29–31, 1999.

54. Ahmad 'Abd Allah, *al-Wa'y al-Qanuni lil-Mar'ah al-Misriyyah* (Cairo, Ittihad al-'Arab, Amideast), 13.

55. El-Dinn, "The Status of Egyptian Women in Personal Status Law," 113.

56. For a more detailed account of Arab women's participation in the labor market, see the report by the International Labor Organization on gender equality in the Arab region at www.ilo.org/public/english/bureau/gender/beijing5/contribu/briefing/arab.htm.

LAMA ABU-ODEH

CHAPTER EIGHT

MUSLIM WOMEN AND LEGAL REFORM: THE CASE OF JORDAN AND WOMEN'S WORK

Amira El-Azhary Sonbol

T his chapter focuses on the legal constraints faced by Jordanian women in their efforts to enter the job market or to open their own businesses. It is based on a larger research project on women and work in Jordan.[1] While the intended focus of that project was Jordanian labor laws, it became clear that these laws were determined to a great extent by gender and family relations and Jordanian personal status laws supporting these relations. The penal codes of modern Jordan also proved to be central to this research because they lie at the heart of gender relations and the philosophy toward women's actions in both the private and the public spheres, which ultimately determine the activities of women and the extent to which they feel controlled by their families and society.

A 1980 study concluded that because of the strong connection between the higher rates of literacy among women and their participation in the economy, a greater emphasis on education for Arab women was essential for their participation in economic development.[2] At the same time, the study pointed to social attitudes toward Arab women as an important determinant in increasing their pursuit of higher education and their participation in politics, business, or other professions.[3] It also noted that it is often social attitudes that pose the greatest obstacles and challenges to the participation of women in the economy.

Given the high literacy rate (79.4 percent) among Jordanian women (as compared to others from Arab states in the region), the conclusion of the 1980 study regarding social attitudes seems highly appropriate. The

Kingdom of Jordan has been in the forefront regarding women's education, taking major steps to extend equal access to education for men and women at both the high school and the university level. Yet this high literacy rate and focus on equal education has not produced a significant increase in women's participation in Jordan's economy or to any significant success in their political participation. Thus, even though the participation of women in the labor force in Jordan has grown significantly during the past decade from 7.7 percent in 1979 to estimates of up to 16 percent in 1994,[4] other Arab women are far ahead of Jordanian women with regard to participation in the economy and careers even though their literacy rates are lower. This is reflected in statistics regarding the wages Jordanian women receive in manufacturing when compared to the wages received by men. Figures from the United Nations show that Jordanian women received 58 percent of the wages received by men in manufacturing in the period from 1995 to 2001, demonstrating an insignificant increase of no more than 1 percent from 1990 figures despite the efforts exerted by the government to improve literacy rates and education among women. This compares very poorly with Egyptian statistics, which show that between 1995 and 2001, there was a significant increase in women's wages, from 68 percent in 1990 to 75 percent of those of men.[5]

On the political front, unlike the women in Kuwait, who failed in their efforts to gain the right to run for office, Jordanian women have this right and have won elections. Three women sat in the seventy-five-member National Consultative Council from 1978 to 1984 and four from 1980 to 1982. In 1989, twelve women ran unsuccessfully for elective office, but in 1993, Tujan Faisal managed to become a member of the Lower House, an occasion met with great optimism for women's future participation in Jordanian and other Arab countries' politics. Jordanian women also ran successfully in elections to municipal councils, nine women winning such seats in 1995, with one elected mayor. In 1999, eight women were elected to municipal seats. The government was active in pushing the women's political agenda, assigning them to cabinet posts, particularly that of minister of social development, a post generally assigned to women in other Arab countries who want to appear as promoting gender equality. Jordan went beyond that by appointing women to head the Ministry of Information in 1984, the Ministry of Trade and Industry in 1993 and 1994, and the Ministry of Planning in 1996. In 1999, Jordan was the first nation in the Arab world to appoint a woman as deputy prime minister. The optimism regarding women's participation in politics, however, soon died down under the impact of severe conservative pressure and opposition, so that while the Upper House of Parliament has had two appointed women members over time, the seventeen women who ran for public office in 1997 all failed in their bid for a seat to the Lower House. The intimidations experienced by women leaders like Tujan Faisal from conservative elements dampened women's enthusiasm to run for office and the general optimistic expectations for future participation by Jordan's women in their country's politics and economy.[6] Both tribalism and conservatism have been faulted for the failure of women in elections. Since women are not economically independent and accept the power of a male provider, they tend not to question the political decisions of their family or tribe. They generally vote for the nominee of the tribe rather than for another woman.[7] An example is Samiha al-Tal, who ran for a parliamentary seat in Irbid and was boycotted by her tribe in favor of their own male nominee. Without her tribe's support, she had no chance of winning.[8]

At the same time, Jordanian women have made great strides in comparison to other Arab women. Perhaps the most impressive accomplishment is the assignment of women to the judiciary since May 1996. At present, the number of women judges is growing; however, none have been assigned to become members of the shari'a court. Furthermore, UN statistics report that by 1977, Jordanian women constituted 6 percent of top government positions, compared with 2 percent for the Arab World and 7 percent for the world average. The contradictions facing Jordanian women can be attributed to several factors, among them the efforts exerted by the monarchy to expand opportunities for women in the administration as well as address income disparities that exist in Jordan. Middle- and upper-middle-class women have greater potential to retain jobs and to run businesses, while poorer women struggle to hold on to employment and continue to receive treatment and salaries unequal to their male counterparts.

At the same time, in the past couple of years there has been significant success in changing Jordanian personal status laws, although those changes were extended selectively and in a limited way. A proposed new personal status law was stalled in parliamentary committees for many years while protracted debates and discussions took place inside the parliament and among various civil groups. It took a royal initiative enacted while the parliament was not in session and acting through a human rights committee to introduce any reforms in personal status laws. The laws are important in addressing some of the serious problems facing Jordanian women, including their previous inability to divorce without their husband's agreement and without going through *shiqaq and niza'* ("discord and conflict"; family dispute court or irreconcilable differences court) court procedures that are expensive and time consuming and that usually end with the wife rescinding all her financial rights. The new laws give women the right to *khul'* (divorce at the insistence of a wife, repudiation of husband) without a husband's agreement. Jordan's khul' laws grant a woman divorce within one month, going beyond Egypt's precedent-making khul' laws enacted in 2000, which call for a three-month waiting period before divorce is granted.[9] The new Jordanian laws also restricted judges' ability to grant leniency in honor crimes.[10] It remains to be seen whether these laws will stand the test of time.

After a careful assessment of the connections between Jordanian society, education, and law, it appears that without a palpable transformation in social attitudes, accompanied by reform of Jordan's various legal codes impacting gender, the investment in women's education or other forms of development will have but little success. Tribalism and social conservatism continue to dominate Jordanian culture, and this translates into male control of women through the family or the larger clan. It is therefore not surprising that most lower-class women who start their own small businesses are either older, married women with children, widows, or single mothers who use their income to supplement the family's finances or save for a rainy day. Some are the daughters of these women and are therefore operating within an accepted family structure. The principle evidenced is that a woman should work only when her family is in need of her income. The Jordanian Islamic scholar Ibrahim al-Qisi propagates the widely accepted view among the *fuqaha'* that a woman's place is in the home raising her children.[11] She should work only if her family needs her income and only in conditions acceptable to Islam:

> A Muslim woman should prefer to bear children and raise them, and watch out for her family's needs rather than work outside the home. However, there is nothing against her going out to work if there is a need as when there is no one to support her, but on condition that her work

be according to conditions laid down by Islam, i.e. that this work be al-
lowable by the *shari'a*, that said work does not take her away from her
husband or children and that it not be in a situation where she would
work with men.[12]

The Qur'anic verse (Sura 33:33) that reads "*wa-qarna fi buyutikunnd*" is
usually quoted to support the notion that female participation in public
enterprise, in office jobs, or in any position that requires interaction with
men is unacceptable, and it continues to be frowned on by both men and
women of the working classes.[13]

Jordan's constitution gives women equal rights and opportunities for
employment, as is clearly stipulated in the constitution's[14] declarations
that "Work is the right of all citizens (*al-'amal haqq li kull al-muwatinin*)"
and "Jobs are based on capability (*'ala asas al-kafa'at wal-mu'ahhilat*)." Personal status laws, however, contradicted the constitution directly by making it possible for a wife to take a job only if her husband approved of it.
("A woman has the right to work with her husband's approval.") The personal status laws draw on the historical social context of the Arab family,
where the power of a husband or father over his wife and daughters is absolute. Feminist appeals to change these laws, combined with pressure
brought on the courts by the proliferation of divorce cases in which husbands attempted to deny their financial duty to their wives based on her
employment status rights, caused amendments to be made to the law.

The amendments also addressed the ongoing debate on *nafaqa*, the
remuneration a wife expects to receive from her husband as part of the
marriage contract. Continued application of nafaqa has come under criticism by those who see this as unfair to the men who support their wives
and children while the wife is allowed to keep the money she has earned
even though, practically speaking, the wife's money is almost always integrated into the household expenses. Therefore amendments to the personal status law made it possible for a wife to get a job without her
husband's approval. In return, though, the husband is no longer responsible for financially supporting his wife. Given the fact that salaries received
by women are generally insufficient to support oneself, the amendments
have provided another form of social censure against a wife who works
without her husband's permission. The husband's superior position over
his wife is thereby undiminished.

As would be expected, judges in court have vacillated when it comes to the question of a woman's right to work without her husband's permission. In 1998, a Jordanian judge found that "the work of a wife with or without the husband's permission does not deny her a nafaqa." This ruling was overturned by a shari'a court judge's determination that "that decision is contrary to what article 68 of the law states."[15] Jordanian judges have also had difficulty with situations in which a husband reneged on his prior approval of his wife's work and asked her to quit her job and in cases where the wife was already employed at the time of marriage, something to which the husband later voiced objections.[16] Matters are further complicated by the tradition of oral contracts between the couple, forcing the courts to take one party's word over the other. This frequently happens in divorce cases where the husband uses his wife's employment as an excuse to divorce her without meeting his financial obligations to her.[17]

The notion that the husband has the right to control whether his wife will work is predicated on the belief that she owes him obedience in exchange for his financial support. Obedience according to the fuqaha'—the basis used by shari'a courts in Jordan to establish gender rules—includes his right to forbid her from leaving the marital home for any except the most necessary purposes, such as going to the hospital or taking care of a sick mother. Jordanian courts have ruled in favor of the husband in work disputes between spouses based on this concept of obedience, even when the case involved government policy and the armed forces.[18] In other words, women who want to extend their years of study, who have the ambition to go to college, who want to get jobs, and who want to open their own businesses are severely constrained by the Jordanian legal system, which reflects and enforces the social traditions that limit women's rights by placing them within the custody of male relatives.

Jordan's constitution declares that women are equal to men and have equal rights, presumably including the right to work: "All Jordanians are equal before the law. There will be no discrimination between [Jordanians] regarding rights and duties based on race, language or religion."[19] Islamic law is often the culprit used to undermine women's rights guaranteed by the constitution. The patriarchal tribal outlook that embraces the shari'a subjugates Jordanian personal status law to the concept that women need the protection of fathers or husbands, which gives husbands the right to determine the degree of his wife's freedom, including her right to work.

This is curious because Islamic principles laid down by the Qur'an actually admonish that women have a right to a share of what they earned as
much as men have a right to a share of what they earned.[20] Furthermore,
the Qur'an calls on the Prophet to "let go" of wives who want to live a life
of idleness and luxury[21] and guarantees a woman's inheritance and her
right to own property. Islamic history tells us that the Prophet Muhammad's first wife, Khadija bint Khuwaylid, was at one time his employer.[22]
Ibn Sa'd's biographical entry describing Khadija bint Khuwailid gives evidence of the active role that women played in the market place: "Muhammad b. 'Umar informed us on the authority of Musa b. Shayba . . . that
Khadija was a woman of substantial honor and wealth and a commerce
that traded with Syria, its value reaching the usual value of the goods of
Quraysh. She hired men and speculated in value of goods (and men?)
(*tadfa' al-mal mudarab*)."[23]

Another of the Prophet's wives, 'Aisha, daughter of Abu Bakr, was a
noted Islamic scholar, whose abilities as narrator of Hadith were recognized and who, at one time, rode into battle on her camel leading the opposition to the caliphate of 'Ali b. Abi Talib. The Prophet's wife Zaynab
bint Jahsh was skilled in handicrafts and fashioned leather items and sold
them. Throughout Islamic history, examples of women's participation in
the economy, owning property, and involvement in intellectual pursuits,
including interpretation of the Qur'an and transmission of Hadith, can be
found.[24]

Discussion in the early books of *fiqh* (jurisprudence) supports the conclusion that Islam neither forbade women from working nor limited their
work to particular areas. Medieval fuqaha' did not debate women's participation in the economy; rather, the questions they discussed involved what
the meaning of obedience to the husband meant, the extent of that obedience, and the responsibilities of the husband toward his wife. Nafaqa
seemed to be the primary concern of the jurists who appraised the husband's financial support as compensation for the wife's fulfillment of her
duties. What these duties were, however, was another matter. Fuqaha' were
concerned mainly with what constituted a good wife. "A woman is a shep-
herd in her husband's home" ("*al-mar'a ra'iyya fi bayt zawjiha*") and "your
husband has a right over you" ("*li-zawjik 'alayki haqq*") are widely accepted
metaphors among the fuqaha' regarding marital relations. They are recip-
rocated by similar words defining the husband's responsibilities toward his

219

wife.[25] Wifely disobedience precipitating denial of nafaqa generally occurred when she refused to live with her husband or to have sex with him. There was no concern expressed regarding her pursuit of a trade or investing her wealth in a business venture, nor was it considered that her place was limited to the home.

The popular prophetic hadith "A woman's work is in her husband's home" is often interpreted to mean that the home is the only place where a woman can work. Since this is the home provided by the husband, then she can only work outside it with his permission. But that interpretation is directly contradicted by other hadiths in which the Prophet points out work that is not acceptable for women to perform and other forms of kasb (earnings) that are legitimate" "Bin Ibrahim related to us on the authority of . . . that the Prophet forbade the wages (kasb) from [the prostitution of] slave girls."[26] There are related hadiths that confirm the type of work that the Prophet pointed to as appropriate for women. "Hashim b. al-Qasim related to us . . . Rafi' b. Rafi' related that the Prophet forbade us of . . . the kasb of slave girls except what she worked with her hands and pointed his fingers to baking, weaving and carding."[27]

This does not necessarily restrict women's work to these skills. Rather, the Prophet's point was that honest income comes from using one's own hands, that is, producing it by oneself rather than through the labor of another, evidenced in the prophetic hadith "the best income (kasb) is an income earned by a worker's sincere hands."[28] There are no Qur'anic references forbidding women to work; the Qur'an forbids only the income generated from "forcing" girls into prostitution: "do not force your young women (fatayatukum) to become prostitutes when they would rather be chaste, in order that you make a profit and enjoy your lives."[29] Thus, it was not women's work per se that seemed to be the problem but rather whether it was moral. Another hadith confirms the premises that all work had to be moral and acceptable to God: "'Abd al-Sammad b. al-Fadl related to us . . . that the Prophet of God forbade earnings from selling a dog, earnings from blood-letting, earnings from prostitution, and earnings from bull stud fees."[30] One can conclude from this that the Islamic work ethic laid out by the Qur'an stipulates that man will be judged according to his moral or immoral acts in earning a living. Therefore, making a living or earning money (kasb) from prostituting girls who may be under one's guardianship (slaves or nonslaves) is considered an immoral act, but working with one's hands in such crafts as baking or spinning is moral.

Shari'a court records dating from the Ottoman period in modern Palestine and Jordan show that Jordanian and Palestinian women have traditionally acted as *waqf* (religious endowments) executors, owned property and administered it, owned or been co-owners of factories (including soap production in Nablus and bakeries in Jerusalem), produced farm products and sold them in the marketplace, and worked as *dallalas* (women vendors). There are no disputes in these historical shari'a court records between husbands and wives regarding her work. There are even a few cases of women suing alone for unpaid day labor, including hard labor in quarries.[31] If anything, a woman's "right" to work does not appear to have become an issue in court or as a discourse until the modern period. Its discussion has gained momentum recently and become quite important in contemporary debates in which traditionalists have increasingly utilized Islam as a means to control women's participation in the public sphere. This debate has been precipitated by the mass mobilization of women in the government and business sectors, a condition that did not exist prior to the modern period. In other words, new policies for utilization of women's work necessitated new legislation to address the changing conditions. The resulting legal codes were an amalgam of various types of laws and philosophies of law that became characterized as shari'a because the basis of the modern personal status laws is grounded in shari'a. Yet the selections from various sources of shari'a law and the infusion of modern laws brought about different family and gender relations than existed prior to modern reforms of the legal system.[32]

Three particular sources of law can be identified as having played an important role in the formation of Jordan's contemporary gender laws. These are the 1) Islamic shari'a (or its interpretation by modern state legislators and court judges), 2) tribal laws once administered through a tribal legal system (*qada' 'asha'iri*) and tribal traditions (*'urf*) that have been integrated into Jordan's laws directly and through legal practices including police actions and executive authority, and 3) European laws that have played an important role in the construction of modern personal status laws through legal diffusion and the application of an underlying gender philosophy reflecting Victorianism and state-gender constructionism.

Shariʻa

Today's Kingdom of Jordan was, until 1918, part of the Ottoman Empire. Like other provinces of the empire, Jordan's legal system was formed of shariʻa courts that applied various *madhahib* (Islamic schools of law, namely, Maliki, Shafiʻi, Hanbali, and Hanafi) and whose interpretation of the law was greatly influenced by local traditions. Because of the importance of the tribes inhabiting the area then known as East Jordan, tribal law was also recognized, and tribes relied on their own legal traditions. When the Ottoman Empire began to introduce its Tanzimat reforms during the nineteenth century, its provinces were expected to follow suit. This took place at differing degrees in the various provinces. In the case of East Jordan, which was basically administered as part of Syria until 1920, this meant the introduction of the Ottoman *Mecelle*, a compilation of laws in effect in the empire that were organized and rationalized according to updated modern categories and placed in one volume "containing shariʻa laws and *ʻadliyya* (codes) laws corresponding (*mutabiqa*) to books of fiqh" according to the *madhhab* of Abu Hanifa al-Nuʻman and as chosen and interpreted by the committees set up by the state to compile the *Mecelle*. A 1917 Ottoman Family Code was applied in Jordan and later became the basis of modern Jordanian personal status laws.

In 1951, the first Jordanian law that sought to organize modern shariʻa courts was passed. Many amendments have been made to these laws since then, but the declared source of the law continued to be the Hanafi madhhab, which was the foundation of the Ottoman *Mecelle* and Family Code. However, those who crafted the Jordanian legal system did not strictly adhere to the Hanafi school of law in matters that pertain to women. Rather, they appear to have resorted to Maliki law when greater patriarchal control was deemed appropriate (as the Hanafi code allowed for a relative loosening of gender controls in this particular instance). A good example concerns guardianship (*wilaya*), which allows fathers, grandfathers, brothers, and even uncles to have direct control over a woman's life before and even after she has reached majority and/or is married. In constructing a law of guardianship, legislators mixed the Hanafi with the Maliki madhhab to compose a much tighter patriarchal law than was applied by *qadis* in earlier Jordanian courts. Hanafi law requires rationality (*'aql*) and puberty (*bulugh*) as a basis for reaching majority; until then, a girl or a boy remains under the power of his or her *waliyy* (guardian). Modern Jordanian personal status laws established the minimum age for the marriage of girls to be fifteen and determined that to be according to the Hanafi code since at fifteen a girl would have reached both rationality and puberty. According to Hanafi law, on reaching majority, a person can contract his or her own marriage without parental approval. This applied to a girl whether she had been previously married or not.[33] This particular aspect of the Hanafi law of guardianship was not applied in Jordanian personal status law, however. Rather, in contradistinction to Hanafi requirements, modern Jordanian personal status laws do not allow a girl who reaches majority to contract her own marriage but stipulate that she has to receive her father's or guardian's approval before a marriage of her choice can take place. If her guardian does not approve of her choice, she may appear before the qadi and ask for permission to be married. The qadi weighs the guardian's arguments and reasons for opposing the union and rules on their validity. In other words, there is no freedom of choice given to the girl without a male's consent. This is fitting with the Maliki requirement that a girl cannot be married without a waliyy, be that the father, grandfather, tribal leader, or qadi. As long as she has not been previously married, she cannot marry herself. In other words, the need for a male waliyy remains a requirement for a girl's marriage even if she has passed the age of legal competency or independence.

Furthermore, Maliki law demands the approval of a waliyy for the marriage of any previously unmarried daughter notwithstanding her age at the time of her betrothal. This is due to the belief that a girl cannot contract her own marriage unless she is experienced, and experience is achieved only through marriage. Therefore, Malikis allow a previously married woman to marry herself without the approval or presence of a waliyy. This is, however, not the way the law works in Jordan, where qadis continue to require a previously married woman to have a waliyy with her at the time she gets married even if it is a second or third marriage and so on. Even a woman who desires a divorce and has yet to reach the age of forty is still required to have her father's approval. Similarly, a girl who is still considered a minor under eighteen years of age cannot ask her husband for a khul' divorce without the approval of her guardian.[34] Such control can only be tribally based since there are no such divorce requirements in any of the madhahib.

In short, Jordan's guardianship laws are a patchwork of Hanafi and Maliki laws as well as tribal 'urf through which the more patriarchal aspects of the madhahib and traditions have been patched together, forming a modern code that gives men control over women, including control of their marriage, divorce, education, and work. These details are important because they explain the genesis of personal status laws. *Talfiq* (patchwork) was utilized to weave together laws from different sources and legal philosophies, emphasizing more "controlling" attitudes toward gender; they were then amalgamated to establish what became known as Personal Status Law.

Tribal Law, or 'Urf [35]

Perhaps the most important remnants of tribalism that have been integrated into Jordan's modern laws involve honor crimes and the payment of *diyya* (blood money). This is not to say that honor crimes are the most serious problem facing Jordanian women today. Lately, "honor crimes" may have become an emblem on Jordan's shoulders, the two—Jordan and honor crimes—being constantly linked in the media, at conferences, and in diatribes against Islam's treatment of women. But, in fact, Egypt's official figures for the year 2000 recognize nearly 1,000 honor crimes per year, and Pakistan admits to many more. Even Italy suffered over thirty honor crimes in 2000, while the Jordanian official figures were twenty-nine.

Still, it is a fact that there are laws in Jordan that allow a man to get away with a minimum sentence, sometimes as little as three months, for killing his sister, daughter, wife, or other close family member in the name of family honor and under the excuse of "surprise" (*yufaji'*). The "surprise" is the discovery of an illicit sexual act taking place that leads to "irrational anger" on the part of the observer who acts under emotional stress caused by the discovery. According to Jordanian law, such circumstances allow the judge to reduce the sentence. Law 340a, b and law 98 of Jordan's penal code provide an interesting combination of tribal law and French penal law, allowing reduced sentencing based on intent. While French laws of intent permit reduced sentencing in crimes of passion, they require strict rules of evidence to prove "surprise" and "intent"—or more properly the lack of intent. The judges and the police in Jordan appear to require less evidence. A plea based on "surprise" has been applied to cases where the intent to commit the crime had been declared prior to the attack. Furthermore, in most honor crimes brought in front of Jordanian courts, the killer never saw the victim participating in an act of sexual intercourse as required by the law. Rather, evidence almost always is ascribed to hearsay or gossip or through family pressure.

In a previous report[36] on the interconnectedness between labor laws, criminal laws, and personal status laws and how together they impede the participation of women in the country's development efforts, I pointed out the serious need for a change in Jordanian criminal laws. My particular concern was with the way the law interprets the word "yufaji'" since this is the main loophole that allows judges to pronounce reduced sentences on the perpetrators of honor crimes, thereby encouraging further honor crimes. The report also questioned the inequality of Jordan's laws in allowing leniency for a husband who commits an honor crime involving his wife but denies the same leniency for a wife who commits an honor crime concerning her husband. Since the publication of the study, a new temporary criminal law has been enacted by the Jordanian government. The meaning of "yufaji'" has been reconsidered, and an interpretation making such "surprise" to be "immediate surprise" has been included in the law. The new law has also extended leniency in sentencing wives. This is a move in the right direction and should withstand parliamentary scrutiny, thereby becoming permanent.

In studying various honor crime cases reported during the past decade, it became clear that many of the crimes committed in which perpetrators received lenient sentences were not due to a dishonorable action by the victim. For example, in 2001, a father killed his twelve-year-old daughter with the help of his thirteen-year-old son because she was leaving the home and going to visit neighbors. When asked why he committed the crime, the father explained that he did it to stop her before she could dishonor him and the family. Furthermore, he explained that he was administering God's law: "We are Muslims, and in our religion, she had to be executed."[37]

In other words, not only was she murdered for a crime she did not commit, but her murder was justified on the basis of Islamic law. The court must have agreed since the father benefited from the leniency provided by Jordanian laws and his sentence was only nine months in prison. This situation is typical of how the state handles gender laws. Even though the laws are not based on the shari'a and are in large measure based on French criminal codes, still the shari'a is used as the justification for allowing such findings by courts and acceptance by the public. Further, the father's justification of the crime is misleading; there are clear requirements set out by the Qur'an and Sunna regarding stringent evidence, confession, and punishment in *zina* (sexual intercourse outside a legal relationship) cases. Even when zina is proven, it is never the woman alone who is punished but also the male. Yet in all these honor crimes, it is always the female who is punished, while the male with whom she is alleged to have committed an honor crime goes unpunished. Furthermore, to prove zina, the requirement of four male or eight female witnesses of the actual act of fornication makes it practically impossible to prove without the confession of the persons involved, confession being another requirement according to prophetic Sunna. This can be seen in the Qur'anic treatment of *li'an*, in which an oath is administered to the wife accused by her husband of giving birth to another man's child and in the hadiths of zina in which the Prophet turned his face four times at four different encounters to a confessor of zina before finally telling those present to take him and do to him what he requested, that is, stoning. It is also present in the Prophet's question of whether a woman accused of zina had been forced into the sexual act. It is her confession that she had been willing that incriminated her.[38] Whether these hadiths are valid or not, the important point here is that nowhere do we see the issue of "surprise" or "intent" included in the Qur'an, Sunna, or Fiqh in regard to zina, which is the only sexual honor crime discussed by the shari'a.

Clearly, Jordan's handling of honor crimes has very little to do with the Islamic shari'a, a fact that needs to be made very clear to the Jordanian public. However, court judges continue to justify drawing connections between Jordanian laws and Islam even though they realize that the basis for their rulings are founded on cultural traditions. As one high-court judge in Jordan expressed to me, "Girls cannot be left to run around loose; society demands that there be control of their actions." Yet Islam stands very strictly against the type of honor crimes that take place in Jordan, Iran, Pakistan, Egypt, and other Islamic countries. If you ask any Muslim girl, she will tell you that Islam came to honor women by putting an end to pre-Islamic tribal practices like *wa'd al-banat* (female genocide), by which Arabs of the *Jahiliyya* (pre-Islamic period) killed their newborn girls so as to preempt any sort of future dishonor that they might commit. "When news is brought to one of them [pre-Islamic men] of the birth of a female child, his face darkens and he is filled with inward grief. With shame does he hide himself from his people because of the bad news he has had! Shall he retain her on contempt or bury her in the dust? Ah! What an evil they decide on?" (Sura 16:59). The Qur'an damns such men in no uncertain terms, and yet fathers who do the same thing today are given allowances by the legal system. Nothing could be more un-Islamic than a pre-Islamic practice, and yet the current justification for committing such a crime is ascribed to Islam, and the courts seem to go along.

In contradistinction, a male's dishonorable act, for example, committing rape or murder, can be negotiated with the victim's clan, and a diyya can be paid to end the matter. Diyya laws (blood-price as compensation for harm caused to another) were codified into law in 1989 following the cancellation of tribal courts in Jordan in 1976. According to these laws, if a girl is raped and the rape is proven, it is not up to the state to prosecute; rather, it is up to the family of the girl who is harmed. Often the victim or her family will hide the crime and not inform the authorities out of fear of facing "yufaji'" or dishonoring the family. In some cases, the perpetrator may compensate for his act by offering to marry his victim, or his clan may offer a substantial amount of money as diyya. This practice is very serious since it appears to encourage rather than impede rape. This environment makes women less willing to venture out and participate in public space for fear of what could happen and the repercussions she could face within her own family and from society. Hence, a daughter's obedience becomes entrenched as a tradition that is in turn supported by the law. Ironically, the male perpetrator of rape, a zina honor crime according to Islam, is not punished according to the requirements of Islam. The perpetrator gets away with it according to modern Jordanian law.

European Codes

European laws made their way into the court and legal systems of Jordan and other Arab countries in a variety of ways. The introduction was part of Ottoman nineteenth-century reforms that adopted European systems sometimes willingly and other times under duress. The Ottoman Civil Code of 1867–1877, modeled after the French and Belgian Civil Code, formed the basis of the Egyptian Civil Code, which was later adopted by Syria and Jordan as the prototype for their civil codes. In this, like in other concerns, the legal system departed from what had been practiced in Ottoman courts before. Where there were no reciprocal laws, European codes were applied directly. Furthermore, European precedents from European courts, particularly French courts, were used as precedents for legal decisions in new Arab national courts. Records of civil cases seem in front of Arab courts in countries that have applied the Civil Code for their modern laws (for example, Egypt or Tunisia) will illustrate the references made to different French collections of law.

European laws were also introduced indirectly into legislation regarding matters of personal status. For example, the Ottoman Family Code became the first step toward modern personal status laws that continue to be applicable in Jordan today. The Ottoman Family Code brought a new outlook toward gender with conceptualizations that reflected Europe's new industrial society and its legal needs. The idea of "family" became the central construct of the new society rather than the individual, clan, or tribe as was previously the case. Family would consist of the nuclear family, father, mother, and children, the father being the recognized head of the group with powers to control and punish its other members. Clans consist of the larger group, with grandparents, aunts, and uncles, while the tribe goes to the level of the *akhmas* (fifths) and beyond, linking widespread clans with lineage toward a common location or forefather. While "family" plays no role in Islamic legal thought, modern laws conceptualized society as a construct of family units in which various individuals play clearly defined roles. The Hanafi code may have been the basis for new personal status laws, but a new form of patriarchy based on the concept of the "family" became the basis of the law, and the state became an effective participant in enforcing personal matters that had not previously been its business.

There are other repercussions to these laws that may not seem to have a direct link to women's entry into the job market but that are quite important in determining gender relations and the powerlessness that women face because of social constraints and legal controls. Thus, laws determining "family" and male legal supremacy within the family have a direct link to "citizenship." They discriminate against the children of Jordanian mothers married to non-Jordanians. According to an 1869 Ottoman *firman* (decree) and following legal practices in Europe at that time, a woman's nationality was defined as "following that of her husband." Children from a mixed-nationality marriage were defined accordingly, that is, following the nationality of the father. In other words, faced with new problems like how to define nationality—moot issues to the Ottoman world as they were to Europe before the nineteenth century—gender became the focus for defining nationality rather than domicile, allegiance, interest, birth, or any other factor that could be used to allow children to take their mother's nationality. Even while states moved to allow women to hold their own nationality rather than automatically losing it if they married a foreign citizen, a woman's right to hold the citizenship into which she was born was not extended to her children. Given the growth in rates of marriages between citizens of different countries, particularly Arab and Islamic countries, these laws work in direct discrimination against women who cannot leave their property to their children from fathers of a different nationality and who cannot take their children home without first going through tiring, time-consuming, and often failed efforts to have their home countries accept their children. The same does not apply to the children of a male resident in Arab countries still following these laws promulgated under colonial rule. Children are welcome in their father's countries and can inherit his property, settle down, hold jobs, and pass their nationality on to their children. The discrimination here is clear, based on Ottoman decisions and European laws, and yet they are always given credibility on the basis of the shari'a.

To conclude, the combination of shari'a law, Western laws, and tribal law in Jordan have created a patriarchal system that is tighter than what was obtained prior to the modern period. This does not mean that women did not live in a patriarchal order before modernity; to the contrary, the system was patriarchal, but the laws by which Jordanian (and other Arab) women live today must be seen as a modern construct rather than a simple continuation of what has been dictated by the shari'a or how courts practiced shari'a law before the modernization of law. It is important that legal systems enforced in the Arab world today be deconstructed and their sources become known so as to facilitate change of both laws and gender culture.

Notes

1. Amira Sonbol, *Women of the Jordan: Islam, Labor and the Law* (Syracuse, N.Y.: Syracuse University Press, 2002).

2. *Arab Women and Education* (Beirut: Monographs of the Institute for Women's Studies in the Arab World, Beirut University College, 1980).

3. *Arab Women and Education*, 13.

4. The 1994 Population Census placed the ratio of women in the workforce at 16 percent.

5. The comparative figures of 78 percent for France, 74 percent for Germany, and 77 percent for England during 1995–2001 are worth noting. United Nations, Statistical Division, "The World's Women 2000: Trends and Statistics," http://unstats.un.org/unsd/demographic/ww2000/table5g.htm.

6. *Feminist News*, November 4, 1997, and Associated Press, November 3, 1997, "Woman Parliamentarian Call for More Women in Office," www.feminist.org/news/newsbyte/november97/1104.html.

7. The tribe will almost always nominate males.

8. Raed Al Abed, "Lack of Awareness and Dull Campaign Tactics behind Women's Failure to Reach the Dome," *The Star* (Jordan's online political, economic, and cultural weekly), November 13, 1997, http://star.arabia.com/971113/JO3.html.

9. 'Abdal-Fattah Murad, *Sharh Tashri'at al-Ahwal al-Shakhsiyya* (Alexandria: N.p., 2003), 152.

10. For a discussion of Jordan's personal status laws, see Sonbol, *Women of Jordan*.

11. Marwan Ibrahim al-Qisi, *Al-Mar'a al-Muslima bayn Ijtihadat al-Fuqaha' wa-Mumarasat al-Muslimin* (Rabat, Morocco: Al-Munazzama al-Islamiyya lil-Tarbiya wal-'Ulum wal-Thaqafa, 1991), 9–25.

12. Al-Qisi, *Al-Mar'a al-Muslima*, 56.

13. I am dependent here on research in the records of the Women's Business and Professional Women's Club of Jordan in Amman, particularly their hot line and interviews with women involved in microfinance projects (here I am particularly indebted to Hind Abdel-Jaber and to 'Arub al-Khayyat).

14. Jordanian constitution of 1952.

15. Court decision quoted in Ahmad Salim Milhim, *Al-Sharh al-Tatbiqi li-Qanun al-Ahwal al-Shakhsiyya al-Urduni* (Amman: Maktabat al-Risala al-Haditha, 1998), 101.

16. Tamyiz court case 41157 dated March 9, 1996.

17. Tamyiz court case 20876 dated June 1979.

18. Tamyiz court case 248/92.

19. Article 6 of the constitution.

20. Qur'an 4:32.

21. Qur'an 33:28.

22. Ahmad Suwayyid, *Nisa' Shahirat min Tarikhina* (Beirut: Mu'assasat al-Ma'arif, 1990), 13.

23. Ibn Sa'd, al-*Tabaqat al-Kubra, vol. 8: Fil-nisa'* (Beirut: Dar Sadir, n.d.), 16.

24. See "Becoming Visible: Medieval Islamic Women in Historiography and History" and other articles in *Women in the Medieval Islamic World*, ed. Gavin Hambly (New York: St. Martin's Press, 1998), 18. On women transmitters of Hadith, see Ruth Roded, *Women in Islamic Biographical Collections: From Ibn Sa'd to Who's Who* (Boulder, Colo.: Lynne Rienner, 1994); on women *faqihat* and teachers during the medieval period, see Jonathan Berkey, *The Transmission of Knowledge in Medieval Cairo: A Social History of Islamic Education* (Princeton, N.J.: Princeton University Press, 1992).

25. Ahmad b. Hajar al-'Asqalani, *Fath al-Bari bi-Sharh Sahih al-Bukhari*, vol. 9 (Cairo: Dar al-Rayyan lil-Turath, 1987), 210–11.

26. Sunan Ibn Dawud, *Bab al-buyu'*, hadith 2973.

27. Musnad Ahmad, hadith 18228.

28. Musnad Ahmad, hadith 8060.

29. Surat al-Nur (24): 33.

30. Masnad Ahmad, *Baqi Musnad al-Nukatharin*, hadith 8039.

31. For a detailed description with examples of this subject, see Sonbol, *Women of the Jordan*, chap. 3, "Women's History and Work."

32. I would like to add that these legal changes were not unique to Jordan. The revision of various laws and legal codes was taking place globally as the movement of people and goods all over the world grew and with it the need to homogenize and standardize laws to facilitate trade and travel.

33. For a discussion of the laws of guardianship and laws regarding minor women and reaching majority, see Amira Sonbol, "Adults and Minors in Ottoman Shari'a Courts and Modern Law," in Sonbol, ed., *Women, the Family and Divorce Laws in Islamic History* (Syracuse, N.Y.: Syracuse University Press, 1996), 236–58.

34. Shari'a court case 24624 (dated during 1990s) published in Abdel-Fattah 'Ayish 'Umar, *Al-Qararat al-Qada'iyya fi'l-Ahwal al-Shakhsiyya hatta 'Am 1990* (Amman: Dar Yamman, 1990), 5.

35. See, for example, Kamal Abdallah al-Hilw and Said Mumtaz Darwish, *Customary Law in Northern Sinai* (Cairo: Printshop of the American University

in Cairo, 1989); Laila Sabagh, *Al-Mar'a fi'l-Tarikh al-'Arabi Qabl al Islam* (Damascus: Manshurat Wizarat al-Thaqafa wa'l-Irshad, 1975); Zafer al-Qasimi, *Al-Hayat al-Ijtima'iyya 'ind al-'Arab* (Beirut: Dar al-Nafa'is, 1981); Muhammad Farid Abu Hadid, *Abu'l-Fawaris 'Antara b. Shadad* (Cairo: Ministry of Education, 1979); and 'Isam el-Sioufi, *Al-Mar'a fi'l-Adab al-Jahili* (Beirut: Dar al-Fikr al-Lubnani, 1991).

36. Amira Sonbol, "Report on Women, Work and Legal Constraints," in *Access to Microfinance and Improved Implementation of Policy Reform: Women in Business Constraints* (Amman: AMIR Project, 2000), 31.

37. Douglas Jehl, "Arab Honor's Price: A Woman's Blood," *New York Times*, June 20, 1999, 4.

38. http://hadith.al-islam.com/Bayan/Display.asp?Lang=eng&ID=978 (accessed July 18, 2001).

BIBLIOGRAPHY

Abduh, Muhammad. 1972. *Al-A'mal al-Kamila*. Edited by Muhammad 'Imarah. Vol. 2. Beirut: Al-Mu'assasa al-'Arabiyya lil-Dirasat wal-Nashr.

Abou El-Fadl, Khaled. 2001. *And God Knows the Soldiers*. Lanham, Md.: University Press of America.

Abu-Odeh, Lama. "Modernizing Muslim Family Law: The Case of Egypt." Unpublished manuscript.

Agreement between the Government of the Hashemite Kingdom of Jordan and the United Nations High Commissioner for Refugees, July 30, 1997, Art. III., New York.

Ahmed, Leila. 1992. *Women and Gender in Islam*. New Haven, Conn.: Yale University Press.

El Alami, Dawoud Sudqi. 1992. *The Marriage Contract in Islamic Law: The Shari'ah and Personal Status Laws of Egypt and Morocco*. London: Graham and Trotman.

El Alami, Dawoud Sudqi, and Doreen Hinchcliffe. 1996. *Islamic Marriage and Divorce Laws of the Arab World*. London: Kluwer Law International.

Amin, Qasim. 1984. *Tahrir al-Mar'a wa-Al-Mar'a al-Jadida*. Cairo: Al-Markaz al-'Arabi lil-Bahth wal-Nashr.

Anderson, Norman. 1976. *Law Reform in the Muslim World*. London: Athlone Press.

Arab Charter on Human Rights. 1994. Reprinted in *Human Rights Law Journal* 18 (1997): 151 (not ratified).

Arab Convention on Refugees. 1994. Resolution No. 5389 (March 26).

Arnaout, Ghassan Maarouf. 1987. *Asylum in the Arab-Islamic Tradition*. Geneva: UN High Commissioner for Refugees.

Asad, Muhammad, trans. and expl. 1984. *The Message of the Quran*. Gibraltar: Dar al-Andalus.

Al-Badiya, Bahithat. N.d. *Al-Nisa'iyyat*. Cairo: Dar al-Huda lil-Tab' wal-Nashr.

Badr, Adnan Ahmad. 1992. *Al-Ifta' wa 'l-Awqaf al-Islamiyya fi Lubnan*. Beirut: Al-Mu'assasa al-Jama'iyya.

Badran, Margot. 1995. *Feminists, Islam, and Nation: Gender and the Making of Modern Egypt*. Princeton, N.J.: Princeton University Press.

Al-Baghdadi, Ibn Ghanim Muhammad. 1890. *Majma' al-Damanat*. Cairo: al-Matba'a al-Khayriyya.

Binjalun, Ahmad Majid. 1977. *Al-Dustur al-Maghrabi: Mabadi'uhu wa-Ahkamuhu*. Casablanca: Dar al-Kitab.

Blausetien, Albert P., and Gisbert H. Flanz, eds. Updated periodically. *Constitutions of the World*. Dobbs Ferry, N.Y.: Oceana Publications.

Böttcher, Annabelle. 1998. *Syrische Religionspolitik unter Asad*. Freiburg: Arnold Bergsträsser Institut.

Brown, Nathan J. 1997a. *The Rule of Law in the Arab World*. Cambridge: Cambridge University Press.

———. 1997b. "Shari'a and State in the Modern Middle East." *International Journal of Middle East Studies* 29, no. 3: 359–76.

———. 1998. "Judicial Review in the Arab World." *Journal of Democracy* 4 (October): 4–9.

———. 2002. *Constitutions in a Nonconstitutional World: Arab Basic Laws and the Prospects for Accountable Government*. Albany: State University of New York Press.

Cairo Declaration on Human Rights in Islam. 1990. Reprinted in UNHCR, *Collection of International Instruments and Other Legal Texts concerning Refugees and Displaced Persons* 120: II (New York: United Nations, 1995).

Calder, Norman. 1984. "*Ikhtilaf* and *Ijma'* in Shafi'i's *Risala*." *Studia Islamica* 58: 55–81.

Cole, Juan R. I. 1993. *Colonialism and Revolution in the Middle East: Social and Cultural Origins of Egypt's 'Urabi Movement*. Princeton, N.J.: Princeton University Press.

Committee on the Elimination of Discrimination Against Women. *Report of the Committee on the Elimination of Discrimination Against Women*, 13th session (17 January to February 1994), General Assembly, Official Records, Forty-ninth Session (4 December 1994), Supplement No. 38 (A/49/38) Libyan Arab Jamahiriya.

Cooper, James, and Sheila McIsaac. 1973. *The Roots of American Feminist Thought*. Boston: Allyn and Bacon.

Cooperation Agreement between the League of Arab States and the United Nations High Commissioner for Refugees, June 27, 2000, Art. I, New York.

Cooperation and Office Agreement between the Office of the United Nations High Commissioner for Refugees and the Government of the State of Kuwait, April 8, 1996, Art. 4 (a), New York.

Cotran, Eugene. 1999–2000. "Women's Rights in Yemen Today." *Yearbook of Islamic and Middle Eastern Law* 6:83.

Coulson, N. J. 1971. *A History of Islamic Law.* Edinburgh: Edinburgh University Press.

Crecelius, Daniel. 1974. "The Course of Secularization in Modern Egypt." In *Religion and Political Modernization,* edited by Donald E. Smith, 67–95. New Haven, Conn.: Yale University Press.

Al-Dasatir al-Misriyya 1805–1971: Nusus wa-Tahlil (The Egyptian Constitutions 1805–1971: Texts and Analysis). 1976. Cairo: Markaz al-Tanzim wa'l-Mikrufilm.

Davison, Roderic H. 1963. *Reform in the Ottoman Empire 1856–1876.* Princeton, N.J.: Princeton University Press.

———. 1990. "The Advent of the Principle of Representation in the Government of the Ottoman Empire." In *Essays in Ottoman and Turkish History, 1774–1923: The Impact of the West,* 96–111. Austin: University of Texas Press.

Devereux, Robert. 1963. *The First Ottoman Constitutional Period: A Study of the Midhat Constitution and Parliament.* Baltimore: Johns Hopkins University Press.

El-Dinn, Amira Bahiyy. 1995. "The Status of Egyptian Women in Personal Status Law." In *The Legal Consciousness of the Egyptian Woman (al-Wa'y al-Qanuni li'l-Mar'ah al-Misriyah),* edited by Ahmad Abdullah, 102–17. Cairo: Ittihad al-Muhamin al-'Arab: Amideast.

Dudziak, Mary L. 2000. *Cold War Civil Rights: Race and the Image of American Democracy.* Princeton, N.J.: Princeton University Press.

Elmadmad, Khadija. 1991. "An Arab Convention on Forced Migration: Desirability and Possibilities." *International Journal of Refugee Law* 3: 461–81.

———. 1999. "Asylum in the Arab World: Some Recent Instruments." *Journal of Peace Studies* 6, no. 1 (January–February): 24–34.

The Encyclopedia of Islam New Edition. 1995. Leiden: E. J. Brill.

Esposito, John L., ed. 1995. *The Oxford Encyclopedia of the Modern Islamic World.* Vol. 2. New York: Oxford University Press.

Fahmi, Khaled. 1997. *All the Pasha's Men.* Cambridge: Cambridge University Press.

Al-Fakahani, Hasan. 1975–1976. *Mawsu'at al-Qada' wal-Fiqh li'l-Duwal al-'Arabiyya.* Vol. 3. Cairo: al-Dar al-'Arabiyya lil-Mawsu'at al-Qanuniyya.

Feminism and Identity. 2002. Cover page. Woman Research Center (January).

Finn, John. 1991. *Constitutions in Crisis: Political Violence and the Rule of Law.* New York: Oxford University Press.

Gallagher, Charles F. 1963. "Toward Constitutional Government in Morocco: A Referendum Endorses the Constitution." In *Morocco,* American Universities Field Staff, North Africa Series, vol. 9, no. 1.

General Committee of the People's Assembly. 1981. "Report of General Committee of the People's Assembly, Presented to and Approved by the Assembly on 15 September 1981." Cairo.

Gerber, Haim 1994. *State, Society and Law in Islam: Ottoman Law in Comparative Perspective.* Albany: State University of New York Press.

Al-Halabi, Ibrahim. 1989. *Multaqa al-Abhur,* edited by Wahbi al-Albani. 2 vols. Beirut: Mu'assasat al-Risalah.

Hallaq, Wael. 1990. "On Inductive Corroboration, Probability and Certainty in Sunni Legal Thought." In *Islamic Law and Jurisprudence: Studies in Honor of Farhat J. Ziadeh,* edited by N. Heer. Seattle: University of Washington Press.

———. 1993. *Ibn Taymiyya against the Greek Logicians.* Oxford: Clarendon.

———. 1994. "From *Fatwas* to *Furu*': Growth and Change in Islamic Substantive Law." *Islamic Law and Society* 1 (February): 17–56.

———. 1997. *A History of Islamic Legal Theories.* Cambridge: Cambridge University Press.

———. 2001. *Authority, Continuity and Change in Islamic Law.* Cambridge: Cambridge University Press.

Hamidullah, Muhammad. 1987. *Muslim Conduct of State.* Lahore: Sh. Muhammad Ashraf.

Hasan, Najat Qassab. 1976. *Qanun al-Ahwal al-Shakhsiyya ma'a al-Ta'dilat al-Sadira fi 31/12/1975.* Damascus: Manshurat al-Muwatin wal-Qanun.

Hasan, Sayyid Abd Allah Ali. 2001. *Al-Muqaranat al-Tashri'iyya bayna al-Qawanin al-Wad'iyya wal-Tashri' al-Islami.* Cairo: Dar al-Salam.

Al-Haskafi, 'Ala' al-Din. 1979. *Al-Durr al-Mukhtar.* Vol. 1. Beirut: Dar al-Fikr.

Al-Hattab, Muhammad. 1969. *Mawahib al-Jalil li-Sharh Mukhtasar Khalil.* Vol. 6. Tarablus, Libya: Maktabat al-Najah.

Al-Hibri, Azizah. 1997. "Islam, Law and Custom: Redefining Muslim Women's Rights." *American University Journal of International Law and Policy* 12, no. 1: 1–44.

Hijab, Nadia. 1988. *Womanpower: The Arab Debate on Women at Work.* Cambridge: Cambridge University Press.

Hill, Enid. 1987. "Al-Sanhuri and Islamic Law." *Cairo Papers in Social Science* 10, no. 1: 1–140.

———. 1988. "Islamic Law as a Source for the Development of a Comparative Jurisprudence." In *Islamic Law: Social and Historical Contexts*, edited by Aziz Al-Azmeh. London: Routledge.

Al-Homsi, Lina. 1996. *Al-Muftun al-'Ammun fi Suriya*. Damascus: Dar al-'Asma'.

Hut, Abd al-Rahman. 1984. *Al-Awqaf al-I'lamiyya fi Lubnan*. Beirut: n.p.

Ibn 'Abd al-Barr, Abu 'Umar Yusuf. N.d. *Jami' Bayan al-'Ilm wa-Fadlihi*. Vol 2. Cairo: Idarat al-Tiba'a al-Muniriyya.

Ibn 'Abidin. 1893. *Al-'Uqud al-Durriyya fi Tanqih al-Fatawa al-Hamidiyya*. Cairo: Al-Matba'a al-Maymuna.

———. 1970. *Sharh al-Manzuma, Majmu' ar-Rasa'il*. Vol. 1. N.p.

Ibn Barhan, Ahmad b. 'Ali. 1984. *Al-Wusul ila al-Usul*, edited by 'Abd al-Hamid Abu Zunayd. Vol. 2. Riyad: Maktabat al-Ma'arif, 341–51.

Ibn Farhun, Shams al-Din. 1883. *Tabsirat al-Hukkam*. Vol. 1. Cairo: al-Matba'a al-'Amira al-Sharafiyya.

Ibn Hajar al-Haytami. 1938. *Al-Fatawa al-Kubra al-Fiqhiyya*. Vol 4. Cairo: 'Abd al-Hamid Ahmad al-Hanafi.

Ibn al-Najjar, Taqi al-Din. 1961–1962. *Muntaha al-Iradat*. Vol. 1. Cairo: Maktabat Dar al-'Uruba.

Ibn Rajab, 'Abd al-Rahman. 1952–1953. *Al-Dhayl 'ala Tabaqat al-Hanabila*. Vol. 1. Cairo: Matba'at al-Sunna al-Muhammadiyya.

Ibn Sa'd. N.d. *Al-Tabaqat al-Kubra. Vol. 8: Fil-nisa'*. Beirut: Dar Sadir.

International Federation of the Rights of Man. 1999. *Rapport Alternatif de la FIDH au Rapport Initial Presente par l'Algerie au Comite sur l'Elimination de la Discrimination a l'Egard des Femmes 19eme Session* (19 janvier–5 fevrier).

Islamic Legal Studies Program of Harvard Law School. 1999. *Newsletter*, January 29–31.

Izzat, Hibah Ra'uf. 1995. *Al-Mar'ah wa-al-'Amal al-Siyasi: Ru'yah Islamiyyah*. Herndon, Va.: International Institute of Islamic Thought.

Jackson, Sherman A. 1996. *Islamic Law and the State: The Constitutional Jurisprudence of Shihab al-Din al-Qarafi*. Leiden: E. J. Brill.

———. 2002. "Jihad and the Modern World." *Journal of Islamic Law and Culture* 7, no. 1: 4–5.

Al-Jaziri, Abd al-Rahman. 1938. "Kitab al-Fiqh 'ala al-Madhahib al-Arba'a." *Qism al Ahwal al-Shakhsiyya*. Vol. 4. Cairo: Matba'at Dar al-Ma'mun.

Johnson, Michael. 1986. *Class and Client in Beirut: The Sunni Muslim Community and the Lebanese State*. New York: Columbia University Press.

Karam, Azza. 1998. *Women, Islamisms, and the State*. New York: St. Martin's Press.

Al-Kasana, 'Ala al-Din. 1982. *Bada'i' al-Sana'i'*. 7 vols. Beirut: Dar al-Kitab al-'Arabi.

Khalid, Muhammad Tawfiq. 1945. *Ba'd al-Khutub wa l-Mudhakkarat*. Beirut: Dar al-Fatwa.

Kharashi, Muhammad. 1985. *Ahkam Qada'iyya fi Fiqh al-Ma'dhuniyya*. Cairo: Jam'iyyat al-Ma'dhunin al-Shar'iyyin.

Kerber, Karoline. 1999. "Temporary Protection in the European Union: A Chronology." *Georgetown Immigration Law Journal* 14: 35–50.

Khadduri, Majid. 1951. "Constitutional Development in Syria." *Middle East Journal* 5, no. 2 (spring): 137–60.

———. 1955. *War and Peace in the Law of Islam*. New York: AMS Press.

———. 1961. *Islamic Jurisprudence: Al-Shafii's Risala*. Baltimore: Johns Hopkins University Press.

Khadduri, Majid, and Herbert J. Liebesny. 1984. *Law in the Middle East: Origin and Development of Islamic Law*. Vol. 1. New York: AMS Press.

Khoury, Philip. 1983. *Urban Notables and Arab Nationalism*. Cambridge: Cambridge University Press.

Koschaker, Paul. 1966. *Europa und das römische Recht*. Munich: C.H. Becksche Verlagsbuchhandlung.

Lewis, Bernard. 1968. *The Emergence of Modern Turkey*. Oxford: Oxford University Press.

Liebesny, Herbert. 1975. *The Law of the Near and Middle East: Readings, Cases and Materials*. Albany: State University of New York Press.

Lombardi, Clark Benner. 1998. "Islamic Law as a Source of Constitutional Law in Egypt: The Constitutionalization of the Sharia in a Modern Arab State." *Columbia Journal of Transnational Law* 37: 81–95.

Majlis al-Shuyukh. 1940. *Al-Dustur: Ta'liqat 'ala Mawaddihi bi-l-A'mal al-Tahdiriyya wa-l-Munaqashat al-Barlamaniyya*. Pt. 3. Cairo: Matba'at Misr.

Makdisi, George. 1981. *The Rise of Colleges*. Edinburgh: Edinburgh University Press.

Malik ibn Anas. 1992. *Al-Muwatta of Imam Malik ibn Anas: The First Formulation of Islamic Law*, translated by Aisha Abdurrahman Bewley. Granada: Madina Press.

Maoz, Moshe. 1992. "Changes in the Position and Role of Syrian Ulama in the 18th and 19th Century." In *The Syrian Land in the 18th and 19th Century*, edited by Thomas Philip, 109–22. Stuttgart: F. Steiner.

Martin, Susan, et al. 1998. "Temporary Protection: Towards a New Regional and Domestic Framework." *Georgetown Immigration Law Journal* 12, no. 4 (summer): 543–88.

Mayer, Ann Elizabeth. 1993. "Moroccans—Citizens or Subjects? A People at the Crossroads." *New York University Journal of International Law and Politics* 26: 63–105.

———. 1995a. "In Search of a Sacred Law: The Meandering Course of Qadhafi's Legal Policy." In *Qadhafi's Libya 1969–1994*, edited by Dirk Vanderwalle, 113–38. New York: St. Martin's Press.

———. 1995b. "Reform of Personal Status Laws in North Africa: A Problem of Islamic or Mediterranean Laws?" *Middle East Journal* 49, no. 3 (summer): 432–46.

———. 1995c. "Rhetorical Strategies and Official Policies on Women's Rights: The Merits and Drawbacks of the New World Hypocrisy." In *Faith and Freedom: Women's Human Rights in the Muslim World*, edited by Mahnaz Afkhami. New York: I. B. Tauris, 105–19.

———. 1996. "Reflections on the Proposed United States Reservations to CEDAW: Should the Constitution Be an Obstacle to Human Rights?" *Hastings Constitutional Law Quarterly* 23, no. 3 (spring): 789–92.

———. 1998. "Islamic Reservations to Human Rights Conventions." *RIMO* 15: 39–40.

———. 1999. "Religious Reservations to the Convention on the Elimination of All Forms of Discrimination Against Women: What Do They Really Mean?" In *Religious Fundamentalisms and the Human Rights of Women*, edited by Courtney W. Howland. New York: St. Martin's Press, 106–16.

———. 2000–2001. "A 'Benign' Apartheid: How Gender Apartheid Has Been Rationalized." *UCLA Journal of International Law and Foreign Affairs* 5 (fall/winter): 252–56.

Mezran, Karim. "Constitutionalism in Libya." In *Islam and Constitutionalism*, edited by Sohail Hashmi and Houchang Chehabi (in press).

Minutes of the Preparatory Committee for Drafting the Constitution [for the Arab Republic of Egypt]. 1971. Cairo: Majlis al-Sha'ab.

Moustafa, Tamir. 2001. "Conflict and Cooperation between the State and Religious Institutions in Contemporary Egypt." *International Journal of Middle East Studies* 32: 3–22.

Al-Murtada, Ahmad ibn Yahya. 1980. *Sharh al-Azhar*. Vol. 2. San'a': n.p.

Al-Mutahhar, Muhammad ibn Yahya ibn. 1985. *Ahkam al-Ahwal al-Shakhsiyya min Fiqh al-Shari'a al-Islamiyya*. Cairo: Dar al-Kutub al-Islamiyya.

Al-Nawawi, Sharaf al-Din. 1925. *Al-Majmu': Sharh al-Muhadhdhabi*. Vol 9. Cairo: Matba'at al-Tadamun.

———. N.d. *Rawdat al-Talibin*, edited by 'Adil 'Abd al-Mawjud and 'Ali Mu'awwad. Vol. 7. Beirut: Dar al-Kutub al-'Ilmiyya.

North, A. M., and Nehal Bhuta. 2001. "The Future of Protection—The Role of the Judge," *Georgetown Immigration Law Journal* 15: 479–83.

O'Kane, Joseph P. 1972. "Islam in the New Egyptian Constitution: Some Discussions in *al-Ahram*," *Middle East Journal* 26, no. 2: 137–48.

Organization of African Unity. 1969. *OAU Convention Governing the Specific Aspects of Refugee Problems in Africa*, Art. I (2), 1001 U.N.T.S. (September 10), 45–47.

Parmentier, Jane C. 1999. "Secularisation and Islamisation in Morocco and Algeria." *Journal of North African Studies* 4, no. 4 (winter): 27–50.

Rahman, Fazlur. 1965. "Concepts Sunnah, Ijtihad, and Ijma' in the Early Period." In *Islamic Methodology in History*. Karachi: Central Institute of Islamic Research.

Al-Ramli, Shams al-Din. 1938. *Nihayat al-Muhtaj ila Sharh al-Minhaj*. Vol. 1. Cairo: Mustafa Babi al-Halabi.

Repp, Richard. 1986. *The Müfti of Istanbul*. London: Ithaca Press.

Roded, Ruth. 1983. "Ottoman Service as a Vehicle for the Rise of New Upstarts among the Urban Elite Families of Syria in the Last Decades of Ottoman Rule." *Asian and African Studies* 17: 63–94.

Rogan, Eugene. 1999. *Frontiers of the State in the Late Ottoman Empire*. Cambridge: Cambridge University Press.

El Saadawi, Nawal. 1980. *The Hidden Face of Eve*. Translated and edited by Sherif Hetata. London: Zed Press.

Sadlan, Salih Ghanim. 1984. *Wujub Tatbiq al-Shari'a al-Islamiyya*. Riyadh: Idarat al-Thaqafa wal-Nashr bi-Jami'at Muhammad b. Sa'ud.

Al-Salah, Taqi al-Din Ibn. 1986. *Adab al-Mufti wal-Mustafti*. Edited by Muwaffaq b. 'Abd al-Qadir. Beirut: 'Alam al-Kutub.

Salim, Latifa. 1984–1986. *Al-Nizam al-Qada'i al-Misri al-Hadith*. Vol. 2. Cairo: Markaz al-Dirasat al-Siyasiyya wal-Istratijiyya.

Salima, Niya [pseud. of Mme. Rachid-Pacha]. 1908. *Les Répudiées*. Paris: Société d'Edition et de Publications.

Schacht, Joseph. 1960. "Problems of Modern Islamic Legislation." *Studia Islamica* 12: 99–129.

———. 1964. *An Introduction to Islamic Law*. Oxford: Clarendon.

Schoenholtz, Andrew I. 2000. "Beyond the Supreme Court: A Modest Plea to Improve Our Asylum System." *Georgetown Immigration Law Journal* 14, no. 2 (winter): 541–42.

Scholch, Alexander. 1981. *Egypt for the Egyptians! The Socio-Political Crisis in Egypt, 1878–1882*. London: Ithaca Press.

Al-Shafi'i, Husayn ibn Muhammad al-Mahalli. 1995. *Al-Ifsah 'an 'Aqd al-Nikah 'ala l-Madhahib al-Arba'a*, edited by Ali Muhammad Mu'awwad and Adil Ahmad Abd al-Jawwad. Aleppo: Dar al-Qalam al-Arabi, 24–29.

Al-Shafi'i, Muhammad b. Idris. 1969. *Al-Risala*. Edited by Ahmad Muhammad Shakir. Cairo: Mustafa Babi al-Halabi.

———. 1973. *Kitab al-Umm*. Edited by Muhammad Zuhri al-Najjar. Vol. 5. Beirut: Dar al-Ma'rifa.

Shaham, Ron. 1997. *Family and the Courts in Modern Egypt: A Study Based on Decisions by the Shari'a Courts 1900–1955*. Leiden: E. J. Brill.

Shakry, Omnia. 1998. "Schooled Mothers and Structured Play: Child Rearing in Turn-of-Century Egypt." In *Remaking Women: Feminism and Modernity in the Middle East*, edited by Lila Abu-Lughod. Princeton, N.J.: Princeton University Press, 126–70.

Shanley, Mary Lyndon. 1989. *Feminism, Marriage and the Law in Victorian England*. Princeton, N.J.: Princeton University Press.

Shaw, Stanford J., and Ezel Kural Shaw. 1977. *History of the Ottoman Empire and Modern Turkey*, Vol. 2. *Reform, Revolution, and Republic: The Rise of Modern Turkey, 1808–1975*. Cambridge: Cambridge University Press.

Al-Shawkani, Muhammad ibn Ali. 1986. *Al-Darari al-Mudiyya: Sharh al-Durar al-Bahiyya*. Vol. 1. Cairo: Maktabat al-Turath al-Islami.

Sherif, Adel Omar. 1998–1999. "An Overview of the Egyptian Judicial System and Its History." *Yearbook of Islamic and Middle Eastern Law* 5: 3–28.

Al-Shirazi, Abu Ishaq Ibrahim. 1988. *Sharh al-Luma'*. Edited by 'Abd al-Majid Turki. Vol. 2. Beirut: Dar al-Gharb al-Islami, 1043–45.

Al-Siba'i, Mustafa. 1962. *Sharh Qanun al-Ahwal al-Shakhsiyya*. Vol. 1. Damascus: Matba'at Jami'at Dimashq.

Siegel, Reva B. 1994a. "Home as Work." *Yale Law Journal* 103: 1073–217.

———. 1994b. "The Modernization of Marital Status Law: Adjudicating Wives' Rights to Earnings, 1860–1930." *Georgetown Law Journal* 82: 2127–211.

Sivan, Emmanuel. 2003. "The Clash within Islam." *Survival* 45, no. 1: 25–44.

Skovgaard-Petersen, Jakob. 1997. *Defining Islam for the Egyptian State*. Leiden: E. J. Brill.

———. 1998. "The Sunni Religious Scene in Beirut." *Mediterranean Politics* 3, no. 1: 69–80.

———. In press. "Levantine State Muftis—An Ottoman Legacy?" In *The Ottoman Intellectual Heritage*, edited by Elizabeth Özdalga.

Sohrabi, Nader. 1995. "Historicizing Revolution: Constitutional Revolutions in the Ottoman Empire, Iran, and Russia, 1905–1908." *American Journal of Sociology* 100, no. 6 (May): 1383–447.

Sonbol, Amira. 1996. *Women, the Family, and Divorce Laws in Islamic History*. Syracuse, N.Y.: Syracuse University Press.

———. 2000. "Report on Women, Work and Legal Constraints for Access to Microfinance and Improved Implementation of Policy Reform: Women in Business Constraints." Amman: AMIR Project.

———. 2002. *Women of Jordan: Islam, Labor and the Law*. Syracuse, N.Y.: Syracuse University Press.

Spectorsky, Susan A. 1993. *Chapters on Marriage and Divorce: Responses of Ibn Hanbal and Ibn Rawah.* Austin: University of Texas Press.

States Parties of Saudi Arabia. 2000. "Consideration of Reports Submitted by States Parties under Article 33 of the Convention." *Initial Report of Saudi Arabia Due in 1998.* CRC/C/61/Add.2 (March 29).

Stowasser, Barbara Freyer. 1998. "What Goes into a Paradigm? Some Reflections on Gender-Issue 'Differences' between Sunni Law Schools, and the Problematic of Their Historical Attribution." *Islam and Christian-Muslim Relations* 9, no. 3: 269–83.

Al-Subki, Taj al-Din. 1906. *Tabaqat al-Shafi'iyya al-Kubra.* Vol. 5. Cairo: al-Maktaba al-Husayniyya.

Suhrke, Astri. 1995. "Refugees and Asylum in the Muslim World." In *The Cambridge Survey of World Migration*, edited by Robin Cohen. New York: Cambridge University Press, 457–60.

Suwayyid, Ahmad. 1990. *Nisa' Shahirat min Tarikhina.* Beirut: Mu'assasat al-Ma'arif.

Swaid, Badawi. 1990. "As-Sunna fi Lubnan." *Ad-Diyar*, October 18–25, 1990 (reprinted in Elizabeth Thompson, ed., *Colonial Citizens* [New York: Columbia University Press, 2000]).

Al-Tahanawi, Muhammad b. 'Ali. 1862. *Kashshaf Istilahat al-Funun.* Vol. 1. Calcutta: W. N. Leeds' Press.

Al-Tahtawi, Rifa'a Rafi'. 1973. *Al-A'mal al-Kamila*, edited by Muhammad 'Imarah. Vol. 2. Beirut: al-Mu'assasa al-'Arabiyya lil-Dirasat wal-Nashr, 563–645.

Talhami, Ghada Hashem. 1996. *The Mobilization of Muslim Women in Egypt.* Gainesville: University Press of Florida.

Al-Tufi, Najm al-Din. 1987. *Sharh Mukhtasar al-Rawda.* Edited by 'Abd Allah al-Turki. Vol. 3. Beirut: Mu'assasat al-Risala.

Tucker, Judith. 1998. *In the House of the Law: Gender and Islamic Law in Ottoman Syria and Palestine.* Berkeley: University of California Press.

Al-Tunisi, Khayr al-Din, 1967. "The Surest Path: The Political Treatise of a Nineteenth-Century Muslim Statesman." Translated by L. Carl Brown. *Harvard Middle Eastern Monographs*, 16. Cambridge, Mass.: Harvard University, Center for Middle Eastern Studies.

UN General Assembly. *United Nations Conference of Plenipotentiaries on the Status of Refugees and Stateless Persons: Convention Relating to the Status of Refugees*, July 28, 1951, G.A. Res. 429(V), 189 U.N.T.S. 137, Geneva.

UN High Commissioner for Human Rights. 1950. *Statute of the Office of the United Nations High Commissioner for Refugees*, December 14, 1950, G.A.

Res. 428, U.N. GAOR, 5th Sess., Suppl. No. 20, at 48 (para. 8) U.N. Doc. A/1775.

UN High Commissioner for Refugees. 1995. Collection of International Instruments and Other Legal Texts concerning Refugees and Displaced Persons 116: II, Geneva.

———. 2001. Statistical Overview of Refugees and Others of Concern to UNHCR. Geneva: UN High Commission on Refugees.

U.N. Protocol Relating to the Status of Refugees, January 31, 1967, 8791 (606) U.N.T.S. 267, done in New York.

U.N. Refugee Act of 1980. P.L. No. 96-212, 94, statutes-at-large, 102 (March 17).

Al-'Utayfi, Jamal. 1980. *Ara' fi al-Shari'a wa-fi al-Hurriyya*. Cairo: Al-Hay'a al-Misriyya al-'Amma li-l-Kitab.

Vogel, Frank, and Samuel L. Hayes III, eds. 1998. *Islamic Law and Finance: Religion, Risk, and Return*. Boston: Kluwer Law International.

Weiner, Myron. 1996. "A Security Perspective on International Migration." *Fletcher Forum on International Affairs* 20, no. 2 (summer/fall): 17–34.

Wensinck, A. J. 1926. *A Handbook of Early Muhammadan Tradition*. Leiden: E. J. Brill.

Al-Zarkashi, Shams al-Din. 1993. *Sharh al-Zarkashi 'ala Mukhtasar al-Khiraqi*. Edited by 'Abd Allah al-Jabrin. Vol. 1. Riyadh: Maktabat al-'Ubaykan.

Ziadeh, Farhat J. 1968. *Lawyers, the Rule of Law and Liberalism in Modern Egypt*. Stanford, Calif.: Hoover Institution on War, Revolution, and Peace.

Zilfi, Madeline C. 1993. "The *Ilmiye* Registers and the Ottoman *Medrese* System Prior to the Tanzimat." In *Contribution à l'histoire économique et sociale de l'Empire ottoman*. Leuvin: Éditions Peeters, 309–27.

Judicial Material

Basic Law of the Sultanate of Oman 1996, Royal Decree No. 101/96 (November 6).

Chalal v. United Kingdom, Eur. Ct. H.R. Report of June 27, 1995, at para. 98.

Cruz Varas and Others v. Sweden, 201 Eur. Ct. H.R. (ser. A), at para. 70 (1991).

Law Regulating the Entry, Stay and Exit of Foreigners in Lebanon, July 10, 1962, Official Journal No. 28-1962.

Ministerial Resolution No. 10 Regarding Organization of Refugees' Department (June 6, 1984).

Political Refugee Act, No. 51, Official Gazette No. 1985 (April 10, 1971).

SC Constitutional Case No. 8 of the eighteenth judicial year, decided on May 18, 1996.

SC Constitutional Case No. 10 for the fifth judicial year, decided on July 3, 1976.

SC Constitutional Case No. 23 for the fifteenth judicial year, decided on February 5, 1994.

SC Constitutional Case No. 74 for the seventeenth judicial year, decided on March 1, 1997.

SC Constitutional Case No. 93 for the sixth judicial year, decided on March 18, 1996.

Saudi Arabia Basic Law of Government, March 1, 1992.

Electronic Sources

The Green Book: Part 3, 28–29. www.greenbook.cjb.net.

International Constitutional Law website. www.uni-wuerzburg.de/law.

The Universal Islamic Declaration. Islamic Council website. www.alhewar.com/ISLAMDECL.html.

UN Treaty. http://untreaty.un.org/ENGLISH/bible/enghlishinternetbible/Part1/charterIV/treaty9/asp.

UN High Commissioner for Refugees. Country Profiles—Iraq. www.unhcr.ch/world/mide/iraq.htm.

———. Country Profile—Lebanon. www.unhcu.ch/world/mide/Lebanon.htm.

———. Country Profile—Libya. www.unhcu.ch/world/mide/Libya.htm.

———. *Statistical Yearbook 2001*. www.unhcr.ch.

———. www.unhcu.ch/reworld.

Hadith Collections

Musnad Ahmad, hadith 8060.

Musnad Ahmad, hadith 18228.

Musnad Ahmad, baqi masnad al-nukatharin, hadith 8039.

Sunan Ibn Dawud, bab al-buyu', hadith 2973.

GLOSSARY

'Ada   Custom
'Adliyya   Justice
Ahl al-hall wa-l-'aqd   Members of the newly established Grand Council
   of Tunisia
'A'ila   Family
'Alayhi al-'amal   Practice
'Alayhi 'amal al-ummah   Judicial practice of the community
'Alim (pl. 'ulama)   Religious scholar
Alladhi jara al-'amal bi-hi fi hadhihi al-mas'ala   The prevailing practice in
   this matter
'Amal   The procedure of the courts; work, practice
Aman   Institution of protection like asylum
'Aql   Rationality
Asahh   More correct
'Asha'iri   Tribal, Bedouin
Ashbah   More similar
al-A'wamm   Common/secular folk
Awjah   More sound
Awqaf   (sing. waqf) Religious endowments

Batil   Invalid
Bey   Ottoman title; ruler of Ottoman Tunisia
Bulugh   Maturity, legal majority

Da'if   Weak

Da'irat al-ifta'   Department of Islamic legal opinions

Dallalas   Women vendors

Dar al-'Ahd   Abode of treaty

Dar al-Harb   Abode of war

Dar al-Islam   Abode of Islam

Dar al-Sulh   Abode of truce

Darura   Necessity

Dhimma   Responsibility or obligation

Diyya   Blood money

Faqih (pl. *fuqaha'*)   Jurist

Fasid   Void

Fatawa (sing. *fatwa*)   Opinions of a mufti that are not legally binding

Fatayat   Young girls

Fatwa (pl. *fatawa*)   Opinion of a mufti that is not legally binding

Fi balad kadha   In such and such region

Fi-hi lafz al-fatwa   Fit for a legal opinion

Firman   Ottoman decree

Fuqaha' (sing. *faqih*)   Jurists

Furu'   Branches

Gharib   Unknown, strange

Halal   Lawful

Haram   Religious sanctuary; forbidden

Hijra   Migration from one's home

Hudud   Penal law

Ifta'   Issuing *fatawa*

Ihram   Ritual consecration

Ijaza   License

Ijtihad   The use of reason to deduce laws from the Qur'an and the Sunna

Ikhtilaf (pl. *ikhtilafat*) Juristic disagreement

'Illa   Effective cause

Istijara   To seek refuge with

Istislah   Preference for public interest

Itlaf ma'sum   Destruction of that which is protected by law

Jihad   Struggle, battle, fight

Jizya   Poll tax paid by non-Muslims

Jumhur al-'ulama   Majority of scholars

Ka'ba   Shrine in Makka and focal point of worship for Muslims

Kasb   Earnings

Kharaj   Land tax

Khilaf   Juristic disagreement

Khul'   Wife-instigated divorce

Kull mujtahid musib   The doctrine that states that each and every *mujtahid* is correct

Kuttab-madrasa   Religious schools

al-La'iha al-Asasiyya   Fundamental ordinance

La yakun la-ha i'tibar   Should not be taken into consideration

Mabsutat   Comprehensive works

Madhaban wa-khilafan   To study a school and its disputations

Madhhab (pl. *madhahib*)   School of classical Islamic jurisprudence

Mafti bi-hi   Decided upon by formal opinion

Majalla   Law code

Majlis al-Shura   Consultative council

Malik   King

Ma'mul bi-hi   Commonly applied

Masalih dunyawiyya   Worldly interests

Mashhur   Widespread

Maslaha   Public interest

Min al-akabir   Distinguished

Mu'abbad   Permanent

Mu'amalat   Social interactions

Mudawwana   Personal Status Code of Morocco

Mufti   A legal scholar who issues fatawa

Muhallal lahu   The husband who has divorced his wife in a *tahlil* arrangement

Muhallil   The second husband in a *tahlil* arrangement

Mujtahid   Muslim jurist who engages in *ijtihad*

Mukhtar lil-fatwa   Chosen for *fatawa*

Mukhtasarat   Abridgements

Mustafti   A person seeking a *mufti*'s opinion

Musta'min   Subject of protection or *aman*

Mut'a   Temporary marriage

Muta'akhkhirun   Modern or recent jurists

Mutadawala   Prevailing usage; regularly applied

Mutaqaddimun   Early jurists

Nafaqa   Expenses, financial support

Nashiz   Adjective used for a disobedient wife

Nasl   Offspring

Niqab   Face veil

Qada'   Justice, jurisprudence, administration of the law

Qadi   Judge

Qanun (pl. *qawanin*)   Positive law

Qanun al-dawla al-tunisiyya   Law of the Tunisian state or dynasty

Qawa'id   General principles

Qiwama   Guardianship

Qiyas   Analogical reasoning that seeks new rules based on commonalities between original and new situations

Ra'ayana   Literally "our flock": subjects of a dynasty, general population

Rahma   Blessing

Rajih   Preferable

Riba   Usury

Sadaq   Dowry

Sahhahahu   That which has been corrected

Sahih   Correct

Sawab   Proper, correct

Shadhdh   Irregular

Shari'a   God's law that humans attempt to deduce through various juridical methods

Shaykh al-Azhar   Rector of al-Azhar University in Cairo, Egypt

Shaykh al-Islam   Grand *Mufti* of Istanbul and head of the Ottoman *'ulama* establishment

Sigha   Written form of a contract

Sihhatuhu   (Its) correctness

Sunna   Words and actions of the Prophet

Tabaqat   Biographies of the 'ulama

Tadfa' al-mal mudaraba   Speculated in value of goods

Tafwidan ila al-sultan   Delegating to the governing authority

Tahlil   A legal arrangement to allow a couple to remarry after divorce

Tahqiq   Verification

Takhayyur   Picking and choosing from different legal sources

Talfiq   A modern process of "patching" together rules from different legal schools of thought

Taqlid   The principle of strict adherence to precedents established by the classical schools of Islamic legal thought

Tarik al-salat   One who refuses to pray

Tarjih   The preference for one legal school over another

Tashhir   To make established or canonical

Tashih   To correct, legalize, or authenticate

Tashri'   Basis of legislation

'Ulama (sing. *'alim*)   Collective term for Muslim religious scholars

Umma   The worldwide community of Muslims

'Urf   Social or tribal custom; customary law; legal convention

Usra   Family

al-Usra al-Muslima   The Muslim family

Usul al-fiqh   Sources or roots of Islamic law as well as the methodology of how to perform *ijtihad*

Wa'd al-banat   Female infanticide

Wajh   Opinion

GLOSSARY

Waliyy   Guardian
Waqf (pl. *awqaf*)   Religious endowment
Wilaya   Guardianship

Yufaji'   He/it surprises

Zakat   Alms
Zani muhsan   Married fornicator
Zina   Illicit sexual relations

INDEX

251

ABOUT THE CONTRIBUTORS

Zeinab Abul-Magd is a graduate student in Middle East History at Georgetown University. She received her B.S. in political science from Cairo University in 1996. Her publications include "Women, Gender and Waqf" in the *Encyclopedia of Women in Islamic Cultures* (2003) and "'Asbab al-Nuzul wa-'Ahkam al-Nisa' fi al-Fiqh al-Shaf'i" (Challenging Orthodoxies—'Asbab al Nuzul and the Misappropriation of the Text) in *Women and Civilization Journal* 1, no. 3 (2002).

Lama Abu-Odeh is associate professor at the Georgetown University Law Center. She received her S.J.D. from Harvard Law School in 1993 after having received degrees from the University of Bristol and the University of York in the United Kingdom and from the University of Jordan. Professor Abu-Odeh has taught comparative family law, Islamic law, and criminal law at Stanford Law School and has served as legal counsel for the Middle East/North Africa division of the World Bank. She has also been a legal adviser for the Jordan Electricity Authority and the Central Bank of Jordan in Amman. Among her publications are "Crimes of Honor and the Construction of Gender in Arab Societies" in Mai Yamani, ed., *Feminism and Islam: Legal and Literary Perspectives* (1996).

Nathan Brown is professor of political science and international affairs at the George Washington University, where he has been a professor since 1987. He was director of the Middle East Studies program there from

1989 to 1994 and from 1996 to 1999. He is also scholar-in-residence at the Middle East Institute in Washington, D.C. Brown received his higher education from Princeton University, earning an M.A. in 1983 and a Ph.D. in 1987. He has published *The Rule of Law in the Arab World: Egypt and the Arab States of the Gulf* (1997), *Peasant Politics in Modern Egypt: The Struggle against the State* (1990), *Constitutions in a Non-Constitutional World: Arab Basic Laws and Prospects for Accountable Government* (2001), as well as numerous articles and book review.

Yvonne Yazbeck Haddad is professor of history of Islam and Christian–Muslim relations at the Center for Muslim–Christian Understanding at the Edmund Walsh School of Foreign Service at Georgetown University. She has taught Middle East history and Islamic studies at the University of Massachusetts, Amherst; Hartford Seminary; and Colgate University. She is a past president of the Middle East Studies Association. Haddad's research interest has focused on twentieth-century Islamic thought and Muslims in the West. Her numerous publications include *Contemporary Islam and the Challenge of History*, *Muslim Communities in North America*, *The Islamic Revival*, *The Muslims of America*, *Women, Religion, and Social Change*, *Muslims on the Americanization Path?*, *Muslims in the West: From Sojourners to Citizens*, and *Muslim Minorities in the West: "Visible" and "Invisible."*

Wael Hallaq has been professor of Islamic law at the Institute of Islamic Studies, McGill University, since 1994. He has also held professorships at the University of Toronto and the State Institute of Islamic Studies in Jakarta, Indonesia. He received his doctorate degree from the University of Washington in 1983 for his dissertation titled "The Gate of Ijtihad: A Study in the Legal History of Islam." One of the preeminent scholars in the field of Islamic law, Hallaq has written numerous books and articles on topics including Islamic legal theory, medieval Islamic philosophy, and contemporary Arabic literature. In 1997, he authored *A History of Islamic Legal Theories: An Introduction to Sunni Usul al-Fiqh* (1997). He is currently editing an eight-volume compendium titled *Themes in Islamic Law* and wrote *Authority, Continuity and Change in Islamic Law* (2000). His works have been translated into Arabic, Indonesian, Turkish, Japanese, and Persian.

Ann Mayer is associate professor of legal studies at the Wharton School, University of Pennsylvania, where she has served since 1977. She received a J.D. from the University of Pennsylvania Law School in 1975, a certificate in Islamic and comparative law from the University of London's School of Oriental and African Studies in 1977, and a Ph.D. in Middle Eastern history from the University of Michigan in 1978. Mayer has written extensively on topics such as comparative law, Middle Eastern law, human rights law, international law, Islamic law, and law and international business. Some of her publications include *Islam and Human Rights* (1998), "Reflections on the U.S. Reservations to CEDAW: Should the Constitution Be an Obstacle to Human Rights?" (*Hastings Constitutional Law Quarterly* 23 [1996]), and "Universal versus Islamic Human Rights: A Clash of Cultures or a Clash with a Construct?" (*Michigan Journal of International Law* 15 [1994]).

Aimen Mir is currently an attorney in the Government and Regulatory Affairs Department of the Washington, D.C., office of Hale and Dorr, LLP. He received his J.D. degree from Georgetown University Law Center, where he served as the managing editor of the *Georgetown Immigration Law Journal*. He also received his M.S. and B.S. degrees in international affairs from Georgetown University. Aimen has represented asylum applicants from the Middle East and other countries before the Immigration and Naturalization Service and immigration courts.

Adel Omar Sherif is a vice president of the Supreme Constitutional Court of Egypt. Justice Sherif was educated at 'Ayn Shams University, where he completed his doctorate in the field of law. He has served on the Council of the State and as a visiting fellow at the Human Rights Law Center of the College of Law, DePaul University, Chicago; the Human Rights Centre of the University of Essex; and the Federal Judicial Center in Washington, D.C., and as a visiting professor at the Faculty of Law, McGill University. He is the author of *Constitutional Adjudication in Egypt* (1988), *Judicial Independence, Requirements and Rewards* (1996) and the coeditor of the following texts from the Kluwer Law International series: *Human Rights and Democracy: The Role of the Supreme Constitutional Court of Egypt*, *The Role of the Judiciary in the Protection of Human Rights*, and *Democracy, the Rule of Law and Islam*.

Jakob Skovgaard-Petersen is associate professor of Islamic studies and head of the Academic Program at the Carsten Niebuhr Institute, University of Copenhagen. He received his M.A. in the history of religion in 1989. After studies in Damascus, Cairo, and Beirut, he received a doctorate for his dissertation "Defining Islam for the Egyptian State: Muftis and Fatwas of the Dar Al-Ifta" (1997). Skovgaard-Petersen's research interests focus primarily on the transformations of religious institutions, thinking, and debate in the Arab world in the twentieth century.

Barbara Freyer Stowasser is professor of Arabic in the Department of Arabic Language, Literature, and Linguistics at Georgetown University. She received her Ph.D. in Islamic studies and Semitic languages from the University of Münster, Germany. Between 1993 and 2003, she served as director of the Center for Contemporary Arab Studies at Georgetown University. She served as the thirty-fourth president of the Middle East Studies Association (1998–1999). Her publications include a book-length study, *Women in the Qur'an: Traditions and Interpretation* (1994); an edited volume titled *The Islamic Impulse* (1987); articles published in American, German, Arabic, and Turkish journals and periodicals; and book chapters in collected volumes. In 2000, The Center for Contemporary Arab Studies published Stowasser's booklet, *A Time to Reap: Thoughts on Calendars and Millennialism*, an exploration of how Islam, Christianity, and Judaism have historically treated periods of apocalyptic imminence.

Nadia Yakoob is currently an attorney at the New York City office of Fragomen, Del Rey, Bernsen & Loewy, P.C., which specializes in immigration law. She received her J.D. from Georgetown University, where she served as the editor in chief of the *Georgetown Immigration Law Journal*. After graduating from law school, she spent a year at the European Court of Human Rights in Strasbourg, France, as a Fulbright researcher, examining human rights prohibitions on the expulsion of aliens. Yakoob received her M.Sc. in international relations from the London School of Economics and her B.A. in political science from the University of California, Los Angeles.